AMERICAN
FISH AND WILDLIFE POLICY:
THE HUMAN DIMENSION

Edited by
WILLIAM R. MANGUN

SOUTHERN ILLINOIS UNIVERSITY PRESS
CARBONDALE AND EDWARDSVILLE

Copyright © 1992 by the Board of Trustees,
Southern Illinois University
All rights reserved
Printed in the United States of America
Designed by Mary Rohrer
Production supervised by Natalia Nadraga

95 94 93 92   4 3 2 1

Library of Congress Cataloging-in-Publication Data

American fish and wildlife policy : the human dimension / edited by
  William R. Mangun.
    p. cm.
  Includes bibliographical references and index.
  1. Wildlife management—Government policy—United States.
  2. Fishery management—Government policy—United States.
  I. Mangun, William Russell.
  SK361.A68 1992
  333.95'0973—dc20   91-47741
  ISBN 0-8093-1821-0   CIP

The paper used in this publication meets the minimum requirements of
American National Standard for Information Sciences—Permanence of
Paper for Printed Library Materials, ANSI Z39.48-1984. ♾

CONTENTS

PREFACE

Wildlife habitat is continually lost because humans exhibit inadequate concern for the basic life support needs of wildlife. Human demands for the resources that animals depend upon for food and shelter seem to be insatiable.

American fish and wildlife policy has been characterized by an emphasis on biological values with an inadequate amount of attention directed to the impact of human activities on the condition of fish and wildlife. It is important for us to understand vital ecological relationships in order to manage fish and wildlife effectively. However, wildlife managers and society as a whole need to devote greater attention to the role of humans with respect to wildlife and the resources upon which their existence depends.

The purposes of this book, therefore, are to help focus attention on the study of the human dimensions of wildlife management and the role of public policy formulation and implementation in wildlife management and to encourage policymakers to adopt an ecological perspective that integrates humans as system parts and not distinct elements that are separate and above them. Rather than presenting a compendium of ecological case studies about wildlife, this volume presents a series of essays that deal with policy issues, management perspectives, and public attitudes about wildlife that shape the world of the wildlife manager.

It would be impossible for me to thank all of the many who helped me put this book together; however, I want to mention a few. I must thank my wife, Jean, for all of her support during preparation of this manuscript. My children Kimberly, Shaun, Emily, and Chris deserve particular thanks for their tolerance in listening to my comments about the condition of wildlife and the need for humans to be more responsible in their actions toward wildlife. I want to thank all of the contributors for their patience during the various drafts of the book chapters.

I am particularly indebted to Lynn Greenwalt, Robert Bartlett, Barbara Knuth, Jean Mangun, and Lynn Llewellyn who performed painstaking reviews and provided critical comments that improved the final product immensely. The willing support of Debra Stewart and Wayne Williams in the preparation of the manuscript is gratefully acknowledged. I want to thank the editorial director of Southern Illinois University Press, Richard DeBacher, for his persistence in persuading me to undertake this project and his continually warmhearted support and guidance throughout its development. Finally, I need to acknowledge the support and assistance of the many professional staff members of East Carolina University who assisted me throughout the various stages of manuscript preparation.

William R. Mangun
East Carolina University

PART 1
INTRODUCTION

FISH AND WILDLIFE POLICY ISSUES

William R. Mangun

Introduction

The human dimensions of wildlife management are an increasing concern for the wildlife manager, dealing with many social and ethical aspects. This book focuses on issues that a changing public is likely to expect from fish and wildlife managers. Changes in demographic patterns are important to wildlife managers. A better-educated populace that is more environmentally aware is likely to demand a larger voice in how wildlife management is to be conducted on public lands. An aging and less mobile population may require improved access to wildlife-associated recreation opportunities. An increasingly urban population is likely to expect more urban-related services (for example, wildlife education programs and urban refuges) with a greater emphasis on nongame species. Population growth in Sun Belt states is likely to lead to greater conflict between traditional rural resource users and risk-averse suburbanites. Finally, greater racial diversity in the human population being served potentially will require accommodation of different values with respect to program offerings.

Policy Perspectives in Wildlife Management

The pervasive approach to wildlife policy in the United States suggests that people are interested in fish and wildlife to the extent that animals serve a purpose for human use and enjoyment. Although the winds of change have begun to blow, the traditional mission of the U.S. Fish and Wildlife Service (FWS) has mirrored such a utilitarian philosophy. Recent agency mission statements stipulated that FWS was "to provide the federal leadership to conserve, protect and enhance fish and wildlife and their habitats for the continuing benefit of people" (U.S. Fish and Wildlife Service 1980).

An alternative policy approach would emphasize the protection and the enhancement of the diversity of wildlife as well as the ecological integrity of their habitats. From that perspective, wildlife policy typically would have goals that direct development away from essential wildlife habitats, encourage forestry and farming practices that benefit wildlife, and provide for the maintenance or establishment of transportation corridors for wildlife in the form of connected habitats that are conserved on the basis of their value to wildlife (Venno 1991).

A more desirable approach for wildlife policy would be one that integrates both perspectives. An integrated wildlife policy would introduce humans into an ecosystem-based policy model or, even further, into a biospheric policy model, rather than reserving humans for separate consideration. The International Joint Commission (IJC) recently adopted such an ecosystem perspective for development of public policy on the management of the Great Lakes. In an assessment of IJC attempts to develop and implement policy, Lynton K. Caldwell (1988:11) concluded that any law or policy that is designed to affect natural resources, nature, or the environment that does not possess a human-inclusive ecosystem perspective is simply inadequate. Furthermore, as Christie and coauthors (1986) correctly stated, an "ecosystem perspective is crucial to human well-being and survival" as well.

The Royal Society of Canada and the National Research Council of the United States (1985) observed that in the Great Lakes Water Quality Agreement implementation of such an integrated policy approach would require "time series of monitored data, maps of key features of the ecosystem and of its use and abuse by humans, models of causal relationship integrating human uses and ecosystem responses, and case studies of management actions to demonstrate what has worked and what has not." Similar types of data would have to be collected for the development and implementation of an integrated wildlife policy approach.

An integrated wildlife policy approach that included both ecological and human considerations would benefit both wildlife and humans. Guidance for the collection and analysis of data necessary for the development and implementation of wildlife policy with a strong ecological focus can be obtained from the National Research Council's Committee on the Applications of Ecological Theory to Environmental Problems (1986). The committee has developed some case studies that deal with wildlife policy issues: for example, studies that address management of North Pacific Halibut, conservation of the spotted owl, and protection of caribou during hydroelectric development. Although the human element is drawn into its analysis, through public input into decision making via impact assessment, more emphasis on human dimensions is required to effect a truly integrated approach. Nielsen and coauthors (1989:429) propose that university natural resource curricula "should place fisheries and wildlife in a management context that gives biology, habitat and the human dimension equal weight." This book should help the reader understand the need for a better integration of ecological considerations of fish and wildlife management with the human dimensions of policy issues.

Fish and Wildlife Policy Process

American fish and wildlife policy has been going through a subtle but accelerating change over the past several decades. For definitional purposes, a fish or wildlife policy can be considered as any purposive course of government action designed to protect or enhance fish or wildlife or their habitat (and, in some circumstances, to regulate or control predator damage). Such courses of action include explicit decisions on the part of government not to take action as well as to take action.

Theodore Lowi's (1964) classic typology of public policy, which categorizes policies as distributive, regulatory, or redistributive, provides us with a working terminology to consider the evolution of fish and wildlife policy.[1]

Until recently, the primary policy emphasis in fish and wildlife agencies was distributive, where agencies provided goods and services to the public. For example, agencies acquired land and maintained fish hatcheries and wildlife refuges to provide fishing and hunting opportunities for citizens. Fish and wildlife agencies also provided animal damage control services to local landowners in order to minimize damage to both landowners and wildlife.

The horizons of wildlife policy broadened as the country's demographic structure evolved from a predominately rural population to a more urbanized society. The present more risk-averse and better-educated population tends to view wildlife in a somewhat different manner. The need for wildlife is now viewed in a less utilitarian manner and a more ecological point of view. Recent studies on public attitudes toward wildlife have indicated that the dominant orientations are "moralistic" and "humanistic" (Kellert 1979, 1980). Consumptive activities like hunting, where the game is "taken" from its wild state and consumed or kept as a trophy, are increasingly challenged by segments of an urban population that have discovered other modes of encountering wildlife. These segments are more interested in nonconsumptive uses of wildlife such as photographing, feeding, or intense observation. Recent literature and national wildlife surveys demonstrate the growth in nonconsumptive wildlife appreciation (More 1979; USDI 1982, 1988; Shaw and Mangun 1985; Shaw et al. 1985).

This attitudinal change is reflected in new legislation and court decisions of a regulatory nature that have reallocated privileges among competing wildlife interest groups. The Endangered Species

Act, the Fish and Wildlife Coordination Act, the Bald Eagle Protection Act, and the Marine Mammal Protection Act, among others, created winners and losers in a regulatory game. In *Palila v. Hawaii Department of Land and Natural Resources* (471 F. Supp. 993–994), for example, the district court affirmed federal authority to regulate endangered species, even a nonmigratory species on state property. James A. Tober (1989:1) characterizes this evolution in policy development as the second great debate over the allocation of property rights in wildlife.

Over time, consumptive wildlife users (both sport and commercial) as well as development interest groups have lost certain privileges, while nonconsumptive wildlife users and environmental interest groups have gained privileges. For example, federal and state endangered species laws prohibit the taking of wildlife species such as the American crocodile or the California condor, as well as the destruction of designated critical habitat required for the continued maintenance of those species. U.S. Fish and Wildlife Service scientific opinions issued under the Fish and Wildlife Coordination Act (16 U.S.C.A. 661–667e, P.L. 85–624) often result in the alteration of major federal development projects. The Marine Mammal Protection Act (16 U.S.C.A. 1361–1407) regulates the use and taking of cetaceans and pinnipeds, with responsibilities divided between the U.S. Fish and Wildlife Service and the National Marine Fisheries Service. Other federal legislation, such as the Clean Water Act (Section 404) (33 U.S.C. 1341–1345, P.L. 92–500) and the Rivers and Harbors Act (Section 10) (33 U.S.C. et seq.), and various state wetland protection regulations limit the types of activities that are permitted in wetlands. Recent proposals for changes in federal wetlands regulations highlight the controversy surrounding the "taking" of development privileges on lands designated as wetlands (Robinson 1991; Schneider 1991).

Redistributive policy is generally considered to occur when resources are taken from an advantaged sector of society and redistributed to a less advantaged sector. In terms of wildlife policy, endangered species and nongame programs could be considered disadvantaged. Three percent of wildlife produce a majority of the revenue and receive a majority of the management attention

(Mangun 1986:24; also see Thompson 1987). In this context, endangered and nongame programs, which represent 97 percent of the species, could be considered disadvantaged. If excise taxes from hunting and fishing equipment, collected under the Federal Aid in Wildlife Restoration Act or Federal Aid in Sport Fish Restoration Act, were used for an endangered species or nongame project, it would constitute redistributive policy. The use of state hunting or fishing license fees for endangered species or nongame-related activities would be another example of redistributive policy. The use of general tax revenues, such as the Missouri sales tax, that are dedicated for conservation purposes also could be interpreted as redistributive policy.

A similar redistributive policy situation occurs when the federal government provides payments in lieu of taxes (PILT) to county governments. Such payments are designed to partially offset losses in tax revenues when federal facilities such as national wildlife refuges (NWR) are established. Money for the payments is derived from a complex array of formulas dealing with revenues from oil and gas production, gravel removal, grazing, and timber harvesting activities conducted on refuge lands as well as from general tax revenues. Although the money is derived from resources belonging to all taxpayers, it is expended in support of habitat protection for migratory or endangered species that tend to benefit a subset of all taxpayers who hunt, observe, or photograph those species. Theoretically, however, one might argue that all taxpayers benefit from the mere existence of wildlife.

Federal, State, and Local Relationships in Wildlife Policy

Traditional Federal-State Relationship

The management of wildlife policy is shared among the states and the federal government. In some instances, the division of authority and responsibility has been formalized in agreements between the federal government and the states. For example, the relationship between U.S. Department of the Interior (USDI) agencies and state government agencies is codified in the *Code of Federal Regulations* (1983: 43CFR, Part 24). In general, state agencies have management authority over all species within their respective boundaries, including species on federal lands. However, the U.S. Fish and Wildlife Service, the Bureau of Land Management, and other federal agencies have responsibilities for migratory species that cross state boundaries and selected other wildlife that are endangered or threatened and are protected under the Endangered Species Act (16 U.S.C.A. 1531–1543, P.L. 93–205) or the Marine Mammal Protection Act (16 U.S.C.A. 1361–1407, P.L. 92–522).

Management responsibility for fish species follows the pattern for wildlife species. However, authority to determine policy for fisheries management is complicated by the involvement of multiple federal agencies, regional cross-jurisdictional authorities, as well as state agencies. State agencies maintain clear responsibility for nonmigratory resident species, such as bass and perch. But the picture concerning anadromous fish that migrate from saltwater into freshwater to spawn is more complex. Management authority for anadromous fish is shared by the U.S. Fish and Wildlife Service, in the Department of the Interior, and the National Marine Fisheries Service (NMFS), in the Department of Commerce, as well as the state governments. Under the Anadromous Fish Conservation Act (16 U.S.C.A. 757a–757g), FWS facilitates state management of the freshwater phase of anadromous fish, including estuaries. The Fishery Conservation and Management Act of 1976 (16 U.S.C.A. 1801–1882) established regional Fishery Management Councils (FMC) composed of NMFS and representatives of state government agencies, with FWS serving in a nonvoting observer capacity, that jointly establish management regulations for the ocean phase of anadromous fish and other saltwater fish beyond estuaries. It should be noted, however, that coastal states have management authority over fishery species within their jurisdictional limits.

The Evolution of State Wildlife Policy

The origins of state wildlife policy in the United States date back to 1639 when the colony of Rhode Island established a closed hunting season for wildlife in order to protect the population of deer (Gottschalk 1978:290). The protection of game for sporting purposes evolved into a situation in which state governments assumed property rights over animals. Such property rights were emphasized through the establishment of state game management agencies to facilitate sportsmen's interests.

State authority to control the use of both resident and migratory species and to distribute favors among constituents was relatively uncontested until the early 1900s. As described in the following section on federal policy, the Supreme Court affirmed a federal management prerogative over migratory species in its decision in the case of *Missouri v. Holland* (Bean 1983).

State wildlife policy has been heavily influenced by the nature of the funding process. Prior to 1936, implementation of state wildlife policies was funded primarily through the imposition of license fees for fishing and hunting privileges and general tax revenues. In 1936, the Federal Aid in Wildlife Restoration Act (16 U.S.C.A. 669–669i), commonly referred to as the Pittman-Robertson Act (P-R), was created by Congress to provide additional revenue to states to restore decimated wildlife populations. In 1950, the Dingell-Johnson Sport Fish Restoration Act (16 U.S.C.A. 777–777k), commonly referred to as the Dingell-Johnson Act (D-J), provided similar assistance to states for sport fish. Under the Pittman-Robertson Act individuals pay an excise tax on the purchase of guns and ammunition. Under the Dingell-Johnson Act anglers pay a similar excise tax on rods, reels, tackle boxes, and other fishing tackle. In 1984, the Wallop-Breaux amendments (P.L. 98–369, 26 U.S.C.A. 1) to Dingell-Johnson provided additional revenues to the states to establish boating access facilities from a share of the federal excise tax on fuel used for motorboating activities. The Wallop-Breaux Act created an Aquatic Resources Trust Fund composed of the Sport Fish Restoration Account and the Boating Safety Account (U.S. Fish and Wildlife Service 1989).

Hunting and fishing tackle manufacturers send the excise taxes directly to the Department of the Treasury which, in turn, apportions them to the U.S. Fish and Wildlife Service. The U.S. Fish and Wildlife Service distributes federal assistance funds for sport-fish and wildlife restoration projects to the states through a complex formula based on each state's size, population, and license sales (Mangun 1986).

The funding process has had tremendous implications for state fish and wildlife policy. Since sporting enthusiasts have provided the bulk of the money, state wildlife programs have strongly favored game species. As noted earlier, changes in demographic structure forced state fish and wildlife agencies to implement more comprehensive management programs that included nongame species. By 1988, all state fish and wildlife agencies established either endangered species or nongame wildlife management programs, or both. However, there remained insufficient funds for such programs. In order to obtain more funds for nongame programs, many state governments established "nongame tax checkoffs." Through such tax checkoffs, taxpayers can contribute a portion of their tax return to a nongame fund (see Harpman 1984; Mangun 1986).

However, state agencies need a more reliable source of income for nongame programs than income tax checkoffs (Applegate and Trout 1984). Nongame checkoffs are subject to competition from other interests such as programs for battered wives or the homeless. The amount of money generated from checkoffs is highly dependent on the state of the economy: the poorer the economy, the less people contribute. Also, if a person does not file a tax return, there often is no means for the taxpayer to designate a contribution. Without more reliable revenue sources for nongame programs, state agencies will continue to emphasize game management programs with a focus on distributive and regulatory policies for game species and funds grudgingly redistributed for nongame-related activities.

Federal Wildlife Policy

Initial federal involvement in wildlife policy simply supported state wildlife management efforts. Formal federal involvement in wildlife policy issues began with the passage of the Lacey Act of 1900 (16 U.S.C.A. 701–702). The Lacey Act prohibited interstate commerce involving wild animals or birds killed in violation of state game laws. The act was designed to assist the states in the enforcement of state game laws by means of federal constitutional authority to regulate interstate commerce (Bean 1983:18) rather than to assert federal prerogative. As the twentieth century progressed, the federal role in wildlife policy expanded considerably, but only in the face of stiff opposition from vested interests of the states.

The basis for federal involvement in wildlife management did not become clearly articulated until 1916. In that year, the United States government signed a treaty with Great Britain, which represented Canada, for the protection of migratory birds. Soon thereafter, Congress established implementation authority for the treaty in 1918 with the passage of the Migratory Bird Treaty Act (MBTA), 16 U.S.C.A. 703–711. The treaty clearly gave the federal government the right to protect migratory species. However, vested state interests quickly challenged the authority of the federal government to interfere with their property rights over game. The Supreme Court upheld the authority of the federal government, in Missouri v. Holland, 252 U.S. 416 (1920), citing the supremacy of the federal treaty-making power. The constitutional authority of the federal government to enter into treaties became the basis, therefore, for national supremacy with regard to migratory species.

As Tober (1989) and Mangun and Mangun (1991) observe, the federal role in wildlife policy grew considerably in the second half of the twentieth century. Citizens who did not have sufficient access through wildlife policy "iron triangles" at the state level (McElveen and Klay 1991) pressed for legislative action at the federal level. The resulting legislative changes established the basis for an enhanced federal regulatory role. The activities of citizen groups and nongovernmental organizations also provided the impetus for redistributive policy efforts to provide funds for nongame programs in the form of the Fish and Wildlife Conservation Act of 1980 (16 U.S.C.A. 2901–2911; see Loomis and Mangun 1987), although this act has remained unfunded because of legislative impasses. Funding proposals for excise taxes on four-wheel drive vehicles, motorhomes, photographic and camping equipment, as well as severance taxes on selected mining activities, could be considered redistributive in nature.

The Wildlife Policy Role for Local Governments

The role of local governments in wildlife policy is relatively unclear and highly limited. Local governments are creatures of their
respective state governments; they receive all enabling authority
from the state. State governments maintain control over resident
wildlife policy issues but typically provide little or no role for local
governments.

Given appropriate oversight, however, it would appear desirable
for state governments to give more attention to increasing the authority and responsibility of local governments in wildlife policy
(Mangun and Mangun 1991). Financial crises at both federal and
state levels and the concomitant competition for scarce fiscal resources is likely to increase opportunities, as well as needs, for
greater local government involvement in wildlife planning and
management. Some state governments such as Maine and Vermont
specifically encourage local governments to give greater consideration to wildlife-related issues in their planning efforts; other states
need to follow their lead (Venno 1991; Vermont Fish and Wildlife
Department 1990). Several strategies are available to local governments to improve their abilities to consider wildlife in decision-
making processes (Knuth and Nielsen 1991).

Expansion of the Wildlife Policy Role for Local Governments

State wildlife agencies and local governments should give greater
recognition to the desires of their citizens for increased opportunities for wildlife appreciation as well as the needs of wildlife in urban
planning. Recent studies (Shaw and Mangun 1985; Shaw et al. 1985;
Schreyer et al. 1989) have noted the correlation between higher
education levels and ecological awareness. In addition, urban residents increasingly are interested in having wildlife-related experiences in and around their neighborhoods (USDI FWS 1982, 1988).

Magill (1988:295) observed that resource professionals have
tended to be insensitive to such nonmaterial experiential needs of
the public. A more politically active and ecologically aware citi-
zenry, however, is likely to demand changes in wildlife policy at

the local level, similar to the demands that they have made for changes in federal policy.

A great deal of ecological information about urban wildlife has become available for use in urban design. Robert Dorney (1986:54) observed that from 1970 to 1985 the new field of urban ecology developed an increasing focus on urban wildlife. Increasing numbers of wildlife ecologists, landscape architects, foresters, and others have studied the manner in which wildlife adapt to life in cities and surrounding areas. Unfortunately, many urban planners do not have the necessary expertise in wildlife ecology to apply such information in planning urban landscapes. Dorney (1986:54) has identified three solutions to the problem. First, architects and engineers need to be better educated about landscape ecology and the economic benefits that can accrue from the proper blending of wildlife into planned urban developments. Second, city planners as well as private engineering firms need to seek out the expertise of wildlife biologists during the design of projects. Third, computer models, such as geographic information systems, could be employed to identify appropriate types of habitat. Such models also could be used to predict the type of wildlife that would inhabit different land-use configurations.

In a handbook outlining how wildlife habitat considerations can be integrated into local planning for Maine communities, Sharri Venno (1991) identified a variety of means for the development of local wildlife policy initiatives. This policy approach is predicated upon an assumption that the conservation of wildlife habitats is important for local governments in order to ensure that their residents will continue to enjoy the benefits of wildlife. First, conservation districts can be established to conserve essential habitat for endangered or threatened species. For example, protection zones can be established around bald eagle nesting sites or deer wintering sites. Second, habitat protection ordinances can be adopted with specific land-use guidelines. Third, mandatory open-space zoning can be employed to maintain wildlife connection corridors. Fourth, wetland protection ordinances can be established to reduce inappropriate development of wetlands. Fifth, shoreland zoning ordinances can be developed to minimize residential and recreational impacts on littoral habitats. Sixth, residential clustering can be encouraged by zoning ordinance. Finally, local governments can acquire important habitat through donations from private landowners, purchase of land trust, or outright fee title purchase. Venno's suggested approaches to enhance the role of local governments in wildlife management are a substantial move in the direction of including the human dimension in fish and wildlife policy while expanding the local role.

Changes in Wildlife Policy Emphasis

The policy role of state and federal fish and wildlife agencies has changed dramatically over the past thirty or forty years; the distributive role has become more regulatory. At one time the fish and wildlife manager was perceived as a "white-hat" distributor of goods and services to traditional constituencies. Wildlife managers maintained refuges and fish hatcheries that provided hunting opportunities and fish for "put and take" programs, for example, the farm pond program (Peek 1986). Wildlife managers also provided services to farmers, cattlemen, and wool growers through animal damage control programs to control populations of blackbirds and coyotes (Cohn 1991). As a result of much of the legislation fostered by the "environmental movement" in the 1960s and 1970s, the role of the fish and wildlife manager gradually changed from a "white-hat" distributor of goods and services to a regulatory "black hat." As a result of responsibilities growing out of the Fish and Wildlife Coordination Act (FWCA [16 U.S.C.A. 661–667e]) and the National Environmental Policy Act (NEPA), fish and wildlife managers at the federal level regularly have conflicts with those agencies with development responsibilities such as the U.S. Army Corps of Engineers (Clarke and McCool 1985) and the Federal Energy Regulatory Commission (Wilds and Lamb 1985).

Through procedural requirements of the Fish and Wildlife Coordination Act, the U.S. Fish and Wildlife Service was mandated to provide scientific opinions concerning the likely impact of federal projects on fish and wildlife and their essential habitat requirements. At one time the FWCA was looked upon as a mere procedural requirement. However, as the environmental movement became stronger and the general public better educated about the ecological consequences of development, scientific opinions rendered under FWCA have become the potential basis for third-party intervention in lawsuits should development agencies choose to ignore the recommendations of the FWS for appropriate mitigation actions.

Environmental legislation of the 1960s and 1970s clearly was the basis for much of the change in the roles and responsibilities of fish and wildlife managers. The major pieces of legislation that fomented change include the National Environmental Policy Act of 1969 (42 U.S.C.A. 4321–4347, P.L. 91–190), the Fish and Wildlife Coordination Act Amendments (16 U.S.C.A. 661–667e, P.L. 85–624), the Endangered Species Act of 1973 and Amendments (16 U.S.C.A. 1531–1543, P.L. 93–205), the Marine Mammal Protection Act of 1972 (16 U.S.C.A. 1361–1407, P.L. 92–522), and the Federal Water Pollution Control Act Amendments of 1972 (33 U.S.C.A. 1251–1376, P.L. 92–500), especially section 404. The NEPA process explicitly required federal agencies (and recipients of federal aid at the state, local, and private levels) to take into consideration the effect of their major development actions on fish, wildlife, and their habitat. Environmental impact assessment requirements at both the federal and state levels have given fish and wildlife biologists a greater role in the management of our society.

Persons whose actions have been constrained by the biological opinions and recommendations of fish and wildlife managers have often labeled these biologists as obstructionists. Although federal agencies simply have to consider the biological opinions of the Fish and Wildlife Service and not necessarily act on those recommendations, often such recommendations become the basis for less environmentally damaging actions (Mangun 1988).

The environmental impact assessment process established by the National Environmental Policy Act of 1970 also is used to identify clearly unacceptable development projects. When this occurs, federal development projects are stopped or held up for a considerable period of time. A good example can be seen in the stoppage of the highly publicized Two Forks Dam Project, in the state of Colorado, with its potentially negative impacts on the "St. Peter's Basilica of trout fishing" and the endangered whooping cranes (Weisskopf 1990).

Conflict over Wildlife Policy

Environmental legislation passed in the "environmental decade" of the 1970s, such as the Endangered Species Act of 1973 and the Marine Mammal Protection Act of 1972, changed the role of federal fish and wildlife administrators enormously. As wildlife species have increasingly become threatened or endangered because of human actions, fish and wildlife managers have been forced to develop policies and programs to control the detrimental behavior of humans. Such controls often make fish and wildlife managers unwelcome actors in the wildlife policy implementation process.

The section 7 consultation process of the Endangered Species Act is one of the efforts designed to limit the actions of humans with respect to threatened and endangered species. Through Section 7 consultations, fish and wildlife biologists make legally enforceable decisions about the use of natural resources. Such decisions stop projects and even affect the ability of individuals and corporations to use their property if there is some federal connection to the property such as a loan guarantee or permit. A private person cannot "take" or harass a listed species, but there is nothing to prevent a private person from building in the habitat of a listed species unless a federal connection exists; even then, it is the federal agency that must consult, not the private landowner.

The designation of "critical habitat" for endangered species, under section 10 of the Endangered Species Act, is also a controversial process. Richard Tobin (1990:175–180) describes the process in detail in *The Expendable Future: U.S. Politics and the Protection of Biological Diversity*. Biologists often must keep secret the location of such habitat, especially with regard to endangered plants, during the habitat designation deliberation process. If a private landowner has the misfortune, or blessing, depending upon your perspective, to have endangered species critical habitat designated on his or her property, he or she may not use that land in any manner that may threaten that habitat or the existence of the endangered species that require that habitat. Because of the dangers of being labeled as antidevelopment or antibusiness, fish and wildlife managers must have a strong sense of dedication and perseverance to fulfill their responsibilities to protect and enhance threatened and endangered species. This is borne out by the controversies surrounding management of the northern spotted owl in the Northwest and the gray wolf and the grizzly bear in the vicinity of Yellowstone National Park.

On a more forceful level, fish and wildlife managers directly regulate the use of endangered species and marine mammals as well as products made from their parts. As a participant to the 1973 Convention on International Trade in Endangered Species of Wild Fauna and Flora (CITES; T.I.A.S. 8249), the United States prohibits the importation of endangered species as well as products made from endangered species listed on CITES. Different levels of trade regulations exist, depending on the threatened status of the listed species and the contribution that trade is assumed to make to that condition. Without explicit use permits from FWS, even zoos and pet dealers are barred from possessing animals on the CITES list.

FWS law enforcement officers also engage in "sting" operations to ensnare violators of fish and wildlife laws. For example, during "Operation Falcon," conducted in the mid-1980s, dozens of people who bought, sold, and used federally protected endangered raptors for sporting purposes were arrested.

The Federal Water Pollution Control Act was amended in 1972 to include explicit provisions for the protection of wetlands. Although authority resides with the Environmental Protection Agency, actual responsibility for implementation of Section 404 permit provisions is delegated to the U.S. Army Corps of Engineers. The Corps of Engineers already had permitting responsibilities associated with Section 10 of the 1899 Rivers and Harbors Act (33 U.S.C.A. et seq.), which was resurrected in the 1960s to regulate the use of wetlands in the United States. Through these acts, federal fish and wildlife managers, as well as state agency managers in those states that have accepted primacy for implementation of section 404 permits, become involved in the issuance of permits for the development of wetlands. Although development may be permitted, fish and wildlife administrators often demand that mitigation lands in like or kind be provided by the developer. Such lands cost developers considerable amounts of money. Even when development is not stopped, fish and wildlife administrators, again, receive considerable rebuke from private citizens because of the difficulties associated with the procedural requirements necessary to obtain development permits.

Time-honored animal damage control programs in which fish and wildlife managers provide much-wanted services to farmers, cattlemen, and wool growers became a highly controversial program as environmental awareness grew among citizens throughout the United States. Although the extermination of blackbirds receives little attention, with the possible exception of situations like Ft. Campbell, Kentucky, in the early 1980s, programs to reduce coyote populations receive severe criticism from groups like Defenders of Wildlife. Toxic collars with Compound 1080 and M–44 control devices are criticized as unacceptable means of controlling predators since the effects cannot be limited to target species. Furthermore, the killing of coyote pups still in the den is also condemned widely by concerned citizens (USDI FWS 1978:86–91; Kellert 1979:46–77). On the other side, cattlemen and wool growers complain vigorously that these methods are scientifically proven and absolutely essential to maintain their profits (USDI FWS 1978).

Despite such contentions, the black-footed ferret is an example of the effect of predicides and other control practices on nontarget species. The black-footed ferret became almost extinct as a result of efforts to control prairie dogs. Collectively, such controversies contributed greatly to a decision by Reagan political appointees to remove the animal damage control (ADC) program from the Department of the Interior and return it to the Animal and Plant Inspection Service of the Department of Agriculture (USDA) where the environmental movement had a less responsive audience.

Controversy over Payment in Lieu of Taxes

One of the greatest sources of controversy between federal, state, and local governments concerns the potential loss of tax revenues whenever a federal land management facility is proposed. The expansion or establishment of national wildlife refuges, national forests, and national parks is often vigorously opposed because of a potential reduction in the local property tax base. Supreme Court decisions in *McCulloch v. Maryland* (4 Wheat. 316 [1819]) and *Van Brocklin v. Tennessee* (117 U.S. 151 [1986]) provide that state governments cannot tax the federal government and that federal property is immune from state tax laws.

In order to compensate state and local governments for lost tax revenues, the federal government shares proceeds from resource development on federal lands and provides payments in lieu of taxes. The payments are designed to lessen the burden of the federal presence in local areas. However, such provisions tend to do very little to mollify local opposition to proposed refuges. Few resources are developed on national wildlife refuges in light of dominant-use provisions of refuge-authorizing legislation. In 1976, Congress enacted the Payment in Lieu of Taxes Act (31 U.S.C.A., 1601–1607) as a revenue-sharing measure for local governments. The act authorizes a minimum payment of seventy-five cents per acre to local governments without consideration of development revenues (Coggins and Wilkinson 1987:190). However, annual appropriations for PILT have been inadequate, running about 75 percent of that mandated by Congress. Such funding inadequacies provoke conflict between federal and local interests when new refuges are proposed.

The National Wildlife Refuge System has a complex PILT procedure applied to it because it was among the first of the revenue-sharing schemes. Congress enacted the Wildlife Refuge Revenue Sharing Act to compensate local governments for the establishment of national wildlife refuges in their districts. The act authorizes payment of 25 percent of the value of revenues generated on refuges, from such activities as mineral extraction, to the appropriate counties. However, it should be noted that there is a complicated formula for determining the amount of payment due to each county in which an NWR is located, and it does not depend on the amount of revenue generated from that particular refuge.

In addition, the Mineral Leasing Act guarantees states 50 percent of the revenues generated from oil and gas leases. However, Alaska is guaranteed 90 percent of such revenues. This fact may help to explain why Alaska state officials are so supportive of efforts to initiate oil development activities on the Arctic National Wildlife Refuge in spite of widespread opposition of numerous conservation organizations across the United States.

Promising Wildlife Policy Strategies

North American Waterfowl Management Plan

The North American Waterfowl Management Plan is a remarkable success story in the development of partnerships to conserve wildlife species. In 1986, the United States and Canada entered into an agreement initiating a massive plan to conserve waterfowl and wetland habitats; they were joined later by Mexico (U.S. Department of the Interior and Environment Canada 1986; U.S. Department of the Interior 1991). The North American Waterfowl Management Plan calls for the conservation of key waterfowl habitat in six important waterfowl regions of the country—Atlantic Coast, Central Valley, Gulf Coast, Lower Mississippi Valley, Lower Great Lakes/St. Lawrence Basin, Prairie Pothole, and Playa Lakes. In those priority areas, "Joint Venture" programs bring together public and private support for conservation efforts. This policy initiative has produced one of the highest levels of cooperative support that has ever been generated for wildlife. However, the amount of revenue that would be required to fulfill all of the partnerships is enormous; it would require an investment of more than $1 billion over one decade. Although any substantial investment in the direction of preserving wetlands would be a promising move in the right direction, the likelihood of such a large investment's materializing is limited, especially in light of federal and state budget difficulties.

Some of the nongovernmental organizations (NGOs) may also weaken their level of support as the "newness" wears off. The remarkable point in the endeavor is the extent of cooperation across the public and private sectors for such a potentially important ecological issue with widespread ecosystem implications, although the focus may be on waterfowl.

The U.S. Prairie Joint Venture is one of the priority initiatives. The goals of this venture are to

1. protect and enhance 1.1 million acres on public and private land in the prairie pothole region by the year 2000, in the north central region of the United States and the south central region of Canada, to increase waterfowl numbers and provide benefits to nongame and threatened and endangered flora and fauna;
2. emphasize habitat protection on private land and work with landowners on soil, water, and wildlife conservation projects;
3. increase waterfowl production on existing wildlife areas; and
4. develop opportunities to balance wildlife, agriculture, and water development needs (FWS 1991b).

By 1990, thirty-seven states, over two hundred conservation groups, and many private corporations entered into North American Waterfowl Plan joint-venture partnerships (FWS 1991a:37). The partnerships have succeeded in protecting, restoring, or enhancing about 554,000 acres. From the East Coast to the West Coast, more than fifty projects have been initiated.

Private-sector initiatives are noteworthy facets of the North American Waterfowl Plan. For example, the Phillips Petroleum Company announced that it would donate $125,000 annually through 1994 to the Playa Lakes Joint Venture to protect twenty-five thousand wet basins in New Mexico, Texas, Oklahoma, Kansas, and Colorado. In addition to those five states and the federal government, this venture also includes Ducks Unlimited (DU) and the National Wildlife Federation, with DU promising to match Phillips's funding contribution for waterfowl enhancement in Canada (FWS 1991a).

Swampbuster Provisions of the 1985 Food Security Act

The 1985 Food Security Act, P.L. 99–198, initiated new regulatory efforts to reduce the rate of destruction and to increase the protection of wildlife habitat. The major provision, which was extended through the 1990 Food, Agriculture, Conservation, and Trade Act, is referred to as the "swampbuster" provision. It focuses on wetlands that provide breeding grounds and wintering habitat for millions of waterfowl. Title XII, section C, of the Food Security Act authorizes the Department of Agriculture to deny federal price supports, payments, and loans to farmers who drain wetlands and subsequently grow crops on the converted land.

Early optimism among fish and wildlife interest groups about the promise of the swampbuster provisions quickly soured as the Department of Agriculture developed loopholes through which farmers were able to escape penalties (Barton 1987:182–183). Controversy over the 1985 "farm bill" centered around the definition of what constitutes a wetland and the timing of when the draining of a wetland was actually initiated. Cohen and coauthors (1991:20) report that after considerable congressional debate, the swampbuster provisions of the 1985 act were modified successfully to accommodate both environmental and agricultural producer concerns in the Food, Agriculture, Conservation, and Trade Act (FACTA) of 1990. Although the definition of a wetland remained unchanged from the 1985 act, FACTA required the USDA to delineate wetlands on certified maps so producers would know exactly which lands were considered wetlands. Instead of requiring a complete loss of agricultural program benefits, a graduated penalty was instituted, based upon the seriousness of the offense. Finally, section 1438 of FACTA provided incentives to producers to either protect or restore up to one million acres of wetlands in long-term conservation easements.

Accommodation of Nongame Interests in Florida Wildlife Policy

Klay and McElveen (1991) report that the Florida Game and Fish Commission (FG&FC) has devised a system to accommodate both game and nongame interests in a win-win situation. Traditionally, game interests have been extremely wary of efforts to develop nongame programs in state fish and wildlife agencies. Game interests feel that because a majority of the funding for fish and wildlife is derived from taxes on equipment and licenses that they purchase, funds should not be spent on nongame programs. Being aware of such concerns, FG&FC staff encouraged the state legislature to develop an alternate source of funds that could be earmarked for nongame programs. In response, the legislature authorized an increase of four dollars in fees for each original license issued for a used car (83–173, Florida Statutes).

About the time the nongame issue became prominent in Florida, the Florida Game and Fish Commission was developing its first comprehensive wildlife management plan (McElveen 1985). Through the comprehensive planning process, FG&FC staff were able to demonstrate clearly how nongame activities would be differentiated from game-based efforts. Most important, the relationship of program activity to funding source could be identified. That allowed the agency to demonstrate that specific nongame initiatives were under way and that the resources for programs in support of fishing and hunting were not being affected; that is, both environmental and game interests were accommodated. Finally, agency staff utilized the planning process to demonstrate the common stake that both game and nongame interests have in protecting and enhancing wildlife habitat. The salience of the last two points is that redistributive wildlife policy initiatives are unlikely to receive a receptive audience within the wildlife community.

Reinvest-in-Minnesota (RIM) Program

The state of Minnesota developed a remarkable policy to protect and restore its fish and wildlife and other natural resources. The program is called "Reinvest in Minnesota" (Minnesota Department of Natural Resources [DNR] 1991). Like the North American Waterfowl Management Plan, RIM began in 1986 and had a heavy emphasis on public and private cooperation and interaction. The RIM program invested tax dollars and private donations in the protection and enhancement of fish and wildlife resources. In line with Aldo Leopold's (1939) land-ethic perspective, the Minnesota DNR focused on the biotic aspects of land stewardship by providing financial incentives to Minnesota landowners to convert poor agricultural land to wildlife habitat. Through wildlife-associated recreation surveys, the Minnesota DNR determined that such recreation provided a billion-dollar-plus fish-and wildlife-based recreation industry in the state. Accordingly, the DNR improved fish and wildlife habitat on public land to provide more opportunities for fishing and wildlife-related recreation.

The four private land programs are managed by the Minnesota Board of Water and Soil Resources (BWSR) through local Soil and Water Conservation Districts (SWCD). The private land programs are Wetland Restoration, Riparian Land Retirement, Marginal Agricultural Land Retirement, and Sensitive Ground Water Areas. The Department of Natural Resources maintains five public land programs to improve existing state land or to acquire new outdoor recreation areas. The public land programs are Wildlife Enhancement, Fisheries Enhancement, Critical Habitat Match, Prairie Bank, and Forest Wildlife Management.

The good news about the Reinvest-in-Minnesota program is that it was highly successful from 1986 to 1991. RIM produced $51.7 million in that five-year period to finance fish and wildlife conservation projects. Private citizens in Minnesota donated and pledged $2.2 million in cash and over $5.7 million in land to the RIM program.

The bad news about the RIM program is that funding for the Prairie Bank, Critical Habitat Match, Fish and Wildlife Enhancement, and RIM Reserve activities will be insufficient to meet program goals in 1992 and 1993 and will, therefore, come to a virtual end. Although there is a high level of interest in the private sector for the RIM program, there are insufficient funds to match private donations or to buy perpetual easements from willing sellers. Even though it may not be continued, the RIM program still represents a remarkable state wildlife policy success story. The program has protected and restored wetlands, cleaned water, saved rare species, improved fishing, provided more wildlife, enhanced natural flood control, protected highly erodible soil, enhanced tourism, fostered local involvement, and stimulated an extensive network of public-private partnerships.

Each of the aforementioned strategies in some way highlights the need for continued movement toward an integration of human dimensions and ecological considerations into wildlife policy.

Management Implications

Although natural resource managers may be trained to be biologists, foresters, geologists, or similar professionals, the policies that they are responsible for developing deal with the control of human actions with regard to the use of natural resources. This means that the scientists who are responsible for the management of fish and wildlife resources and their habitats need to acquire public policy analysis and management skills beyond their specializations in order to adequately address the human dimension of policy issues. In order to accomplish this formidable feat, fish and wildlife managers will need to be able to communicate effectively. They will have to develop the skills that will permit them to be "convincing, knowledgeable, a careful listener, a good writer, and an easing public figure" (Anderson 1985:234). That fact is substantiated repeatedly in each of the chapters that follow in this book.

From a social science perspective, it also means that fish and wildlife agencies will need to collect more data about demographic changes and then assess the data to determine their implications for management purposes. Much of the data collection will have to be on a localized basis (for example, local user surveys to determine needs and interests not being served by current practices), while other attributes may be determined from national surveys. Such social science information is important for fish and wildlife managers for several reasons:

1. *Self-interest* (that is, to generate the political support necessary to further fish and wildlife programs)
2. *Equity* (that is, to serve changing and diverse populations most effectively in the most ethical manner while taking into consideration the needs of animals)

3. *Efficiency* (that is, to provide better information for the allocation of scarce resources)
4. *Minimization of conflict.*

Conclusion

Changing demographic patterns across the United States are placing new and different demands on wildlife managers. Wildlife managers need to monitor social change in order to anticipate demands for services and to be more responsive to their constituents. National and regional participation surveys like the ones identified in chapter 8 serve as valuable tools to assist managers in integrating human and ecological dimensions into wildlife policy. Monitoring changes in societal patterns also helps managers anticipate future demands for services as well as ecological threats to wildlife as is noted in chapter 11, the concluding chapter that deals with futures issues in wildlife policy.

Wildlife policy has changed from a distributive emphasis of providing goods and services to a more regulatory emphasis as wildlife habitat has diminished and animal populations have declined. Greater concern for nonconsumptive wildlife-associated recreation has created pressures for a redistribution of resources away from consumptive uses as is noted in chapter 6 on funding wildlife activities and, again, in chapter 8 with regard to nonconsumptive wildlife-related recreation. A variety of demographic, ecological, and fiscal pressures also have emphasized the need for local governments to assume a more active role in wildlife management.

This introductory chapter has provided a description of the nature and evolution of fish and wildlife policy in the United States. It also established the policy framework for the rest of the book by identifying many key laws and policies whose impacts are dealt with in greater detail in later chapters, with an emphasis on the human dimension. The chapter began with a description of the wildlife policy process and how it has evolved over the past one hundred years in the United States. Theodore Lowi's (1964) typology of public policy was then employed to categorize various phases in the evolution of wildlife policy. The subsequent chapters in this book describe various wildlife policy issues and how the profession of wildlife management is evolving to address those issues. Students of public policy should be interested in determining how these issues correspond to the various stages of Lowi's policy typology.

Acknowledgments

I want to gratefully acknowledge the extensive comments and valuable observations that I received from Lynn Greenwalt, Barbara Knuth, Lynn Llewellyn, Robert Bartlett, and Jean Mangun throughout earlier drafts of this chapter.

Note

1. According to Dubnick and Romzek (1991:202), *distributive policies* are actions that deal with the processing of claims or entitlements for some specific segment of society; *regulatory policies* are actions that involve selecting winners and losers in the allocation of some social good or highly valued scarce resource; and *redistributive policies* are actions that involve expropriating some highly valued resource from one group and appropriating it to another.

References

Anderson, Stanley H. 1985. *Managing Our Wildlife*. Columbus, Ohio: Charles E. Merrill.

Applegate, James R., and J. R. Trout. 1984. "Factors Related to Revenue Yield in State Tax Checkoffs." *Transactions of the Forty-ninth Annual North American Wildlife and Natural Resources Conference* 49:199–204.

Barton, Katherine. 1987. "Federal Wetlands Protection Programs." Pp. 179–198 in Roger L. Di Silvestro, ed., *Audubon Wildlife Report 1987*. New York: Academic Press.

Bean, Michael J. 1983. *The Evolution of National Wildlife Law*. 2d ed. New York: Praeger Publishers.

Caldwell, Lynton K. 1988. *Perspectives on Ecosystem Management for the Great Lakes: A Reader.* Albany: State University of New York Press.

Christie, W. J., M. Becker, J. W. Cowden, and J. R. Vallentyne. 1986. "Managing the Great Lakes Basin as a Home." *Journal of Great Lakes Research* 12(1):2–17.

Clarke, Jean N., and Daniel McCool. 1985. *Staking Out the Terrain: Power Differentials among Natural Resource Management Agencies.* Albany: State University of New York Press.

Coggins, George C., and Charles F. Wilkinson. 1987. *Federal Public Land and Resources Law.* 2d ed. Mineola, N.Y.: Foundation Press.

Cohen, Wendy L., Andrew W. Hug, Abeba Taddese, and Kenneth A. Cook. 1991. "FACTA 1990: Conservation and Environmental Highlights." *Journal of Soil and Water Conservation* 46(1):20–22.

Cohn, Jeffrey P. 1991. "Ferrets Return from Near-Extinction." *Bioscience* 41(3):132–135.

Dorney, Robert S. 1986. "Bringing Wildlife Back to Cities." *Technology Review* 89(7):48–54.

Dubnick, Melvin J., and Barbara S. Romzek. 1991. *American Public Administration: Politics and the Management of Expectations.* New York: Macmillan.

Gottschalk, John S. 1978. "The State-Federal Partnership in Wildlife Conservation." Pp. 290–301 in H. P. Brokaw, ed., *Wildlife and America.* Washington, D.C.: U.S. Council on Environmental Quality.

Harpman, D. A. 1984. An Economic Analysis of the Nongame Checkoff. Master's thesis, Department of Agricultural and Natural Resource Economics, Colorado State University, Ft. Collins.

Kellert, Steve R. 1979. *Public Attitudes Toward Critical Wildlife and Natural Habitat Issues—Phase I Report.* Washington, D.C.: U.S. Fish and Wildlife Service.

————. 1980. *Activities of the American Public Relating to Animals—Phase II Report.* Washington, D.C.: U.S. Fish and Wildlife Service.

Klay, William Earle and James D. McElveen. 1991. "Planning as a Vehicle for Policy Formulation and Accommodation in an Evolving Subgovernment." *Policy Studies Journal* 19(3–4):527–533.

Knuth, Barbara A., and Larry A. Nielsen. 1991. "People, Patches, and Politics: Considering the Human Dimension in Landscape Management." Pp. 83–96 in Daniel J. Decker, Marianne E. Krasny, Gary R. Goff, Charles R. Smith, and David W. Gross, eds., *Challenges in the Conservation of Biological Resources: A Practitioner's Guide.* Boulder, Colo.: Westview Press.

Leopold, Aldo. 1939. "A Biotic View of Land." *Journal of Forestry* 37(9):727–730.

Loomis, John B., and William R. Mangun. 1987. "Evaluating Tax Policy

Proposals for Funding Nongame Wildlife Programs." *Evaluation Review* 11(6):715–738.

Lowi, Theodore J. 1964. "American Business, Public Policy, Case Studies and Political Theory." *World Politics* 16(4):677–715.

Magill, A. 1988. "Natural Resource Professionals: The Reluctant Public Servants." *The Environmental Professional* 10:295–303.

Mangun, William R. 1986. "Fiscal Constraints to Nongame Management Programs." In J. B. Hale, L. B. Best, and R. L. Clawson, eds., *Management of Nongame Wildlife in the Midwest: A Developing Art*. Chelsea, Mich.: Northcentral Section, The Wildlife Society.

———. 1988. "Environmental Impact Assessment as a Tool for Wildlife Policy Management." Pp. 51–62 in Robert V. Bartlett, ed., *Policy Through Impact Assessment: Institutionalized Analysis as a Policy Strategy*. Westport, Conn.: Greenwood Press.

Mangun, William R., and Jean C. Mangun. 1991. "Intergovernmental Dimensions of Wildlife Policy." *Policy Studies Journal* 19(3–4):519–526.

McElveen, James D. 1985. "Florida's Comprehensive Planning System." *Transactions of the Fiftieth North American Wildlife and Natural Resources Conference* 50:279–288.

Minnesota Department of Natural Resources. 1991. *Reinvest in Minnesota: Annual Report*. St. Paul, Minn.

More, Thomas A. 1979. *The Demand for Nonconsumptive Wildlife Uses: A Review of the Literature*. General Technical Report NE–52. Broomall, Pa.: North East Forest Experiment Station, U.S. Forest Service.

National Research Council. Commission on Life Sciences. Committee on the Applications of Ecological Theory to Environmental Problems. 1986. *Ecological Knowledge and Environmental Problem-Solving: Concepts and Case Studies*. Washington, D.C.: National Academy Press.

Nielsen, Larry A., Barbara A. Knuth, and Ronald R. Helinski. 1989. "Thinking Together: Uniting the Human-Dimension Responsibilities of Universities and Agencies." *Transactions of the Fifty-fourth North American Wildlife and Natural Resources Conference* 54:426–431.

Peek, James M. 1986. *A Review of Wildlife Management*. Englewood Cliffs, N.J.: Prentice-Hall.

Robinson, Bert. 1991. "'Wetlands,' a Fighting Word to Many Who See U.S. Blocking Development." *The Philadelphia Inquirer*, 23 July, pp. 1A, 13A.

Royal Society of Canada and the National Research Council of the United States. 1985. *The Great Lakes Water Quality Agreement: An Evolving Instrument for Ecosystem Management*. Washington, D.C.: National Academy Press.

Schneider, Keith. 1991. "Administration Proposes Opening Vast Protected Areas to Builders." *The New York Times*, 3 August, pp. 1, 25.

Schreyer, Richard, Richard S. Krannich, and Donald T. Cundy. 1989. "Public Support for Wildlife Resources and Programs in Utah." *Wildlife Society Bulletin* 17:532–538.

Shaw, William W., and William R. Mangun. 1985. *Nonconsumptive Use of Wildlife in the United States.* U.S. Fish and Wildlife Service Resource Publication 154, Washington, D.C.

Shaw, William W., William R. Mangun, and James R. Lyons. 1985. "Residential Enjoyment of Wildlife by Americans." *Leisure Sciences* 7(3):361–375.

Thompson, Bruce C. 1987. "Attributes and Implementation of Nongame and Endangered Species Programs in the United States." *Wildlife Society Bulletin* 15:210–216.

Tober, James A. 1989. *Wildlife and the Public Interest: Nonprofit Organizations and Federal Wildlife Policy.* Westport, Conn.: Praeger Publishers.

Tobin, Richard J. 1990. *The Expendable Future: U.S. Politics and the Protection of Biological Diversity.* Durham, N.C.: Duke University Press.

United States Code of Federal Regulations. 1983. Title 43, Part 24, "Department of the Interior Fish and Wildlife Policy; State-Federal Relationships." Washington, D.C.: U.S. Government Printing Office.

U.S. Department of the Interior (USDI FWS). Fish and Wildlife Service. 1978. *Predator Damage in the West: A Study of Coyote Management Alternatives.* Washington, D.C.: U.S. Government Printing Office.

———. 1982. *1980 National Survey of Fishing, Hunting, and Wildlife-Associated Recreation.* Washington, D.C.: U.S. Government Printing Office.

———. 1988. *1985 National Survey of Fishing, Hunting, and Wildlife-Associated Recreation.* Washington, D.C.: U.S. Government Printing Office.

———. 1991. *Wetlands Stewardship: Highlights of the Department of the Interior's 1990 Wetlands Activities.* Washington, D.C.: U.S. Government Printing Office.

U.S. Department of the Interior and Environment Canada. 1986. *North American Waterfowl Management Plan.* Washington, D.C.: U.S. Fish and Wildlife Service.

U.S. Fish and Wildlife Service (FWS). 1980. *Service Management Plan.* Washington, D.C.: U.S. Government Printing Office.

———. 1989. Federal Laws and Treaties of Interest to the U.S. Fish and Wildlife Service. Washington, D.C. Mimeo.

———. 1991(a). *Fish and Wildlife '90: A Report to the Nation.* Washington, D.C.: U.S. Government Printing Office.

———. 1991(b). "U.S. Prairie Pothole Joint Venture." Washington, D.C.: U.S. Government Printing Office.

Venno, Sharri A. 1991. *Integrating Wildlife Habitat into Local Planning: A Handbook for Maine Communities.* Miscellaneous Publication 712. Orono, Maine: Maine Agricultural Experiment Station, University of Maine.

Vermont Fish and Wildlife Department. 1990. *How to Include Fish and Wildlife*

Resources in Town and Regional Planning. Waterbury, Vt.: Vermont Fish and Wildlife Department.

Weisskopf, Michael. 1990. "EPA Chief Blocks Dam's Approval." *Washington Post*, 25 March, p. A4.

Wilds, Leah J., and Berton L. Lamb. 1985. "Conflict Resolution and Negotiation in the Licensing Process." Pp. 444–449 in F. W. Olson, R. G. White, and R. H. Hamre, eds., *Proceedings of the Symposium on Small Hydropower and Fisheries*. Bethesda, Md.: American Fisheries Society.

2

Toward a Comprehensive Paradigm of Wildlife Management: Integrating the Human and Biological Dimensions

Daniel J. Decker
Tommy L. Brown • Nancy A. Connelly
Jody W. Enck • Gerri A. Pomerantz
Ken G. Purdy • William F. Siemer

Introduction

The practice of wildlife management has experienced many changes over the last fifty years. The literature provides a chronicle of the changes that the profession has embraced in some cases and endured in others. Reflecting on the history of wildlife management in North America, one cannot help but be struck by the persistence of some concepts, philosophies, and biological principles (for example, carrying capacity, wise use, ecological succession, competition, habitat) that have generally become the conventions of wildlife management. Many of the basic precepts of wildlife management today were first presented by Leopold (1933) in *Game Management*.

Although the conventions of wildlife management have served the management profession well over most of its brief history, some have become increasingly inadequate to deal with contemporary problems and challenges. The primary shortcoming has been the exclusivity regarding the weight given biological dimensions in management decisions. The professional literature indicates that human dimensions have emerged over the past twenty years as pervasive and often primary considerations, yet this is seldom reflected in published conceptions of the management process. The integration of the human dimensions into wildlife management has been hampered by several factors (Decker et al. 1987). We believe the major impediment has been the lack of a generally accepted way of thinking about current practices that encompasses both human and biological dimensions. We believe that the profession needs to reexamine its traditional biologically dominated perspective in view of contemporary needs and situations.

Fortunately, a point has been reached in both the development of human dimensions knowledge and the evolution of management experience where the role of human and biological dimensions can be integrated in a comprehensive, conceptual paradigm for contemporary wildlife management. The paradigm we offer for consideration may be only a first approximation to that which will emerge as experience is gained in its application. Nevertheless, it is a step toward more responsive, adaptive management for the benefit of people and the wildlife resource.

In this chapter we will review conceptions of wildlife management by examining the definitions and models that have been espoused in textbooks. Using Nichols and Applegate (1987) as a base resource for identifying important wildlife literature, we selected the general wildlife management texts from their listing and added four more recent volumes for our review purposes. Besides being profoundly important in influencing philosophies and attitudes in the profession, textbooks may be the best source of insight into the contemporary definitions of a field at any point in time because they typically represent a synthesis of current thinking. We will follow the review with a discussion of an omnibus concept of natural resource management that serves as the foundation for the specific paradigm of wildlife management we propose.

What Is Wildlife Management?

Leopold (1933) established the foundation for the development of the field with his landmark book *Game Management*. The definitions and concepts he articulated prevailed, largely unaltered, for nearly a half century. Leopold's (1933:3) definition of "game" management was a simple and straightforward reflection of the time: "the art of making land produce sustained annual crops of wild game for recreational use." The use of three words—game, crops, and use—plainly indicate the utilitarian philosophy underlying the practice for about the next forty years. Leopold viewed game management as a production function of land. By explicating the biological and ecological understandings of the day in the context of producing wildlife, he put wildlife husbandry on a level similar to that of agriculture. That is, application of the relevant scientific knowledge in wildlife management was akin to technological innovations in agriculture. His book was the cornerstone for what thereafter was referred to as the scientific basis of wildlife management; it also firmly established the "biological bias" (Decker et al. 1987) that persists to this day among many wildlife professionals.

Of course, Leopold's contribution was multifaceted. His compelling articulation of wildlife values and a land ethic stressing stewardship and harmony with nature are enduring and powerful aspects of the profession. The fact that no other significant text devoted to wildlife management was produced for forty-five years after Leopold's *Game Management* attests to the utility of that work and to the conservative nature of the field.

In 1941, the first edition of Gabrielson's book *Wildlife Conservation* was published; a second edition was published in 1959. Less a discourse on wildlife management than on conservation of natural resources generally and related policy up to that time, the book does not contain a straightforward definition of wildlife management. Nevertheless, Gabrielson's view can be gleaned from some of his statements:

> It recognizes the reality and operation of ecological communities and that man's activities often greatly disturb them; thence that it is often desirable from the human viewpoint to work with these communities

and attempt to modify or manage them in man's interest. (Gabrielson 1959:110)

In its present state, wildlife management is an effort to apply to urgent problems the ecological and biological data that are now available, always with the consciousness that existing tools, methods, and processes may have to be discarded as new and better information becomes available. (Gabrielson 1959:117)

Gabrielson (1959) devoted chapters to "Resident game," "Migratory birds," "Fur animals," "Nongame birds and mammals," and "Rare and vanishing species." Thus, the discussion of nongame and rare and endangered animals in wildlife texts began. This theme would be covered in more detail by other authors in subsequent texts.

Although management per se was not a topic of new textbooks until the late 1970s, the raw material for books on biology and ecology related to management was being produced by researchers at universities, U.S. Fish and Wildlife Service facilities, and state agencies. During the period from the early 1960s to the early 1970s, wildlife scientists made important contributions to the field by synthesizing the accumulation of relevant biological and ecological knowledge (for example, Dasmann 1964). It seemed to be a period of reaffirmation of the biological basis for management that Leopold had espoused, but with much greater empirical support due to the intervening thirty to forty years of research in wildlife science.

Dasmann (1964) described his text on wildlife biology as "an introduction to the principles of wildlife biology on which the art of wildlife management is based" (Dasmann 1964:iii). Dasmann strongly reinforced the notion that wildlife management was largely a biologically based endeavor, a practice of applying ecological concepts and principles to the purpose of producing or preserving viable populations of wildlife. He also emphasized a philosophy that was markedly broader than that in *Game Management* (see Dasmann 1964:10), reflecting the general movement of the profession to a more encompassing notion of management of animals other than game for purposes other than hunting and trapping.

The trend toward quantitative approaches was marked by another contribution in the early 1970s with the release of *Wildlife Ecology* (Moen 1973). This text helped the wildlife manager understand the quantifiable energetic relationships between the organisms being managed and their dynamic environment. The consideration of an animal as an energy budgeter responding to its environment to attain a long-term balance between energy intake and loss gave the manager a different window through which to study, quantify, and understand the animal-habitat relationships that had been observed for decades.

Thus, books published in the field between the early 1960s and the mid-1970s reinforced the view that wildlife biology and ecology were the bases for the practice of wildlife management and reflected the recognition of nonconsumptive uses and users as legitimate beneficiaries of management.

The hiatus in management-focused texts (as distinguished from the historical overviews [for example, Allen 1954 and Trefethen 1975] and supporting texts on wildlife biology/ecology) ended in 1978. Between 1978 and 1986, six texts and one collection of papers focusing on wildlife management were published: *Wildlife Management* (Giles 1978); *Wildlife Conservation: Principles and Practices* (Teague and Decker 1979); *Wildlife Ecology and Management* (Robinson and Bolen 1984); *Principles of Wildlife Management* (Bailey 1984); *Managing Our Wildlife Resources* (Anderson 1985); *Introduction to Wildlife Management* (Shaw 1985); and *A Review of Wildlife Management* (Peek 1986). Thus, the textbook literature expanded markedly in less than ten years. But how consistent were notions about wildlife management communicated through those texts? How was the profession or its practice defined?

Review of the texts produced during the "era of proliferation" (1978–1986) indicates that in recent times four views of wildlife management have existed. They have broadened from the founding purpose of producing game for hunting. At the risk of oversimplifying, we will attempt to summarize these views from the least to the most comprehensive:

1. Producing wildlife
2. Producing wildlife of recreational interest for recreational use
3. Manipulating wildlife to meet societal goals for the wildlife resource
4. Manipulating wildlife and people to meet societal goals for the wildlife resource

Ideas from the texts that contributed to the expanding comprehensiveness of the concept of wildlife management will be presented to illustrate the groundwork of others to predispose the
profession to adopt a broader concept. The ideas will not be discussed in chronological order of text publication date. Rather, the
period 1978 to 1986 is viewed as an era of significant maturation
during which wildlifers were attempting to redefine their profession and out of which a synthesis of their individual ideas may
provide the best indication of the status of their collective thinking.

Although the most recently published text we will consider,
Peek (1986) built the first span to bridge from Leopold's game
management to more contemporary management. "Thus, an up-
to-date definition resolves to this: wildlife management is the art of
making land produce wildlife. And we don't have to have a reason
for this because we have the obligation" (Peek 1986:3). Regarding
the notion of obligation, in Peek's view, "It should go without
saying that a wildlife biologist's primary obligation is to the resource
rather than to the agency or to the people who pay his or her
salary" (Peek 1986:4). Peek also stated: "Wildlife management has
elaborated itself extensively since the 1930s, yet the fundamental
practices of guiding populations and habitats plus effective interaction with the public are still the roots of the profession" (1986:23).
He later adds that "change in wildlife management is relatively
slow, perhaps best correlated with the degree of general understanding of the public of the important issues" (Peek 1986:24). He
went on to indicate that "one of the most chronic problems in
wildlife management is the lack of public support for many sound
programs. Perhaps one of the major reasons for this has been a
basic inability of professional biologists to articulate their stands
effectively." He presented information on public attitudes toward
wildlife but did not integrate such information into the process of
wildlife management. Thus, Peek pointed out the importance of the
public but did not include human dimensions within the purview of
management. Rather, he viewed the biologist as knowing what is
right for the resource and the problem as being the public's lack of
understanding or agreement.

Shaw (1985) and Anderson (1985) also emphasized the biological aspects in their renditions of wildlife management. Shaw expressed his view as follows: "Wildlife management is carried on through the application of biological principles toward maintaining, increasing, or reducing wildlife abundance according to specific management objectives" (1985:14). He also explained that "wildlife values, both economic and otherwise, are essential to justify wildlife management" (1985:14). He believed that one needed to understand the "whys" of management before delving into the "hows." People's values relative to wildlife were the prevailing "whys" as he identified them. Though devoting considerable text to values and attitudes, he presented a limited set of examples from the human dimensions literature and did not weave them into a single conceptual model of wildlife management.

Anderson (1985:3) stated, "Wildlife management is the art and science of manipulating populations and habitats for the animals' and for human benefit." He explained further that "wildlife management is, therefore, a complex procedure of inventorying and evaluating habitats and populations, determining people's goals, and superimposing those goals on the natural system" (1985:4). Anderson (1985:21) recognized that human dimensions were important but seemed to relegate such dimensions to the status of context rather than being a part of that which is managed. Thus, he did not integrate the biological and human dimensions.

In 1979 the Wildlife Society published *Wildlife Conservation: Principles and Practices* (Teague and Decker 1979), a collection of papers essentially analogous to chapters in a text that surveys the field of wildlife conservation, replacing the earlier publication *A Manual of Wildlife Conservation* (Teague 1971). The book was divided into two sections, (*a*) Wildlife and Man and (*b*) Wildlife Management, indicating a distinction between human considerations and the wildlife resource and wildlife management per se. The distinction was noted in a chapter titled "The Roles of Social Science in Wildlife Management," where Teague (1979:59) concluded that

> most wildlife management problems start out as biological problems but eventually become people problems. Despite much publicizing and bemoaning of this early recognized fact, we have continued to stockpile

scientific evidence for wildlife management, but failed to apply human ecology to the behavior of human organisms as they are related to wildlife work. . . . Because we are dealing with a social science problem, we should use concepts and procedures that have been developed in the social sciences. . . . These working tools of the social scientists are at hand but gathering dust in the wildlife management workshop.

In a subsequent chapter of the same book, Burger addressed "Principles of Wildlife Management." He defined wildlife management as "a blending of science and art, aimed at achieving sound human goals for wildlife resources by working with habitats, wildlife populations, and people" (Burger 1979:89). Burger briefly discussed biological principles and then referred to the "people factor." He noted,

Although wildlife management is aimed at achieving human goals, the human element largely was ignored until recent years. Early management efforts were directed almost entirely at game species. Yet even here there is little evidence that the hunter constituents were polled or queried as to their wishes; by and large, professional wildlifers and agencies set their own goals for game populations, with at least the implications of "we know best." (1979:95)

Burger concluded by restating a definition of wildlife management that reflected the biological emphasis but ended with a recognition that an "examination of the human element as it applies to management goals is both useful and overdue" (1979:97).

Thus, *Wildlife Conservation: Principles and Practices,* as an official publication of The Wildlife Society, broached the subject of human dimensions in a tentative and nonintegrative way. A paradigm encompassing the human and biological dimensions of wildlife management was not offered.

Robinson and Bolen (1984:2) defined wildlife management as "the application of ecological knowledge to populations of vertebrate animals and their plant and animal associates in a manner that strikes a balance between the needs of those populations and the needs of people." The definition is broad from the standpoint of what constitutes wildlife, but restricts management to the nonhuman dimension. The authors noted, "Wildlife management is changing, but its past remains relevant. The practice of wildlife management is rooted in the intermingling of human ethics, attitudes, and written laws" (1984:2). The authors also implied that the needs of society and animals other than game species should be taken into account and that the wildlife manager will be called upon to know not only what and how to manipulate a population or community of organisms but also why such manipulation is warranted.

Robinson and Bolen recognized the growth of interest in urban wildlife, nongame wildlife, and endangered species. They presented case studies where social and economic considerations were being melded with ecological dimensions. Nevertheless, in their own conception of management they maintained the exclusive biological emphasis by not integrating the human and biological dimensions. Thus, although providing the broadest discussion of human values for wildlife up to that time, Robinson and Bolen did not tie those elements together such that a new, more comprehensive model resulted.

Bailey defined wildlife management as "the art of making land produce valuable populations of wildlife" (1984:6). Bailey (1984:6) explained that the practice "involves direct population management (control of harvest, transplanting) and indirect management of populations through habitat manipulation to favor or inhibit target species." Bailey emphasized the biological aspects, but he acknowledged human dimensions. At one point he explained, "Most principles presented in this text are biological principles. Sociological principles . . . are not as well covered" (Bailey 1984:6).

Despite the narrow definition offered by Bailey, he discussed wildlife values as part of the context of wildlife management. Further, his concluding chapter, "The Art of Wildlife Management," repeatedly referenced human dimensions. He depicted wildlife management as a cyclic, incremental process having both biological and sociological elements of apparently similar importance. Bailey's paradigm (figure 2.1) had three categories of responses to management—wildlife population, habitat, and user satisfaction. He viewed management as part of a broader undertaking of wildlife conservation, which he defined as "a social process encompassing

Figure 2.1. Wildlife management as a cyclic, incremental process (taken from Bailey 1984).

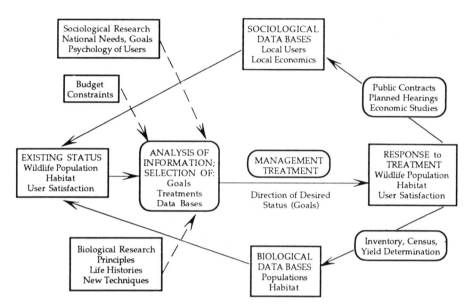

both lay and professional activities that define and seek to attain wise use of wildlife resources and maintain the productivities of wildlife habitat" (Bailey 1984:9). Bailey called attention to this broad notion of wildlife conservation to make the important point that "wildlife management is not practiced in a vacuum" (1984:20).

In summary, Bailey offered two significant contributions to the development of a broadened paradigm. First, he emphasized that contemporary management has a context more complex than the simple game and crop elements originally identified by Leopold. Second, he presented wildlife management as a cyclic, incremental process having biological and sociological dimensions; however, he did not elaborate the integration of those dimensions.

The first text produced during the "era of proliferation" was *Wildlife Management* (Giles 1978). It is discussed last because it presented the most comprehensive concept of the topic. Exciting from an integrative perspective, it was the first text to address management as a process or set of processes that attends to more than the biological aspects in a significant way. Other texts tended to consider human dimensions as part of the context of management (that is, goals of management rather than part of the process).

Giles (1978:5) described wildlife management as a decision science and defined it as "the science and art of making decisions and taking actions to manipulate the structure, dynamics, and relations of populations, habitats, and people to achieve specific human objectives by means of the wildlife resource" (1978:4). Giles portrayed wildlife populations, habitat, and people as a triad in which each element is equal and interactive. He encouraged a systems approach whereby activities that constitute management are viewed as interactive systems and wildlife management itself is seen as a system within society as a whole. Giles also reminded us that "animals exist, with or without humans; but the wildlife resource is a human construct" (1978:14).

Giles proposed that "Management of People" in their relationship to wildlife can be viewed as a subsystem, bringing the human dimension front and center as a primary consideration in a comprehensive approach. Giles acknowledged the biological emphasis of traditional wildlife management but attempted to move the profession toward a more comprehensive paradigm. He noted, "In the past, wildlife managers have been poorly educated (if at all) to deal with the human dimensions of the developing science of wildlife management. They have been disinclined, for many reasons, to work with the human subsystem. Many still harbor the false notion that little factual information is known about people-management processes" (Giles 1978:211). He went on to advise, "Wildlife management, when done well, is a sensitive balancing of populations, habitats, and people. These three elements must coexist in the minds of managers and those involved in the management agency. In all cases, if this triad is out of balance, the user will be poorly served, or even hurt" (1978:211–212). Giles gave several examples of strategies and tactics that could be employed to manage people.

Thus, *Wildlife Management* represented an important step in broadening the thinking of existing and aspiring wildlife managers to include the human dimensions in their conceptual framework. It was an attempt to help managers consider how the growing body of research on the human dimensions could be incorporated into their practice.

So, What Is Wildlife Management?

So what, exactly, is wildlife management? Although several contemporary concepts exist, the perspectives offered by the authors whose works were included in the overview demonstrated two general points:

1. An evolution of sorts in thinking has occurred among wildlife professionals, but it has not been pervasive. Wildlife has come to mean more than game; management has broadened to meet the needs and desires of more than consumptive users; management needs are recognized outside the rural and wilderness environments; and management has come to reflect the breadth of values society holds for all wildlife, not just those species of immediate recreational, aesthetic, or economic value. Simultaneously, the values and attitudes that were assumed for traditional clientele, and espoused throughout the professional training and socialization of many aspiring wildlife managers, could not be assumed to apply for all elements of the new, expanded clientele. Thus, since 1980, the profession has been reexamining some of the fundamental precepts it has followed faithfully for decades.

2. The importance of human dimensions has become more generally recognized. Nevertheless, the traditional biological emphasis is strong and dominates the texts available on wildlife management. This probably reflects two related factors: (a) textbook authors are products of primarily biological training themselves and generally may not be well prepared academically to deal with the human dimensions concepts that pertain, even if their importance is recognized, and (b) research, experience, and conceptualization of human dimensions have only recently developed to the point where useful generalizations and theoretical frameworks can be offered. A dilemma facing the profession, however, is the resistance of some biologists to the notion that wildlife management is more than the artful application of biological and ecological principles. These are essential elements today as they always have been, but do not provide a sufficient basis for contemporary wildlife management.

The discussion thus far has attempted to illuminate the factors and conditions leading up to and, we believe, justifying the need for a more comprehensive paradigm of wildlife management. We have purposefully sidestepped a discussion of the major social and policy issues influencing wildlife conservation and management during the past fifty-plus years. We have used the examination of texts as indices to those issues as they have affected management thinking. Some texts reflected the changes more accurately than others, but overall it is clear that substantial, if not pervasive, adaptation of the profession has occurred, presumably as a response to larger social issues.

Toward a Comprehensive Paradigm of Wildlife Management

The review of textbooks demonstrated that Leopold's concept of game management was not seriously challenged for forty years and a single definition or conceptual framework to guide the practice was lacking during the last ten years. Regarding the latter point, some would argue that such diversity is healthy for the profession, but others might argue persuasively that it is debilitating and symptomatic of lack of discipline.

Perhaps a middle-ground perspective is that the lack of a single definition for the last ten years reflects the reality that the discipline has been in a relatively revolutionary period. The profession may temporarily be experiencing "growing pains" that are symptomatic of maturation through the adolescent stage of people, organizations, and professions (or disciplines). Perhaps the profession has not yet fully accepted the possibility that the infant fathered by Leopold has matured considerably, particularly over the last ten to twenty years. This is the outlook from which we wish to share a vision of the basic elements of wildlife management that we believe will serve the profession well for the near future, and we hope not to seem pretentious in so doing.

Despite our belief that the lack of conformity in definition of wildlife management is an artifact of a maturation process for the discipline and therefore is not inherently "bad," we nevertheless concur with the position of Krueger and coauthors (1986:50):

Resource managers could better guide the management process, especially when the public is directly involved, if they agree to similar concepts about how management should be approached. Such a conceptual model must be rational and logical in sequence and yet be sufficiently robust to accommodate initial errors in decisions. The model must be self-correcting and adaptive to social and biological changes over time, and thus encourage proactive as opposed to reactive management.

It is in this spirit that we have developed a paradigm that has ten primary elements (figure 2.2). We have built upon and adapted the general resource management model by Krueger and coauthors (1986) to create one that depicts the comprehensiveness of the wildlife management process as we have experienced it in New York. Although the paradigm differs from that of Giles (1978), we have adopted Giles's (1978:4) definition (cited previously herein) for contemporary wildlife management. Like Krueger and his coauthors (1986), we view management as a dynamic, goal-oriented process that functions within a management environment having cultural, economic, political, and ecological components.

The concept of a *management environment* draws together aspects of context that were identified in several texts discussed earlier. The cultural component includes the traditions, religions, values, and philosophies of the general public, specific constituencies, and resource managers. This component typically contributes most to the establishment of goals. Social values inherent in the cultural component provide the principal motivation for wildlife management. Management is conducted because the end products of the process are believed to have value to part or all of society.

The economic component includes all the processes of the marketplace as well as unpriced values that can influence decisions about wildlife management. The economic impact of management contributes to the societal perceptions of the value of management and thereby helps to define societal values.

The political component has two aspects: the laws of governance and the personal values of the individuals who enact, enforce, or interpret laws and policies. The first aspect is usually defined by the legislative statutes and administrative codes that give agencies the responsibility and authorization for management. The second

Figure 2.2. A comprehensive paradigm of wildlife management.

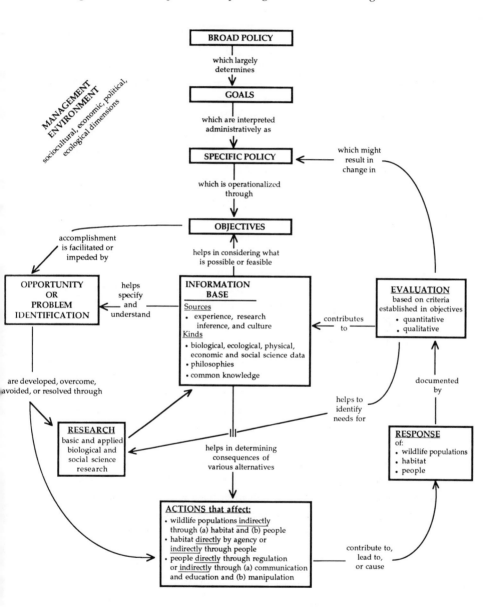

aspect is poorly defined because the biases of government officials are dynamic and undocumented.

The ecological component includes the ecosystem where wildlife populations of interest live, grow, reproduce, and die. Management programs that focus on particular species often alter the abiotic and other biotic parts of the ecosystem. The ecological component defines the upper boundaries of what management can expect to achieve in terms of resource production.

Wildlife managers must consider simultaneously the cultural, economic, political, and ecological components of the management environment. As Krueger and coauthors (1986:51) noted, "Historically, resource agencies have focused most attention on the ecological component; it is now apparent, however, that the other elements must be given greater attention. In some cases, resource management has been driven principally by components other than the ecology of the system being managed."

The ten primary elements of the process are interactive. The first three are hierarchical. *Broad policy* emerges from the management environment and reflects the equally broad values of society that result in the recognition of wildlife as a resource and establishes a relative priority for attention to be directed toward wildlife. Broad state and federal policy largely determines goals for management of the wildlife resource. *Goals* are broad statements of intent about the purpose of management, often stated as general conditions that should be attained for wildlife and people. Goals are then interpreted administratively within an agency as specific policies. *Specific policies* typically set institutional bounds on management (managers sometimes regard these as constraints because they often limit the scope and perceived effectiveness of their efforts) and serve as general operational guidelines for those responsible for achieving goals on behalf of society. Specific policy may, for example, delineate the animal species that will be considered for management attention.

Objectives are established within the bounds set by specific policy. Objectives provide a measurable definition of the goal that is expected within a particular time frame. *Opportunity or problem identification* determines the avenues available to facilitate objective achievement and overcome the barriers likely to impede such achievement. To develop opportunities fully or to overcome, avoid, or resolve problems usually requires a management action, but sometimes actions necessarily must be preceded by research. Basic and applied biological and sociological *research* builds the information base such that the opportunities and problems are better understood and actions can be better developed.

Actions immediately come to mind when people think of wildlife management; but as the paradigm illustrates, actions are only one element of management. The typology of actions presented include those that affect

1. wildlife populations indirectly through (*a*) manipulation of habitat and (*b*) people;
2. habitat directly by an agency and indirectly through citizens; and
3. people directly through regulation or indirectly through (*a*) communication and education (both formal and nonformal) and (*b*) manipulation (for example, economic, incentives, recognition, special opportunities or experiences).

Actions are undertaken to make something happen—a response. *Response* is an important major concept because it is the short-term outcome of actions. Responses of wildlife populations, habitats, and people are the foci of evaluation to assess the achievement of objectives. *Evaluation* measures the response of the management environment to the actions implemented in terms of the parameters stated in the objectives (in essence those parameters become the criteria against which success is measured) and provides intelligence for fine tuning or redirecting the process. The latter step is essential if goals and objectives are to be revised, new problems identified, and alternate actions implemented that better address the current situation. Evaluation is integral to the feedback link that allows management to be an adaptive, responsive process.

The nine primary elements discussed above are supported by and contribute to the *information base* that includes published and unpublished data, collective experience, and theory from biology, ecology, sociology, psychology, economics, political science, administrative science, communications science, and humanities. The information base has two characteristics: source and kind. Sources include but are not necessarily limited to experience (and intuition), research (including evaluation), inference through theory and modeling/simulation, and culture. Kinds of information include biological, ecological, economic, and social science data; common knowledge; and prevailing philosophies.

The dynamic complexity of contemporary wildlife management is apparent from the model. Equally apparent is the difficulty of operationalizing the model in state or federal agencies. Applying the paradigm effectively will take some significant changes in how agencies are staffed. For example, Krueger and coauthors (1986) presented the idea that because of the complexity of management of a natural resource, a team representing several disciplines is required. A team approach has merit because of the number of disciplines that are helpful when addressing many management problems and the depth of knowledge in any one discipline needed to overcome the problems frequently encountered. The authors also call our attention to a significant reality (1986:51): "Operating within the management environment described is the resource manager, who is traditionally trained in applied ecology. These individuals often find themselves forced to function within cultural, economic, and political arenas as opposed to the biological foci of their education." They later added, when referring to management on a regional, state, or multistate scale, "it is unlikely that one person could conduct successful management, or that universities could purport to prepare a single person to do so. At this scale, the concept of the 'manager' should instead be changed to that of a 'management team' that is comprised of several individuals who represent disciplines such as ecology, sociology, economics, administration, political science, educational communication, law enforcement, and management science" (Krueger et al. 1986:51). The low probability of a team approach being widely accepted in the near future notwithstanding, the approach emphasizes the integration of biological/ecological and human dimensions.

The case of black bear management in the Catskill region of New York (see Decker et al. 1985; Decker and O'Pezio 1989) may help to illustrate the model. Black bear management by the New York State

Department of Environmental Conservation (DEC) between 1970 and 1988 reflects the use of a comprehensive, integrated approach (similar to the cycle depicted in figure 2.2), even though the elements of such an approach had not been articulated beforehand by management policymakers.

The *broad policy* for all wildlife in New York, as stated in the environmental conservation law, indicates that managers should maintain wildlife populations consistent with biological carrying capacity and human land use. From this broad policy, the *goal* for black bear management in the Catskill region was developed: to optimize sustained recreational use of bears from populations that are compatible with man and the habitat. Based on DEC's *evaluation* of the situation in 1976, a *specific policy* was established to increase the bear population. This policy was operationalized as an objective to increase the black bear population between 60 and 80 percent during the subsequent two-year period.

However, a *problem was identified* as a potential impediment to meeting the objective. Previous research found that hunting was the major cause of mortality. Given the *information* that hunting was limiting the bear population, DEC proposed a two-year moratorium on bear hunting in the Catskills as a management *action*. During this time, baseline sociological and ecological *research* was conducted. Sociological research indicated that the pre-moratorium bear population was well within the wildlife acceptance capacity (Decker et al. 1981; Decker and Purdy 1988) of area residents. The ecological study identified areas where bears could potentially expand into new range.

In *response* to the two-year hunting moratorium the bear population increased by 80 percent, thus meeting the management objective. Managers' *evaluation* of the bears' physical condition suggested that the population increase had not exceeded biological carrying capacity. After the population had stabilized at this higher level, further evaluation was planned to determine whether the larger population remained within the wildlife acceptance capacity of area residents.

In the management cycle that followed, specific objectives were revised to reflect additions and modifications to the information base, such as the results of the second sociological study (Decker et al. 1985). Since 1970, at least three cycles of bear management have occurred that parallel the flow depicted in figure 2.2 (Decker and O'Pezio 1989).

Conclusion

The model presented herein represents our best effort to depict a comprehensive paradigm of contemporary wildlife management. It is robust in its inclusion of: (1) a wide range of values for the wildlife resource; (2) a full spectrum of information considerations; and (3) recognition that targets of management action include wildlife populations, habitats, and people (individuals, groups, organizations, and institutions). The model illustrates the need for feedback and feedback mechanisms that make management a dynamic, adaptive, responsive, and pro-active process. The model also integrates the biological and human dimensions into a complementary process that more realistically portrays the interaction of these dimensions in day-to-day practice. Thus, we hope the paradigm suggested will either prove to be a more useful conceptual framework for wildlife management than the available alternatives or stimulate someone to improve it or offer a better alternative.

Acknowledgments

We thank Ray Oglesby of Cornell University for his critical manuscript review and Margie Peech and Renée Shiffler for their assistance in manuscript preparation. This chapter is a contribution of New York Federal Aid to Wildlife Restoration Project W–146–R.

References

Allen, Durward L. 1954. *Our Wildlife Legacy*. New York: Funk & Wagnalls.
Anderson, Stanley H. 1985. *Managing Our Wildlife*. Columbus, Ohio: Charles E. Merrill.

Bailey, James A. 1984. *Principles of Wildlife Management.* New York: John Wiley & Sons.

Burger, George V. 1979. "Principles of Wildlife Management." Pp. 89–97 in Richard D. Teague and Eugene Decker, eds., *Wildlife Conservation: Principles and Practices.* Washington, D.C.: The Wildlife Society.

Dasmann, Raymond F. 1964. *Wildlife Biology.* New York: John Wiley & Sons.

Decker, Daniel J., Tommy L. Brown, Deborah L. Hustin, Stephen H. Clarke, and John O'Pezio. 1981. "Public Attitudes Toward Black Bears in the Catskills." *New York Fish and Game Journal* 28(1):1–20.

Decker, Daniel J., Tommy L. Brown, and George F. Mattfeld. 1987. "Integrating Social Science into Wildlife Management: Barriers and Limitations." Pp. 83–92 in Marc L. Miller, Richard P. Gale, and Perry J. Brown, eds., *Social Science in Natural Resource Management Systems.* Boulder, Colo.: Westview Press.

Decker, Daniel J., and John O'Pezio. 1989. "Consideration of Bear-People Conflicts in Black Bear Management for the Catskill Region of New York: Application of a Comprehensive Management Model." Pp. 181–187 in Marianne Bromley, ed., *Bear-People Conflicts. Proceedings of a Symposium on Management Strategies.* Yellowknife, Northwest Territories, Canada: Northwest Territories Department of Renewable Resources.

Decker, Daniel J., and Ken G. Purdy. 1988. "Toward a Concept of Wildlife Acceptance Capacity in Wildlife Management." *Wildlife Society Bulletin* 16:53–57.

Decker, Daniel J., Robert A. Smolka, Jr., John O'Pezio, and Tommy L. Brown. 1985. "Social Determinants of Black Bear Management for the Northern Catskill Mountains." Pp. 239–247 in Samuel L. Beasom and Sheila F. Roberson, eds., *Game Harvest Management.* Kingsville, Tex.: Caesar Kleberg Wildlife Institute.

Gabrielson, Ira N. 1959. *Wildlife Conservation.* New York: Macmillan.

Giles, Robert H., Jr. 1978. *Wildlife Management.* San Francisco: W. H. Freeman.

Krueger, Charles C., Daniel J. Decker, and Thomas A. Gavin. 1986. "A Concept of Natural Resource Management: An Application to Unicorns." *Transactions of the Northeast Section—The Wildlife Society* 43:50–56.

Leopold, Aldo. 1933. *Game Management.* Madison: University of Wisconsin Press.

Moen, Aaron N. 1973. *Wildlife Ecology: An Analytical Approach.* San Francisco: W. H. Freeman.

Nichols, Ted C., and James E. Applegate. 1987. "The Essential Volumes of a Wildlife Professional's Library." *Wildlife Society Bulletin* 15(4):584–591.

Peek, James M. 1986. *A Review of Wildlife Management.* Englewood Cliffs, N.J.: Prentice-Hall.

Robinson, William L., and Eric G. Bolen. 1984. *Wildlife Ecology and Management.* New York: Macmillan.

Shaw, James H. 1985. *Introduction to Wildlife Management.* New York: McGraw-Hill.

Teague, Richard D., ed. 1971. *A Manual of Wildlife Conservation.* Washington, D.C.: The Wildlife Society.

Teague, Richard D., and Eugene Decker, eds. 1979. *Wildlife Conservation: Principles and Practices.* Washington, D.C.: The Wildlife Society.

Trefethen, James B. 1975. *An American Crusade for Wildlife.* New York: Winchester Press.

PART 2
CONFLICT AND INNOVATION
IN WILDLIFE POLICY

3

INTERAGENCY
CONFLICT AND COORDINATION
IN WILDLIFE MANAGEMENT

Ann H. Harvey

Under the system of wildlife management that has evolved in the United States, individual wildlife populations often come under the simultaneous jurisdiction of several agencies. This results from both the nature of the wildlife resource—animals are mobile and do not recognize jurisdictional boundaries—and the legal and administrative arrangements under which wildlife is managed. A complex assortment of laws, treaties, compacts, and cooperative agreements apportions responsibility for wildlife and habitat among numerous federal and state agencies. Although the states have traditionally been the primary regulators of wildlife, the federal role in wildlife regulation has steadily expanded since the passage of the Lacey Act in 1900 (Bean 1983; Coggins and Ward 1981). Federal agencies are also responsible for managing wildlife habitat in the national parks, national forests, and other federal public lands.

Whenever authority over wildlife or its habitat is shared, a layer of institutional and political complexity is added to the already difficult biological tasks of wildlife management. Agencies are often unable to accomplish their objectives for a wildlife population without the cooperation of those agencies that share authority. Effective wildlife management demands that the agencies possess not only technical knowledge and expertise but also the ability to work productively with other agencies.

Although many laws and agency policies recognize the need for interagency coordination and cooperation, they have often been secondary concerns of managers preoccupied with their own missions and goals (Keiter 1989). But as wildlife habitat is fragmented and populations decrease in size, the need for cooperative management is becoming more apparent. Land under the control of one agency often does not encompass the complete seasonal ranges of wide-ranging or migratory wildlife. Wildlife reserves are often too small to provide sufficient habitat to support viable populations over the long term. As populations decline, they become increasingly vulnerable to genetic, demographic, and environmental perturbations that can drive them toward extinction (Gilpin and Soulé 1986). Ensuring the survival of wildlife populations under conditions of ecological and political fragmentation demands a coordinated effort by numerous agencies and individuals (Salwasser et al. 1987).

Even when agencies attempt to work cooperatively, a variety of obstacles can impede their efforts. In many cases, interagency conflicts among wildlife agencies stem not from disagreements over the technical and biological aspects of wildlife management but rather from organizational factors that may have little to do with wildlife issues. Competition for authority, legitimacy, or resources, incompatible goals, conflicting values, inflexible organizational structures, and external pressures on the agencies all can contribute to interagency conflict.

This chapter examines several interrelated variables that are important sources of conflict in interagency settings: agency values and cultures; organizational structures; formal and informal goals; and external forces such as client and constituent groups, legislators, and commissions. A case study involving joint management of a wildlife population by one state and two federal agencies is used to illustrate the influence those factors can have on cooperative efforts. The chapter concludes with an overview of proposals to improve interagency cooperation in wildlife conservation.

Factors Affecting Interagency Cooperation

Agency Values and Cultures

Over the course of their history, agencies develop distinctive values that may be fundamentally different from those of other agencies managing the same resources. Values are not merely preferences but are normative standards for making morally, rationally, or aesthetically proper choices (Twight 1983). Analyzing an agency's values can be difficult since core values are not always expressed in policy statements, values change over time as an agency evolves, and all persons within an agency do not share the same degree of commitment to its prevalent values. Even though underlying values are not always stated explicitly in agency policies, their influence is extensive (Henning and Mangun 1989). Strongly held values can act as an ideological filter, preventing an agency from perceiving and responding to forces in its environment (Twight 1983). An agency can, through a system of selection, appraisal, and incentives, ensure that most of its employees share the agency's predominant value orientation. Over time most agency employees come to "internalize" the values of the organization and to accept them as their own (Simon 1976). The values, beliefs, and interpretations shared by the organization's members make up a distinctive agency culture, which helps to create an organizational identity. Agency cultures and values are such a pervasive part of organizational life that they may become invisible to the members of the organization.

Agencies' values, beliefs, and traditions play a large role in determining their attitudes toward other agencies. When the value orientations of two agencies differ, the agencies are likely to view a problem differently and may discount public demands that contradict their preferred response. Once an organization has developed a particular value orientation and ideology, it may become very resistant to new facts or theories that challenge its doctrines (Clark and Westrum 1987).

Values and tradition become especially important when agencies are faced with scientific uncertainty, as they very often are in wildlife cases (Coggins and Ward 1981; Romesburg 1981). When scientific information is lacking (and often even when it is available), managers rely on tradition and values for guidance in making decisions. Resolving value-based disagreements can be a daunting task for agencies attempting to coordinate their management efforts.

Organizational Structures

Governmental wildlife and habitat management agencies in the United States are, for the most part, organized as standard hierarchical bureaucracies, with subdivisions along geographical and functional lines. That organizational structure is designed to provide efficiency, reliability, and predictability by assigning tasks to specific units of the organization, concentrating power and authority at the top, and governing behavior by formal rules. In large, complex, and geographically dispersed agencies, the extensive formal structures serve as a mechanism for controlling and coordinating all parts of the organization. Kaufman (1967) examined this aspect of the U.S. Forest Service, finding an elaborate system of "preformed decisions" that were very effective in producing relative uniformity of behavior among geographically scattered subunits of the agency.

That mechanistic type of organizational structure is well suited to carry out the routine daily activities of the agencies. But for a variety of reasons it can hinder effective organizational responses to new and complex problems that may arise in the wildlife arena (Clark et al. 1989). First, organizational structure is an important determinant of how an organization collects information and thus how it perceives its environment. Subunits within the organization selectively screen out information, and their ability to pass relevant data to decision-making centers depends on communication channels and lines of authority within the organization (Pfeffer and

Salancik 1978). Second, organizational structure is a key element in determining how decision making is carried out and thus how the organization responds to perceived problems (Clark et al. 1989). Large mechanistic agencies rely heavily on standard operating procedures and rules for dealing with problems, and they are usually reluctant to depart from them, even when confronted with a nonroutine problem. Instead of trying to anticipate changes and searching for new and creative solutions, an agency may try to use its existing system of categorized decision making, whether or not it is suited to the task at hand. When several agencies are involved, their relative sensitivity to a problem is likely to vary, depending on their screening mechanisms, the efficiency of their communication channels, and their value orientations. Decision makers who are unaware of a problem because of these factors may be unwilling to cooperate with other agencies who do perceive a problem.

A commitment to existing organizational structures and operating procedures can also be a hindrance to interagency cooperation. An agency may see another agency's actions as a threat to its own established programs and procedures, and rather than cooperating, it may attempt to eliminate the competing organization from its domain (Clark and Westrum 1987).

Goals

An obvious potential source of conflict between agencies is the set of goals, both formal and informal, under which each agency operates. If two agencies' mandates or other formal goals are incompatible, cooperation will naturally be difficult. But even if agencies' formal goals for a shared program are not directly contradictory, implementation conflicts may arise. First, the goals of public agencies are often stated in general terms, providing managers with little concrete direction (Warwick 1975). Second, many public agencies have multiple goals, some of which may be internally contradictory (Yaffee 1982). Third, the link between the stated ends of an organization and the means to accomplish them may be obscure. Interagency conflicts may arise from incompatible interpretations of vague mandates, commitment by the agencies to some goals at the expense of others, or disagreements among the agencies about the correct way to reach shared goals.

A less obvious but equally important source of interagency conflict is each agency's unwritten "organizational maintenance" goals (Simon 1976). They include goals such as ensuring organizational stability and predictability, defending agency domains, avoiding conflict, and keeping controllers and constituent groups satisfied. These unofficial rules and goals evolve within organizations as a means of ensuring their own institutional survival and protecting their autonomy and discretion. Members of an organization often become committed to the goals of organizational survival, sometimes more so than to the organization's substantive objectives.

Commitment to the goal of maintaining managerial discretion and autonomy is often an obstacle to cooperation among land management agencies (see Sax and Keiter 1987). Any perceived encroachment on authority, autonomy, or turf by another agency is likely to be strongly resisted. When agencies are focused on "power" goals as opposed to "task" goals, the task goals may be compromised (Clark and Harvey 1991).

External Influences

Every public agency is subject to a variety of pressures and constraints imposed upon it by outside actors. They include lawmakers and other "controllers" with authority over the agency, as well as groups who receive benefits or services from the agency (clients) or who take an interest in the agency's activities even though they have no economic ties to it (constituents). The interactions among agencies, their client and constituent groups, and lawmakers or other controllers are important influences on an agency's ability and willingness to cooperate with other agencies.

The degree of influence that controllers or interest groups have over an agency depends on both the characteristics of the agency and the characteristics of the outside force. Some agencies are very susceptible to outside pressure, while others are not. An agency with an independent source of funding (from license fees or user fees) is likely to be less sensitive to pressures from legislators than one operating on legislatively appropriated general funds (Wamsley and Zald 1976). In addition, an agency may be shielded from legislative interference by an overseeing board or commission. An interest group's power depends on factors such as its size and cohesiveness, the intensity of concern among its members, its goals, and its access to resources that it can use to influence the agency.

Interest groups can be an important source of power for an agency in its dealings with its legislative and executive superiors as well as with other agencies (Clarke and McCool 1985; Culhane 1981). Recognizing this, many agencies cultivate interest-group support. An agency's efforts to institutionalize client or constituent support, however, can result in the agency's becoming unresponsive to the demands of other interest groups or other agencies.

Bighorn Sheep Management in the Teton Range: A Case Study

To provide an illustration of the ways in which the factors discussed above can influence agency responses to a shared problem, this case study examines management of a remnant population of Rocky Mountain bighorn sheep (*Ovis canadensis canadensis*) in the Teton Range, Wyoming, by three agencies: the National Park Service (NPS), the U.S. Forest Service (FS), and the Wyoming Game and Fish Department (WGF). Although the agencies generally agree that the population may be at risk because of its small size and isolation, their efforts toward cooperative management have been sporadic. Interagency conflicts, stemming more from organizational factors than from biological disagreements, have hindered an effective and coordinated effort to ensure the population's long-term viability.

Management of the Teton bighorn sheep population presents biological challenges of a type that are becoming increasingly common as habitat is fragmented and populations decline to critically low numbers. The bighorn population is small (about one hundred animals), isolated from neighboring populations, and restricted, especially in winter, to marginal habitat on the crest of the Teton

Range. The boundary between Grand Teton National Park and Targhee National Forest runs along the Teton crest, subdividing the bighorns' habitat. The bighorns cross freely back and forth between the two jurisdictions. The Wyoming Game and Fish Department claims responsibility under Wyoming state law for the animals themselves.

Before white settlement of the area, bighorns were more numerous, migrating seasonally from alpine summer ranges to lower-elevation winter ranges. But human settlement inhibited the bighorns' use of their lowland seasonal ranges, restricting them year-round to rugged terrain high in the Tetons. Neighboring bighorn populations declined or were extirpated early in the settlement era, resulting in isolation of the Teton population. The bighorns were further stressed by large numbers of domestic sheep that were grazed throughout the Tetons during the early decades of the 1900s (Whitfield 1983).

Although the bighorns' mountain habitat is now protected within a national park and a national forest wilderness area, the population is far from secure. The most extensive study of the population conducted to date concluded that the population is highly susceptible to extinction (Whitfield 1983). This concern stems from several factors. Small population size and isolation can lead to inbreeding and other deleterious genetic effects (Allendorf and Leary 1986). In an examination of the relationship between population size and persistence in bighorn sheep populations, Berger (1990) found that populations of fifty to one hundred sheep persisted for about sixty years, while 100 percent of the populations with fewer than fifty individuals went extinct within fifty years. Bighorns are notoriously susceptible to catastrophic disease epidemics, especially when under stress. The Teton bighorns' reliance on marginal winter habitat contributes to high lamb mortality. The population is thought to be static or declining.

The bighorns still face a variety of stresses, including heavy recreational use of both sides of the Teton crest, domestic sheep grazing in some portions of bighorn habitat in the Targhee National Forest, and an annual trophy ram hunt regulated by the Wyoming Game and Fish Department. An additional threat could arise from nonnative mountain goats (*Oreamnos americanus*) that are dispersing into the Tetons from a population introduced to the south by the Idaho Fish and Game Department in the early 1970s. The goats began dispersing from the transplant site in the mid-1970s and have been sighted in or near Grand Teton National Park every year since 1978. Although overwintering goats have not been confirmed in the park, the possibility exists that they could become year-round residents there. If they do, they could further stress the bighorns by competing for forage on the critically important winter range.

Several disagreements over appropriate management have arisen among the agencies (Harvey 1987). For example, when the Wyoming Game and Fish Department proposed in 1976 to open an annual trophy ram hunt in the national forest portion of the big-horns' range, the Park Service formally requested that the hunt not be opened (USDI NPS 1976). The NPS expressed concern that hunting would condition the bighorns to avoid humans and that the combined effect of hunters and nonconsumptive recreationists would adversely affect their number and distribution. Despite the NPS's objections, the hunting season was opened as planned and has been held each fall since.

Domestic livestock grazing permitted by the Forest Service has also been a point of disagreement. Although the scale of the activity has been relatively small (about thirty-five hundred ewes with lambs are grazed each summer on allotments in the Tetons), both the NPS (USDI NPS 1986:123) and the WGF are concerned about possible detrimental effects the domestic sheep might have on the forage needed by bighorns during the winter. The agencies are also concerned about the possibility of disease transfer from domestic to wild sheep, which in other areas has led to catastrophic die-offs of bighorn populations. Because of those concerns, the WGF has suggested that domestic sheep be removed from bighorn habitat (WGF 1989). Although some FS managers share the WGF's concerns, others assert that more research is needed to demonstrate competition between the domestic and wild sheep (Harvey 1987) and that potentially disease-transmitting contact between wild and domestic sheep in the Tetons is so rare as to be insignificant. The boundaries of one allotment have been modified to keep domestic sheep out of an area of known overlap, but beyond that the grazing issue remains unresolved.

The appearance and potential establishment of mountain goats in the Teton Range has been another source of interagency conflict. To the Park Service, the goats are an exotic species that may threaten park resources, but to the WGF, they are a game species that may someday provide attractive opportunities for hunting in the Tetons. The NPS is particularly concerned because goats are not native to the Teton Range and could cause significant changes in an ecosystem that has evolved without them (USDI NPS 1986). NPS policy calls for controlling or eradicating exotic species whenever such species threaten park resources (USDI NPS 1988). According to the NPS, habitat suitable for mountain goats exists throughout the Teton Range; if the goats become established there, they could compete with the bighorns for the limited winter range, further threatening the bighorns' survival. The NPS recognizes that controlling goats only inside the boundaries of the park would not solve the problem, since suitable habitat for goats exists on national forest lands adjacent to much of the park's west boundary. Unless the FS were to cooperate in a goat control program, goats could continue dispersing into the park, as well as occupying bighorn habitat in the national forest.

In 1985, the NPS proposed that the three principal agencies and other interested groups form an interagency team to develop and implement a cooperative plan for managing both the bighorn sheep and the mountain goats (USDI NPS 1985). The FS's response to the NPS proposal was cautiously cooperative, expressing the agency's willingness to participate in the development of a cooperative plan. The WGF's response, however, was less favorable. The WGF asserted that wildlife in Wyoming is the property of the state, that the state considers mountain goats a game animal, and that the distribution of goats in the Tetons is a "naturally occurring outgrowth of the plant in Idaho" (WGF 1985). The WGF expressed doubts about the mountain goats' posing a threat to the Teton bighorns and suggested that more site-specific research is needed. Finally, the WGF objected to the idea of developing cooperative interagency plans for the animals, saying that the state would address management of the goats through its own strategic plan process "when the need arises" (WGF 1985). Faced with opposition from the WGF, the Park Service did not pursue the idea of an interagency team any further.

Since then, management of the bighorn population has continued to be "low intensity, undirected, and independent," as the Park Service (1986:125) described it. Recently, however, a few encouraging actions have been taken. The NPS's revised Backcountry Management Plan for Grand Teton National Park states that new trails will not be built in bighorn habitat and that bighorns' sensitivity to recreational use will be a major limiting factor in establishing recreational use levels (USDI NPS 1989). Targhee National Forest and WGF biologists visited the Teton crest together in 1988 to evaluate possibilities for bighorn habitat enhancement. And in June 1990, a Forest Service biologist organized a working group of biologists from all three agencies to discuss the population's status and strategies for restoring the herd to healthy numbers. Despite its earlier rejection of the Park Service's proposal to form an interagency planning team, the Wyoming Game and Fish Department has participated in the biologists' working group.

The working group, which met twice in its first year, has begun to outline a strategic plan for managing the bighorn population. At the meetings, the issues of improving and expanding winter range and minimizing contact between domestic and wild sheep received particular attention. The hunting issue was also discussed, and although some of the WGF biologists questioned the biological justification for hunting such a small population, others within the agency said that without data indicating that the hunt is detrimental to the population the state game commission would not close the hunt.

In this case, disagreement over biological questions plays a role in interagency conflict, but it is not the primary factor blocking an effective interagency effort. All three agencies have access to the same scientific data on the population, all agree that the population is small, static or declining, and below desirable population levels, and all recognize that they cannot manage the population effectively without the cooperation of the other agencies. Nevertheless, their progress toward integrating their management has been limited. The organizational factors discussed earlier have all contributed to the agencies' difficulties in cooperatively addressing the bighorn issue. Value differences affect the way the agencies perceive the problem and influence their preferred responses to it; agency structures inhibit progress toward cooperation; and clients and constituents pressure the agencies to continue grazing and hunting. The most significant obstacle to cooperation in this case, however, has been a concern with unofficial organizational goals, especially that of maintaining agency discretion and authority. The WGF's refusal to join the proposed cooperative planning effort for the Teton bighorns in 1985 was based in large part on the department's concern with maintaining state control over wildlife and preventing federal incursions into the state's domain.

The disagreement between the NPS and the WGF over hunting stems in part from the conflict between the NPS's preservationist/ noninterventionist values and the WGF's utilitarian/hands-on values. Central to the WGF's value orientation is a strong belief that hunting is not just an important form of recreation but a vital tool for regulating wildlife population numbers. The WGF's decision to open the hunt reflects the agency's faith in the traditional methods for managing bighorns, even though the scientific rationale for removing the largest rams from marginal populations has been questioned (Morgan 1973; Geist 1975). Another strongly held value of the WGF is a belief in state control over wildlife. The agency's commitment to this position goes beyond a simple bureaucratic desire to defend its domain, although turf protection certainly plays a role in WGF's stance. The WGF believes in states' authority over wildlife as an important and valuable tradition, and it resists any perceived federal attempts to move into this domain as a threat not only to its own authority but also to the wildlife resource.

The National Park Services's values are distinctly different from those of the WGF. The predominant NPS philosophy with regard to wildlife is to allow natural processes to function with as little human interference as possible, except where active management is needed to restore natural conditions. The NPS is also dedicated to providing for human use and enjoyment of the parks, a mission that sometimes conflicts with its preservationist values. The Forest Service has a utilitarian orientation and a tradition of hands-on management of resources (Robinson 1975). The disparity in the agencies' fundamental values contributes to the conflict in this case.

The three agencies' formal goals for the bighorn population are quite compatible and do not provide obvious grounds for inter-agency conflict. All the agencies have mandates to ensure the con-tinued survival of wildlife populations, and all want to see the Teton bighorns persist into the future. But conflicts arise from the agencies' desires to simultaneously continue other uses of bighorn habitat and from their different opinions about the threats current activities such as grazing, recreation, and hunting pose to the big-horn population. The agencies' goals for the mountain goats are less congruent, and they may prove to be grounds for interagency conflict in the future if goats become established in Grand Teton National Park.

All three of the agencies involved in this case are large, well-established bureaucracies organized along standard hierarchical lines. The structures of the three agencies ensure organizational stability and continuity, reinforce the agencies' cultures and value orientations, and contribute to a resistance to change. The agencies all generally prefer to resolve demands for change within the con-text of existing organizational structures. The commitment to ex-isting structures and procedures seems to be more pronounced at the upper levels of the agencies' hierarchies. For example, the WGF's rejection of the NPS's 1985 proposal to form an interagency planning team came from the state office in Cheyenne, not from the district office that deals directly with the bighorn population. The 1990 interagency working group, on the other hand, was initi-ated by direct contacts among field-level biologists from the three agencies.

The federal agencies involved in the bighorn case face a some-what different external environment than does the WGF. The NPS and the FS depend on legislative and budgetary committees of the Congress for authority and funding, while the funding and oversight system under which the WGF operates (funding primarily from hunting license fees and a commission with almost full executive powers over wildlife management) was deliberately set up to shield the department from the political influence of the state legislature. The WGF's primary constituency—license-buying hunters—is relatively uniform and cohesive in its interests, while the federal agencies have a variety of local client and constituent groups and a diffuse and diverse national constituency. The WGF's autonomy and its strong ties with its primary constituents may contribute to the agency's reluctance to give up any of its discretion in cooperative efforts with the federal agencies. The Forest Service's long-standing commitment to the livestock permittees using allotments in the Tetons also contributes to the agency's reluctance to curtail grazing for the bighorns' benefit.

Although a number of different groups could be affected by decisions concerning the bighorns or their habitat (including recreationists, outfitters, livestock operators, hunters, and environmental groups), public awareness of the bighorn problem is low, leaving the agencies relatively free from outside scrutiny and pressure. In the absence of vocal public opinion, and faced with a variety of constituent groups, the agencies have some leeway in deciding what course of action to follow. The result is that the bighorn issue has been low on the agency agendas and, until quite recently, few actions have been taken for the bighorns' benefit, despite the consensus that the population is critically small. The agencies have been reluctant to restrict human use of bighorn habitat partly because of the anticipated negative reactions such action might provoke (see Culhane 1981). According to agency officials, an increase in public concern over the bighorns would be an important factor in convincing them to allocate more resources to the problem (Harvey 1987).

The formation of the biologists' working group, and the participation of the WGF in it, is a significant step. It remains to be seen, however, whether the biologists can convince their respective agencies to take action for the bighorns' benefit, especially where doing so might mean restricting other activities such as livestock grazing, recreation, and hunting.

Improving Interagency Cooperation

Conservationists and organizational scholars have proposed a variety of ideas for improving coordination and cooperation between land and wildlife management agencies. The proposals fall into three basic categories: clarifying authority, clarifying goals, and improving interagency coordination mechanisms. Some researchers advocate voluntary administrative reform, while others argue that because of the disparate mandates and interests of the wildlife and habitat agencies and their historical preoccupation with maintaining their managerial discretion, reliance on voluntary cooperation is unrealistic. They believe that more comprehensive reform, including new legislation, is needed to force agencies to cooperate in conserving viable populations of wildlife (Coggins 1987; Grumbine 1990).

Defensiveness over perceived threats to authority and discretion can contribute to the resistance agencies may feel toward cooperative efforts (Keiter 1989). Without new legislation or some other strong external pressure, the agencies are unlikely to voluntarily concede authority to another agency or change their goals to make them more compatible with those of neighbors. Proposals for clarifying authority relationships generally take two distinct approaches. The first is to keep existing agencies and jurisdictions as they are but to make authority relationships between them more explicit. The second is to create new land-managing bodies for specific regions or ecosystems, with authority over the agencies within their jurisdictions. The first approach is illustrated by legislative proposals to strengthen the NPS's authority over other federal agencies in order to combat external threats to the parks. An example is the Park Protection Act that passed the House of Representatives in both the Ninety-seventh and Ninety-eighth Congresses. That legislation would require the Interior Secretary to determine, before proceeding with an action on lands adjacent to park boundaries, that the action would not have a significant adverse effect on the values for which the park unit was established. The second approach is illustrated by the national reserve concept, wherein a new regional planning authority is established for a specific area and endowed with the authority to regulate land use and preempt land-use decisions made by other agencies within the reserve. The first national reserve, Pinelands National Reserve in New Jersey, was established by Congress in 1978.

Many proposals for clarifying goals would also do so within specific geographic areas, by setting boundaries within which stated goals would have precedence over all others. Examples of this are biosphere reserves (Dyer and Holland 1988), proposed "greater ecosystem areas," and proposed "conservation networks" (Salwasser et al. 1987). Within the designated areas several agencies may have jurisdiction, and none is given authority over the actions of the others. In theory, all the agencies are working toward the same goals, which are set by legislation or other formal recognition of the purposes of the designated area. By making it clear that goals for preservation of biological diversity, for example, are paramount to all other goals within the designated area, conflict between agencies working toward different ends should be lessened. In practice, agencies whose original mandates are incongruent with the goals established for the designated area are unlikely to change without legislation or other strong incentives.

Proposals for improving interagency coordination mechanisms usually focus on voluntary actions that could be taken by the agencies, rather than imposing new requirements on them from outside. Some of the suggestions focus on improving the exchange of information among agencies, some focus on conflict anticipation and resolution, and some focus on establishing new organizational structures to improve interagency cooperation. Examples include constructing regional data bases on species and habitats of concern (Grumbine 1990), establishing flexible task-oriented "parallel organizations" to address shared problems outside the constraints of large bureaucracies (Clark et al. 1989), using coordinators to help agencies integrate management (Mangun 1989), training agency personnel in conflict management, and providing incentives to encourage employees to participate in coordination activities.

The array of proposals under discussion reflects a growing recognition on the part of conservation advocates, legislators, and agencies of the need for more effective approaches to solving cross-jurisdictional problems. Despite such recognition, attempts to enact or implement most of the ideas are likely to generate strong political and institutional resistance. If the new coordinating mechanisms are strong and binding on the agencies, opposition to their enactment will be fierce; on the other hand, if they are not binding, they may be ineffective in overcoming agency resistance to cooperation. Nevertheless, both improved interagency cooperation and increased agency commitment to upholding wildlife protection statutes will be required if viable populations of wildlife, particularly large migratory species, are to persist. Under our existing system of small reserves with inward-focused management, interagency rivalry, and lack of commitment to wildlife, we will surely see serious declines in wildlife numbers and diversity over the next decades. These proposals are at least a start in exploring ways to make institutional structures and processes more compatible with ecological realities.

References

Allendorf, Fred W., and Robb F. Leary. 1986. "Heterozygosity and Fitness in Natural Populations of Animals." Pp. 57–76 in Michael E. Soulé, ed., *Conservation Biology: The Science of Scarcity and Diversity*. Sunderland, Mass.: Sinauer Associates.

Bean, Michael J. 1983. *The Evolution of National Wildlife Law*. Rev. ed. New York: Praeger Publishers.

Berger, Joel. 1990. "Persistence of Different-sized Populations: An Empirical Assessment of Rapid Extinctions in Bighorn Sheep." *Conservation Biology* 4(1):91–98.

Clark, Tim W., Ron Crete, and John Cada. 1989. "Designing and Managing Successful Endangered Species Recovery Programs." *Environmental Management* 13(2):159–170.

Clark, Tim W., and Ann H. Harvey. 1991. "Implementing Recovery Policy: Learning As We Go?" Pp. 147–163 in Kathryn A. Kohm, ed., *Balancing on the Brink of Extinction: The Endangered Species Act and Lessons for the Future*. Washington, D.C.: Island Press.

Clark, Tim W., and Ron Westrum. 1987. "Paradigms and Ferrets." *Social Studies of Science* 17:3–33.

Clarke, Jeanne Nienaber, and Daniel McCool. 1985. *Staking Out the Terrain:*

Power Differentials Among Natural Resource Management Agencies. Albany: State University of New York Press.

Coggins, George Cameron. 1987. "Protecting the Wildlife Resources of National Parks from External Threats." *Land and Water Law Review* 22(1):1–27.

Coggins, George Cameron, and Michael E. Ward. 1981. "The Law of Wildlife Management on the Federal Public Lands." *Oregon Law Review* 60:3–183.

Culhane, Paul J. 1981. *Public Lands Politics: Interest Group Influence on the Forest Service and the Bureau of Land Management.* Baltimore: Johns Hopkins University Press.

Dyer, M. I., and M. M. Holland. 1988. "Unesco's Man and the Biosphere Program." *BioScience* 38(9):635–641.

Geist, Valerius. 1975. "On the Management of Mountain Sheep: Theoretical Considerations." Pp. 77–98 in J. B. Trefethen, ed., *The Wild Sheep in Modern North America.* Alexandria, Va.: Boone and Crockett Club.

Gilpin, Michael E., and Michael E. Soulé. 1986. "Minimum Viable Populations: Processes of Species Extinction." Pp. 19–34 in Michael E. Soulé, ed., *Conservation Biology: The Science of Scarcity and Diversity.* Sunderland, Mass.: Sinauer Associates.

Grumbine, R. Edward. 1990. "Viable Populations, Reserve Size, and Federal Lands Management: A Critique." *Conservation Biology* 4(2):127–134.

Harvey, Ann H. 1987. "Interagency Conflict and Coordination in Wildlife Management: A Case Study." Master's thesis, University of Michigan, Ann Arbor.

Henning, Daniel H., and William R. Mangun. 1989. *Managing the Environmental Crisis: Incorporating Competing Values in Natural Resource Administration.* Durham, N.C.: Duke University Press.

Kaufman, Herbert. 1967. *The Forest Ranger: A Study in Administrative Behavior.* Baltimore: Johns Hopkins University Press.

Keiter, Robert B. 1989. "Taking Account of the Ecosystem on the Public Domain: Law and Ecology in the Greater Yellowstone Region." *University of Colorado Law Review* 60:923–1007.

Mangun, William R. 1989. "Environmental Impact Assessment as a Tool for Wildlife Policy Management." Pp. 51–61 in Robert V. Bartlett, ed., *Policy Through Impact Assessment: Institutionalized Analysis as a Policy Strategy.* Westport, Conn.: Greenwood Press.

Morgan, James K. 1973. "Slamming the Ram into Oblivion." *Audubon* 75(November):16–19.

Pfeffer, Jeffrey, and Gerald R. Salancik. 1978. *The External Control of Organizations: A Resource Dependence Perspective.* New York: Harper and Row.

Robinson, Glen O. 1975. *The Forest Service: A Study in Public Land Management.* Baltimore: Johns Hopkins University Press.

Romesburg, H. Charles. 1981. "Wildlife Science: Gaining Reliable Knowledge." *Journal of Wildlife Management* 45:293–313.

Salwasser, Hal, Christine Schonewald-Cox, and Richard Baker. 1987. "The Role of Interagency Cooperation in Managing for Viable Populations." Pp. 159–173 in Michael E. Soule, ed., *Viable Populations for Conservation.* Cambridge: Cambridge University Press.

Sax, Joseph L., and Robert B. Keiter. 1987. "Glacier National Park and Its Neighbors: A Study of Federal Interagency Relations." *Ecology Law Quarterly* 14:207–263.

Simon, Herbert A. 1976. *Administrative Behavior.* 3d ed. New York: Free Press.

Twight, Ben W. 1983. *Organizational Values and Political Power: The Forest Service Versus the Olympic National Park.* University Park: Pennsylvania State University Press.

U.S. Department of the Interior. National Park Service (USDI NPS). 1976. Letter from Jack Neckels, Acting Superintendent, Grand Teton National Park, to Earl Thomas, Acting Director, Wyoming Game and Fish Department, 29 April.

———. 1985. "Draft Natural Resources Management Plan and Environmental Assessment, Grand Teton National Park." Washington, D.C.

———. 1986. "Natural Resources Management Plan and Environmental Assessment, Grand Teton National Park." Washington, D.C.

———. 1988. "Management Policies." Washington, D.C.

———. 1989. "Backcountry Management Plan, Grand Teton National Park." Washington, D.C.

Wamsley, Gary L., and Mayer N. Zald. 1976. *The Political Economy of Public Organizations.* Bloomington: Indiana University Press.

Warwick, Donald P. 1975. *A Theory of Public Bureaucracy: Politics, Personality, and Organization in the State Department.* Cambridge, Mass.: Harvard University Press.

Whitfield, Michael B. 1983. "Bighorn Sheep History, Distributions, and Habitat Relationships in the Teton Mountain Range, Wyoming." Master's thesis, Idaho State University, Pocatello.

Wyoming Game and Fish Department (WGF). 1985. Letter from Francis Petera, Assistant Director for Operations, to Dick Hartman, Wyoming State Planning Coordinator, 14 August.

———. 1989. "Targhee Bighorn Sheep: A Field Evaluation for Potential Habitat Improvements in the Darby and Fox Creek Drainages." Cheyenne.

Yaffee, Steven L. 1982. *Prohibitive Policy: Implementing the Federal Endangered Species Act.* Cambridge, Mass.: MIT Press.

4

DEVELOPING POLICY FOR
PUBLIC ACCESS TO PRIVATE LAND:
A CASE STUDY

Philip S. Cook • *Ted T. Cable*

Introduction

Wildlife management is an unusual mix of public and private resource management. Wildlife is a public resource, owned by all citizens, yet the habitats upon which wildlife depends are not always publicly owned, and wildlife often moves freely between publicly and privately owned lands. Likewise, the public has the right to use wildlife for recreational purposes (for example, hunt, trap, watch), but they may not be able to exercise that right because the wildlife may be on privately owned lands. Fifty-seven percent of the land area of the United States is occupied by privately owned farms, ranches, and forests (Wunderlich 1979), and 75 percent of the wildlife in the United States uses agricultural land as part of its habitat (Horvath 1976); consequently, public agencies that are responsible for maintaining wildlife-related recreational opportunities must rely to a large degree on privately owned lands to fulfill their agencies' missions. Wildlife-related recreational opportunities may be decreasing because federal, state, and local agencies have decreased public land acquisitions (Propst et al. 1985), and landowners are becoming more restrictive about recreational access to private lands (Cordell et al. 1985).

Recent decreases in the public's participation in hunting have been blamed, in part, on decreased access to land (Wright et al. 1988; Meinen 1989). Several reasons are cited for this trend of more restrictive public access to private land. First, landowners are posting their land against trespass more often because of concerns about liability for accidents and vandalism by recreationists (Cordell et al. 1985). Second, the leasing of recreational access rights to private individuals or groups has become common in many areas of the country (Cordell et al. 1985). While increasing recreational opportunities for the specific lessees, the lease arrangements do not supply opportunities for the general public. Third, purchases of rural land by urban dwellers for exclusive use by the owners is increasing (Gramann et al. 1985). Those lands provide recreation for the owners but not for the general public.

One strategy for addressing the dilemma of public access to a public resource that exists largely on private lands is the intervention of states to encourage the provision of public access to wildlife on private lands. The leasing of public access rights directly by the state is an approach that has received much attention in the wildlife and recreation management literature (for example, Gottschalk 1977; Wright and Kaiser 1986; Sampson 1986; President's Commission on Americans Outdoors 1987; Wright 1988) and has been implemented by numerous states. Typically, in public access programs, states lease recreational access rights from private landowners, and, in turn, the public purchases permits from the state to gain access to the leased lands. For example, North Carolina has a hunter access program with three million acres under lease, and hunters pay an eight-dollar fee to use the lands (Cordell et al. 1985). By far the majority of state access programs are designated for hunting, but land is also leased for other recreational purposes. The state of Michigan, for example, leases land for snowmobile use (Manning 1973).

Most state-sponsored access programs have been successful in opening land to the public without causing problems for landowners or the state (Holecek 1983; Barry 1984; Meinen 1989; Mooney 1989). For example, Michigan's Public Access Stamp Program for hunters grew from 93,513 leased acres and 23,000 users in 1977 to 188,691 leased acres and 73,000 users in 1982 (Holecek 1983). Wisconsin has nearly 250 landowners and 100,000 acres enrolled in its program (Mooney 1989). However, a recently proposed public access program in Kansas was not implemented because it failed to gain significant political support.

The reasons for the failure of the Kansas public access proposal are not altogether clear, but the objectives of this chapter are to analyze the public access issue in Kansas and to suggest causes of the proposal's failure. The analysis is organized as follows: (1) introductory facts about Kansas's land ownership and recreational access patterns; (2) a history of the state's public access proposal; (3) an examination of the benefits and costs of a public access program to recreationists, landowners, and the state; (4) an examination of the positions of various interest groups on the public access issue; and (5) reasons for the failure of the state-sponsored program.

Public Access to Private Land in Kansas

Background

Over 97 percent of the land in Kansas is privately owned, and 94 percent of the total land base is in agricultural production. All public land in Kansas accounts for only 1,123,456 acres, and only 88,011 of those acres are developed for public recreational use; consequently, publicly provided recreational opportunities are limited (Kansas Park and Resources Authority 1985).

Despite the lack of public land, Kansans are active participants in wildlife-related recreation. The U.S. Fish and Wildlife Service (1988) estimated that 86 percent of Kansans participate in wildlife-associated recreation. Kansas hunters spend 3.4 million hunter-days afield (U.S. Fish and Wildlife Service 1988), and Kansas's pheasant harvest consistently ranks within the top three states nationally every year (Kansas Department of Wildlife and Parks 1988).

Recreationists traditionally have had little trouble in gaining access to private land by asking permission from landowners. In recent years, however, this system has begun to break down as more landowners have closed their land to recreationists. The percentage of Kansas landowners that reported they allowed no outsiders to hunt on their land rose from 27 percent in 1980 to 37 percent in 1985 (Meinen 1989). Also, more landowners have moved off their rural properties, making it more difficult for recreationists to locate the owners of lands that they wish to use.

The State's Public Access Proposal

A state program of recreational access to private lands was first discussed by the Commission on the Future of Kansas Agriculture, established by the secretary of the State Board of Agriculture to make suggestions to improve Kansas agriculture and enhance the incomes of rural Kansans. In 1987, the commission's report recommended an effort to encourage farmers to diversify their incomes by leasing lands to recreationists.

The secretary of the Kansas Department of Wildlife and Parks (KDWP), as the lead agency, along with the secretary of the Kansas Board of Agriculture, developed a recreational access program to provide greater access to private lands and supplemental income for landowners. In October 1988, the proposal was made public. The original proposal included three options: a General Access Program, a Community Wildlife Association Program, and an Outfitter/Guide Program.

The General Access Program, the primary approach, was a voluntary leasing program whereby landowners and tenants could offer their land to the access program during a special sign-up period. The KDWP would evaluate each parcel and offer the landowner a per acre payment based upon established criteria, such as the quality of the parcel's habitat, the parcel's potential for recreation, and the amount of access control retained by the landowner.

The KDWP planned to lease 300,000 acres the first year and 600,000 acres over the first five-year period. The KDWP estimated that lease fees would be less than five dollars per acre per year.

Public users of the General Access Program lands would be required to purchase a special permit from the KDWP, or a licensed vendor, to gain access to the enrolled lands. The KDWP estimated the permit fee would be approximately twenty-five dollars per year and expected 60,000 to 100,000 permits to be purchased each year. The money from the permits would be deposited into a special account used to pay the lease fees and administrative expenses of the program.

Under the Community Wildlife Association Program, groups of landowners or tenants could form associations that would allow larger blocks of land to be open for access and would give landowners the opportunity for more participation in the administration and promotion of their areas. The program would operate much like the General Access Program. The KDWP would lease the land, but a special permit would be required by users of each association's land. Part of the permit fees would be returned to the association to cover promotional costs.

The Outfitter/Guide Program was a relatively small part of the initial proposal. The program would allow people to become certified guides or outfitters, and landowners could earn income by either becoming guides or outfitters or by leasing their land to a guide or outfitter. Individual members of the public would contract services with a guide or outfitter. The KDWP would provide big-game-hunting outfitters with a limited number of big-game permits.

The KDWP and the Board of Agriculture considered enabling legislation necessary for the successful implementation of the public access program. In January 1989, S.B. 375 was introduced in the Kansas legislature and referred to the Senate Committee on Agriculture, and H.B. 2367 was introduced and referred to the House Committee on Energy and Natural Resources. Both bills contained provisions for the General Access Program and the Community Wildlife Association Program, but neither bill addressed the Outfitter/Guide Program. In addition to the enabling legislation, the governor's budget for fiscal year 1990, introduced in the 1989 legislative session, recommended $2.2 million and seven new positions to initiate the public access program.

During the 1989 legislative session, both legislative committees held hearings on the bills; however, neither bill received approval from its respective committee. It was agreed that there should be an interim committee appointed to study the concept and make a recommendation to the 1990 legislature. Neither the money nor the positions were included in the final state budget.

In June 1989, the interim committee, the Special Committee on Energy and Natural Resources, held the first of two hearings about the public access proposal. State officials and members of private interest groups testified at the hearing. By this time, the KDWP had scaled back its original proposal for a statewide program to a pilot project for testing the feasibility of the full-fledged program. Under the pilot program, the KDWP would lease up to 100,000 acres in one region of the state for the General Access Program and form two Community Wildlife Associations, leasing up to 150,000 acres. One association would be in eastern Kansas and the other in western Kansas. The KDWP requested $1.6 million and five new positions for the pilot project.

The Special Committee on Energy and Natural Resources recommended that H.B. 2587, authorizing the establishment of the pilot project, be introduced in the 1990 legislative session. In January 1990, H.B. 2587 was introduced in the legislature and referred to the House Committee on Energy and Natural Resources. No hearings or votes on this bill were held during the 1990 legislative session.

The funding for the pilot program was included in a separate appropriations bill and was referred to the Joint Committee on State Building Construction. The committee tabled the proposal, effectively killing the pilot program and any large-scale public access program for the state.

Benefits of the Proposed Public Access Program

Recreationists

The obvious benefit of a public access program to recreationists would be the increased availability of recreational opportunities.

Under the original proposal, 300,000 to 600,000 acres would be opened for public access, significantly increasing the 88,011 acres of public land now developed for public recreation. The KDWP estimated hunter-days would increase from 3.0 million to 3.6 million because of the increased access to land (Meinen 1989).

Recreationists might also benefit by having the state in the leasing market. Fees for gaining access to private land not enrolled in the program would be influenced by the state-controlled access fee. If state fees were lower than private lease fees, private lessors might be influenced to lower their fees, thus benefiting recreationists. Although private leasing for recreation is not well developed in Kansas, it is feared that private leasing would inflate user fees and price many low-income recreationists out of the market (Kansas State University Cooperative Extension Service 1987). State leasing would provide an alternative to private leasing and consequently influence private lease prices.

Recreationists also would benefit by having to spend less time searching for land on which to recreate and by not having to locate landowners to ask permission for access. Recreationists also would benefit from improved wildlife habitat management on private lands. Lease payments would provide landowners with an economic incentive to provide and protect wildlife habitat, and the state could enter into additional cooperative management programs with landowners.

Landowners

The most direct economic benefit for landowners would be the opportunity to earn income for leasing their land. Whereas private leasing also would produce income, under a state-sponsored leasing program many landowners' concerns about access to their land would become the responsibility of the state. The state would assume the duty of care (liability) for accidents and injuries to recreationists on the leased land. Although a 1989 change in Kansas's recreational use statutes decreased the duty of care for landowners, even if they charge fees to visitors, leasing to the state would relieve landowners of almost all legal liability.

The state would also assume responsibility for controlling access to the land. While some landowners might regard this as a negative aspect of the program, the landowners would benefit from not having to take the time to grant individual access permits to numerous persons. The state also would assume responsibility for vandalism caused by recreationists and be responsible for enforcing all laws.

State

A public access program would benefit the state's economy. The lack of recreational areas may not only be a constraint to participation by residents, but it also has been cited as a hindrance to expanding nonresident tourism (Manske 1989). For hunting alone, the KDWP estimated a yearly increase of eighty thousand hunter-days (21.7 percent increase) by out-of-state hunters if the public access program were implemented (Meinen 1989). Using U.S. Fish and Wildlife Service hunter-day values, the increase would mean $4.3 million per year in additional income for the Kansas economy from out-of-state hunters. The increase in income from resident hunters would amount to $10.4 million. The increase in income would benefit the state and local economies.

The public access program also might decrease the pressure on or need for the state to buy lands in the future. Efforts to increase public ownership of land in Kansas have always faced formidable public opposition. The public access program would provide a way to increase recreation without the state's purchasing land.

Costs of a Public Access Program

Recreationists

For the recreationist using the state program, the cost of a public access program would be the cost of a permit. However, the program also might result in increased costs to those not using the state program. Landowners who presently allow hunting at no cost or at rates below what the state would charge might raise their fees in response, thus costing the recreationist more.

There might be another cost to recreationists. Under the present system of asking a landowner's permission for access, many recreationists gain access simply by lending a hand to the landowner. If the landowner chose to lease his or her land to the state, the recreationist would be required to obtain a permit. The public access system might cost some recreationists their long-standing personal relationships with landowners.

Landowners

Landowners participating in the public access program would lose control over who has access to their land. Although the state would assume responsibility for vandalism, the landowner would still have to deal with the inconvenience of filing a claim and might not be compensated for lost time or materials while the claim was being reviewed.

State

Although the program is supposed to be self-supporting, there would be initial start-up costs, as well as potential costs associated with increased liability for accidents, repairing vandalism by users, and enforcing trespass and other recreation laws. Although the potential for increased liability costs is great, no state that currently has a public access program has experienced significant problems with liability (Meinen 1989).

The Roles of Private Interest Groups

Interest groups play important roles in public policy making (Edwards and Sharkansky 1978; Reich 1988). Numerous private interest groups had a stake in the success or failure of the public access program. During the two years of debate about public access, several groups held public meetings, polled their members, adopted official positions, or testified at legislative hearings.

Agricultural-related enterprises are the largest industry in Kansas, and the Kansas Livestock Association and the Kansas Farm Bureau are the two largest private groups representing agriculture in the state. The Kansas Livestock Association (KLA), a 10,000-member trade organization, represents the cattle-ranching industry in Kansas. Kansas is the nation's leading beef-producing state; consequently, ranching interests wield much political clout. The KLA openly opposed the public access proposal based on "the belief that it would compete with landowners already leasing land to sportsmen and be a burden for adjoining, non-participating landowners" (Kansas Livestock Association 1990:26).

The Kansas Farm Bureau (KFB) is a 106,000-member organization that provides services to agricultural families and businesses. The KFB is the main advocacy group for the protection of farmers' rights. It adopted a rather ambiguous position about the public access issue. The KFB stated that it supported the present system of asking landowners' permission for access to their land, obtaining a clear understanding of which lands could be accessed, and respecting the landowners' property. They further declared that if a program were to become workable in Kansas it must create the opportunity for Kansas farmers to earn income, it must not remove management decisions from the hands of farmers and ranchers, it must guarantee to farmers control over access to their leased lands, it must assign liability for damages and injuries to the state, and it must be for leasing only, not acquisition. The KFB's policy was not directly opposed to the proposed program but did contain reservations about taking access management away from landowners.

The Kansas Wildlife Federation (KWF) is the largest sportsmen's group in the state with eight thousand members. The KWF held two public hearings and surveyed conservationists and recreationists in the state. The KWF adopted a resolution in support of the program and encouraged the state to earmark some of the program funds for permanent wildlife habitat protection and land acquisition.

At the interim committee hearing in June 1989, numerous other groups testified about the public access proposal. Those in favor of the proposal were the Kansas Department of Forestry, the Governor's Office, Southeast Kansas Tourism, Inc., Prairie Packers, Convention and Visitor's Bureau of El Dorado, Kansas, Kansas Audubon Council, Sierra Club, Kansas Natural Resources Defense Council, Kansas Field Trials Association, and the Kansas Canoe Association. No groups other than the KLA and the KFB opposed the public access program.

The Failure of the Public Access Proposal

Policy making is an inexact process, and although models for it exist (for example, Edwards and Sharkansky 1978; Williams 1980), the reasons for a particular policy's success and another's failure are not always clear (Hogwood and Peters 1985). The reasons for the failure of the Kansas recreational access proposal are not well documented, but several political, social, and economic factors could have contributed to its demise.

First, recreational access was not a well-defined public problem in Kansas when the state introduced its program. Correctly identifying a problem or need is a crucial first step in policy making (Edwards and Sharkansky 1978). Neither demographics nor the public's perception of population pressure on recreational opportunities appears to have forced the state to introduce the program.

Most states that have introduced public access programs have tremendous population pressures on their recreational lands. For example, Michigan, which has a successful program, ranks fourteenth in population density (159.6 persons per square mile) among the fifty states (U.S. Bureau of the Census 1986). Ninety percent of Michigan's population lives in the southern third of the state where 97 percent of the land is privately owned (Holecek 1983). By contrast, Kansas ranks thirty-eighth in mean population density with 30 persons per square mile (U.S. Bureau of the Census 1986). The median population density in Kansas's 105 counties is only 10.1 persons per square mile, and only 6 counties have population densities in excess of 100 persons per square mile (Helyar 1988). Although 97 percent of Kansas is privately owned, the population density does not put extreme pressure on the land resource.

Public opinion influences the success of policy making (Edwards and Sharkansky 1978), and often the most successful ideas are public ideas (Moore 1988). The state's recreational access proposal was not an idea generated by recreationists in the general public, and it has not received overwhelming support from recreationists. Some evidence suggests that the lack of recreational opportunities is not a major barrier to participation in recreation by Kansans.

In 1987, a survey about barriers to recreation was conducted among eastern Kansas residents (Cook et al. 1990). Eastern Kansas is the most densely populated area of the state. The study found that the lack of facilities and overcrowding were cited by less than 1 percent of recreationists as barriers to more participation in current recreational activities. Those results must be viewed with caution, however, because the study did not investigate activities in which recreationists may want to participate but cannot because they do not have access to any facilities. However, for activities in which recreationists currently participate, lack of access is not a major barrier.

The major barriers to participation are work-related conflicts and time. A state-sponsored program might have reduced the amount of time required to locate or get to a recreation site, but recreationists would not necessarily have used the extra time to recreate more. The same survey found that only 58 percent of recreationists said they would participate in their current activities more often if they had more access to private land.

Recreationists did not give overwhelming financial support to the idea of public access either. In the same survey (Cook et al. 1990), when asked "how much would you be willing to pay to gain recreational access to all private lands in Kansas," 23 percent of respondents reported they would not pay at all. In a 1988 statewide survey of Kansas hunters (Cable 1991), only 37.4 percent said they would be willing to pay an entry fee to gain access to privately owned hunting areas in Kansas. Despite having some support among recreationists, survey results did not indicate a mandate for more public access.

Although the amount of land being closed to public access or being leased privately is increasing in some states, a 1988 survey of 1,658 landowners in twenty-two randomly selected counties in Kansas (Hildebrandt 1989) found that 40 percent still allow some recreational access to their land and only 7.5 percent charge any kind of fee for access. In a survey of hunters who use windbreaks, Cable (1991) found that 68.2 percent of the sites that hunters used most often were located on land not owned by the hunters and access was free. Only 2.3 percent reported leasing land. The old system of asking permission to gain free access is still widely accepted in Kansas, and private leasing has not taken hold.

Although leasing land to recreationists was first proposed by agricultural interests and provides an opportunity for landowners to earn income, they opposed a state-sponsored public access program. Hildebrandt (1989) found that only 7 percent of landowners were interested in the state public access system, 66 percent were not, and 27 percent were undecided. Kansas has a history of strong protection of private property rights and opposition to government ownership or control of land. The loss of access control and giving that control to the state government were intolerable to many landowners, and agricultural interest groups, such as the KLA and the KFB, used the abridgment of private property rights as a rallying point against the state-sponsored leasing program. Landowners did not believe that the benefits of earning lease income would outweigh the cost of relinquishing access control.

Public bureaucracies often create policy in their own self-interest (Williams 1980), and the self-interested actions of state agencies may also have contributed to the defeat of the public access proposal. Although the secretaries of the KDWP and state Board of Agriculture drafted the proposal together, the board did not vigorously support the program. When the proposal was submitted to the board and its legislative body, neither took any action (Brownback 1989). The KDWP and the board have not traditionally been allies. The board protects the interests of Kansas agriculture, and the KDWP has fought with it over issues such as wetland conversions and water use. In the end, the board sided with its agricultural constituency by not supporting the state program.

The KDWP also acted in its own self-interest by proposing a large-scale program with extensive KDWP involvement. Alternative strategies for increasing recreational opportunities, such as tax incentives to landowners who allow access, could have been proposed, but the alternatives might not have provided the KDWP with as large a budget or as much influence over recreation management as the public access program would. Also, an increase in participation in hunting would mean an increase in revenues from license fees and increased political support for the KDWP.

Economic constraints also have a tremendous influence on an agency's policy-making ability (Edwards and Sharkansky 1978), and the start-up funding of the public access program was another stumbling block. The governor's budget proposed that pilot projects be funded by money from the state's Economic Development Initiatives Fund. This fund has traditionally been used to attract businesses and jobs to the state. Although the public access program would have increased overall economic activity associated with recreation, it probably would not have created jobs in the private sector or attracted businesses from out of state. Legislators did not consider the recreational leasing program to be a proper use of the economic development funds (Joseph 1990).

Lessons Learned

There are no fail-safe rules for policy making, but the failure of the public access proposal in Kansas may provide some instructive lessons for other states. The first lesson is in problem definition. Wildlife management agencies need to be sure that there is an access problem and that the public perceives that the problem exists. Lack of a grassroots movement for more access may have doomed the policy in Kansas.

Second, agencies should look at many alternatives. State agencies tend to adopt programs that other states have tried (Williams 1980); however, political, social, and economic factors may not be the same in all states. In Kansas, public attitudes toward government interference with private property rights may make any sort of state-sponsored public access program infeasible.

Third, agencies may need to try incremental approaches to policy change. Some states accept change and innovative policies more readily than others (Walker 1969; Gray 1973; Clarke 1980), and the size of the group whose behavior is being changed and the extent of the change will affect the acceptability of new policies (Sabatier and Mazmanian 1981). Landowners and recreationists are both large, poorly defined groups, and the traditional system of asking permission for access is well entrenched in both groups. Both factors make innovative policy difficult to implement in Kansas. Also, Kansas is not ranked highly for its innovative land-use policies (Clarke 1980); therefore, an incremental approach to the idea of public access may work better.

Despite having a proposal that looked toward the future, Kansas was unable to put in place a program to provide public access to private land for recreation. Kansas, like many other western states, is just beginning to feel the pressures of an increasing population on its recreational resources (Wright and Kaiser 1986). When the timing is right, determining policies to deal with this new management problem may require solutions unique to each state and previously untested.

References

Barry, S. J. 1984. "Public Access: Private Property Protection." *Parks and Recreation* 19(5):42–46, 75.

Brownback, S. 1989. "Testimony Before the Special Committee on Energy and Natural Resources." Topeka, 16 June.

Cable, T. T. 1991. *A Profile of Kansas Hunters*. Report of Progress 626. Manhattan: Kansas State University Agricultural Experiment Station.

Clarke, S. E. 1980. "Determinants of State Growth and Management Policy." Pp. 151–163 in T. R. Dye and V. Gray, eds., *The Determinants of Public Policy*. Lexington, Mass.: D. C. Heath.

Cook, P. S., E. Udd, and R. Hildebrandt. 1990. "Outdoor Recreation on Private Lands: Information Sources and Site Selection Behavior." *Abstracts from the Symposium on 1990 Leisure Research*, p. 31. Alexandria, Va.: National Recreation and Park Association.

Cordell, H. K., J. H. Gramann, D. E. Albrecht, S. Withrow, and R. W.

McLellan. 1985. "Trends in Recreational Access to Private Rural Lands." *Proceedings of 1985 National Outdoor Recreation Trends Symposium II, vol. 1—General Sessions*, pp. 164–183. Clemson, S.C.: Clemson University.

Edwards, G. C., III, and I. Sharkansky. 1978. *The Policy Predicament: Making and Implementing Public Policy.* San Francisco, Calif.: W. H. Freeman.

Gottschalk, J. S. 1977. "Wildlife Habitat—The 'Price-less' Resource Base." *Transactions of Forty-second North American Wildlife and Natural Resource Conference* 42:237–245.

Gramann, J. H., T. M. Bonnicksen, D. A. Albrecht, and W. B. Kurtz. 1985. "Recreational Access to Private Forests: The Impact of Hobby Farming and Exclusivity." *Journal of Leisure Research* 17(3):234–240.

Gray, V. 1973. "Innovation in the States." *American Political Science Review* 67:1174–1185.

Helyar, T. 1988. *Kansas Statistical Abstract 1987–1988.* Lawrence, Kans.: Institute for Public Policy and Business Research.

Hildebrandt, R. 1989. *Public Access to Private Kansas Lands for Recreational Purposes.* Department of Forestry Res. Rep. No. 89–512-D. Manhattan: Kansas Agricultural Experiment Station.

Hogwood, B. W., and B. G. Peters. 1985. *The Pathology of Public Policy.* New York: Oxford University Press.

Holecek, D. F. 1983. "Michigan's Land Leasing Program for Public Hunting." *Transactions of Forty-eighth North American Wildlife Natural Resource Conference* 48:108–115.

Horvath, W. J. 1976. "Habitat Programs and Recreation Opportunities on Private Agricultural Land: Opportunities and Constraints." *Transactions of Forty-first North American Wildlife and Natural Resource Conference* 41:504–512.

Joseph, B. 1990. "Pilot Recreational Access Program Tabled by Legislative Committee." *Kansas Sportsman* 37(2):7.

Kansas Department of Wildlife and Parks. 1988. *A Plan for Kansas Wildlife and Parks: Strategic Plan.* Topeka: Kansas Department of Wildlife and Parks.

Kansas Livestock Association. 1990. "1990 KLA Policy Resolutions." *Kansas Stockman* 75(3):26–27.

Kansas Park and Resources Authority. 1985. *State Comprehensive Outdoor Recreation Plan.* Topeka: Kansas Park and Resources Authority.

Kansas State University Cooperative Extension Service. 1987. *Proceedings of Lease Hunting: Pros and Cons, 1987 Telenet Conference.* Manhattan: Kansas State University Cooperative Extension Service.

Manning, R. E. 1973. "A Study of the Michigan Program of Private Land Leasing for Snowmobile Use." *Proceedings of the 1973 Snowmobile and Off Road Vehicle Research Symposium*, pp. 176–182. East Lansing: Michigan State University Experiment Station.

Manske, B. 1989. "Testimony Before the Special Committee on Energy and Natural Resources." Topeka, 16 June.

Meinen, R. L. 1989. "Kansas Department of Wildlife and Parks Notes on House Bill 2367: Recreational Access Program." Topeka, 16 February.

Mooney, R. 1989. "New Relief for Hunter Hassles." *Farm Journal* 113(3):i–viii.

Moore, M. H. 1988. "What Sort of Ideas Become Public Ideas?" Pp. 55–83 in R. B. Reich, ed., *The Power of Public Ideas.* Cambridge, Mass.: Ballinger.

President's Commission on Americans Outdoors. 1987. *The Report of the President's Commission on Americans Outdoors.* Washington, D.C.: Island Press.

Propst, D. B., H. K. Cordell, D. H. Holecek, D. B. K. English, and S. Chen. 1985. "Trends in Consumer Expenditures and Public Investments for Outdoor Recreation." *Proceedings of 1985 National Outdoor Recreation Trends Symposium II, vol. 1—General Sessions,* pp. 201–221. Clemson, S.C.: Clemson University.

Reich, R. B. 1988. "Policy Making in a Democracy." Pp. 123–156 in R. B. Reich, ed., *The Power of Public Ideas.* Cambridge, Mass.: Ballinger.

Sabatier, P. A., and D. A. Mazmanian. 1981. "The Implementation of Public Policy: A Framework for Analysis." Pp. 3–35 in P. A. Sabatier and D. A. Mazmanian, eds., *Effective Policy Implementation.* Lexington, Mass.: D. C. Heath.

Sampson, N. 1986. "Assessing the Availability of Private Lands for Recreation." *Parks and Recreation* 21(7):34–38, 59.

U.S. Bureau of the Census. 1986. *State and Metropolitan Area Data Book.* Washington, D.C.: U.S. Government Printing Office.

U.S. Fish and Wildlife Service. 1988. *1985 National Survey of Fishing, Hunting, and Wildlife-Associated Recreation.* Washington, D.C.: U.S. Government Printing Office.

Walker, J. L. 1969. "The Diffusion of Innovation in the American States." *American Political Science Review* 63:880–889.

Williams, B. A. 1980. "Organizational Determinants of Policy Change." Pp. 49–59 in T. R. Dye and V. Gray, eds., *The Determinants of Public Policy.* Lexington, Mass.: D. C. Heath.

Wright, B. A. 1988. "The National Private Land Ownership Study: Establishing a Benchmark." *Human Dimensions in Wildlife Newsletter* 7(3):16–17.

Wright B. A., H. K. Cordell, T. L. Brown, and B. Sale. 1988. "Advancing the Theory and Methods of Studying Recreational Access to Private Lands in the United States." *Proceedings of the Second Social Science in Resource Management Conference,* pp. 22–23. Urbana-Champaign, Ill.: Institute for Environmental Studies and Department of Psychology, University of Illinois.

Wright, B. A., and R. A. Kaiser. 1986. "Wildlife Administrators Perceptions of Hunter Access Problems: A National Overview." *Wildlife Society Bulletin* 14(1):30–35.

Wunderlich, G. 1979. *Facts about U.S. Landownership.* USDA Economic Statistics and Cooperative Service Information Bulletin No. 422. Washington, D.C.: U.S. Government Printing Office.

5

IMPLEMENTING
ENDANGERED SPECIES POLICY

Debra A. Rose

Introduction

The politicization of policy implementation has attracted growing awareness and attention. Variations in the character of implementation have been attributed to different policy *types*, with particular emphasis upon the adversarial relationships thought to be characteristic of social or protective regulation. While such distinctions are analytically useful, attention must also be paid to variations among distinct policy *issues* in explaining the character of policy implementation. Environmental policy, in particular, poses a unique set of implementation problems and dynamics for students of public policy and administration, which can be illustrated by examining implementation of the Endangered Species Act (ESA) of 1973. The uncertain and rapidly changing information base, the number and intensity of potential interests affected, and the clash of values involved in the act's implementation have made battles over its continued existence and relevance unusual in their scale,

94

openness, and longevity. Most important, from an analytical stand-point, is that the battles have been waged, not during the initial policy-making stage, but during implementation. Although the arti-ficiality of the traditional politics-administration dichotomy has long been recognized, the fact that ESA implementation has been much more political than its passage implies the need for further modifications in our approach to the policy process.

The Policy Process and the Politics of Implementation

The expanding federal role in the economic and social life of the nation has led to increasing interest in policy implementation and to a rejection of the distinction between politics and administration. On the one hand, the growing complexity, intractability, and inter-dependence of the problems targeted by government action have increased the likelihood of program failure and the demands of effective implementation. On the other, the prominence of bureau-cratic discretion, administrative rule making, public participation, and judicial review has blurred the functional and institutional lines separating implementation from other stages in the process. As a consequence, it is now generally recognized that implementation is no less political than policy making and may even be described as a policy process unto itself (Maynard-Moody 1989).

While those effects are common, several analysts have argued that their impact varies according to the forms and targets of policy. Lowi (1964) and Ripley and Franklin (1976) distinguish between distributive, redistributive, and regulatory policy, arguing that open conflict is much more characteristic of regulatory policy than of the other types. This distinctiveness arises from its high visibility, high awareness on the part of potential losers and gainers from policy application, and a large degree of intervention by both the Congress and the executive branch, partly in response to appeals from those affected (Lowi 1964; Ripley and Franklin 1976:chapter 5). Ripley and Franklin (1976) and Bryner (1987) also single out agencies charged with protective regulation, whose broad man-dates and limited resources, coupled with explicit delegation of legislative powers by Congress, have left them with broad discretion and subject to contradictory political pressures (Ripley and Franklin 1982; Bryner 1987: chapters 1 and 2). Reagan also points to the conflictual nature of protective, or social, regulation, focusing on the growing specificity of legislation, the concentration of the costs of implementation, and increased public participation (1987:chapter 5).

Sabatier and Mazmanian (1980) also point to the importance of the problem itself in affecting the success of program implementation. The tractability of the problem includes not only the number and intensity of the interests affected and the degree to which their behavior is expected to change but also "difficulties in measuring changes in the seriousness of the problem, in relating such changes back to modifications in the behavior of target groups, and in developing the technology to enable target groups to institute such changes" (Sabatier and Mazmanian 1980:541–543). The authors argue that the impact of the problem on program effectiveness occurs totally apart from the difficulties universally associated with the implementation of government programs (Sabatier and Mazmanian 1980:541). It is much more likely, however, that much of the difficulty in implementation is a function of the problem's impact on the policy process itself. The authors themselves point out that the absence of measurable improvements will lead to declining political support, the absence of available technology will lead to conflict over compliance requirements and deadlines, the diversity of regulated behavior increases bureaucratic discretion, and the quantity and degree of change required further expands political conflict (Sabatier and Mazmanian 1980:541–544).

Given those effects, it is likely that the nature of the policy process will vary according to specific issue areas as well as policy types. Environmental policy in particular has been subject to the implementation problems discussed above, demonstrating to the extreme the effects of unavailable information and technology, bureaucratic discretion, expanded conflict, and incremental adjustment. Surprisingly, few analysts have made explicit distinctions among issue-areas, although many make such a distinction implicitly. Mann (1982:5) notes, "The implementation of environmental policy is an especially thorny task because of the inevitable implications of some policies for other sectors of society and the economy." Ripley and Franklin use environmental regulation as an example of the conflicts generated by policy application (1976:112–116), and Bryner describes environmental regulation as one of the three issue-areas most strongly marked by the problems of bureaucratic discretion and dispute because of its dependence on scientific and technical information that is by nature incomplete and changing (1987:1–2).

But the distinctiveness of environmental policy implementation lies also in its placement in the wider policy process. Jones points out that the Clean Air Act of 1970 was a nonincremental response to public demands for environmental protection in which legitimation preceded policy formulation. The push of public opinion forced government action before the requisite information and technology were available, thus increasing the likelihood of policy failure and public backlash against its implementation (Jones 1974:438–464). The same can be said, of course, of all the major environmental legislation of the 1970s. While Jones focuses on the sequence of policy formulation, the nature of the initial environmental statutes also illustrates the blurring of formulation and implementation. Implementation has been overwhelmingly characterized by policy revision, political conflict, and discretionary application and enforcement, in large part because the bargaining and the negotiation normally considered to belong to the policy-making stage have instead taken place through implementation.

A case study of the implementation of the Endangered Species Act of 1973 illustrates each of these issues. The nonincremental nature of the policy itself, while somewhat unique to government policy in general, is largely typical of the country's major environmental statutes. Lack of experience with any systematic effort to preserve endangered species allowed for relatively quick and conflict-free passage of the act, but continual changes in information, technology, and the interests affected by implementation quickly generated extensive controversy. Subsequent involvement not only by Congress and the environmental interests responsible for the act's passage, but also by commercial and development interests in almost every sector of society, state and local governments, the judiciary, and even environmental organizations favoring different interpretations and applications of the law, represents not merely a continuation of earlier struggles but rather a playing out of battles inevitable in the American system but largely missing from the policy-making stage. The effects of this process on endangered species preservation have been magnified by the extensive discretion vested in the Interior and Commerce departments and have led to incremental implementation of a nonincremental policy by reinforcing the tendency toward bureaucratic conservatism and by encouraging frequent program adjustments by Congress.

Implementing the Endangered Species Act

The 1973 Endangered Species Act was passed "to provide a means whereby the ecosystems upon which endangered species and threatened species depend may be conserved, to provide a program for the conservation of such endangered species and threatened species," and to implement the Convention on International Trade in Endangered Species and other international agreements (Committee on Merchant Marine Fisheries 1988:1–2). The ESA was not the first attempt by the federal government to protect wildlife species; the Lacey Act of 1900 authorized the federal government to assist in enforcement of state wildlife laws through its power to regulate interstate commerce, in this instance wildlife products taken illegally in their state of origin. The Lacey Act also authorized the Department of Agriculture to take all necessary measures to preserve and restore populations of game and non-game wild birds. The Endangered Species Preservation Act of 1966 authorized the secretary of the interior to conserve, protect, restore, and propagate species of native fish and wildlife threatened with extinction, primarily through the National Wildlife Refuge System. The Departments of Agriculture and Defense were also directed to protect endangered species when such a task was consistent with their primary functions. The 1969 Endangered Species Conservation Act required that determination of endangered status follow the rule-making procedures specified by the Endangered Species

Act and extended protection to species threatened with worldwide extinction (Bean 1983a:17–18, 319–324; Rohlf 1989:19–22).

While the 1973 ESA builds on the previous statutes, it represents more than a minor adjustment to them. First, it extends protection to all wildlife species, not just those important to commercial and sport interests. Second, the act prohibits the taking of endangered species, an area previously left to state discretion. Third, the act protects threatened, as well as endangered, species and includes species threatened in only a portion of their range. Fourth, it extends the international dimension through provisions for the implementation of CITES, which became effective in the same year. Fifth, the act mandates consultation and cooperation with the states in conservation programs. Sixth, the act requires all federal agencies to further the goals of endangered species protection and prohibits them from undertaking or licensing any project that would adversely affect listed species. Seventh, the act makes generous provisions for public participation and judicial review. Finally, the act requires the pursuit of any and all measures necessary to conserve and restore endangered and threatened species and, for the first time, provides the resources to undertake these tasks (Bean 1983a:331–334; Rohlf 1989:23–24).

The burden of implementing and enforcing the Endangered Species Act falls primarily to the Fish and Wildlife Service of the Department of the Interior, although its authority over some marine species is shared with the National Marine Fisheries Service of the Commerce Department. The FWS is required to list endangered and threatened species through informal rule-making procedures, determine the range and possible uses of habitat critical to species preservation and recovery, develop recovery plans for the species in cooperation with state agencies and scientific authorities, consult with other federal agencies to assess the impact of planned projects on species status and develop recommendations for mitigating any adverse impact, and develop and enforce regulations on taking or commerce in listed species. Because each of those tasks imposes limitations on the behavior of individuals, firms, and other government agencies, it can best be described as protective regulation.

The nature and purposes of the act make administrative discretion inevitable. That discretion is considerably expanded by the enormity of the task and the limited resources of the FWS, which force it to choose among species, habitats, recovery measures, and enforcement targets. It is especially true of the listing process, which follows the procedures of informal rule-making. Initial listings or changes in status can be initiated either by the secretaries of the interior and commerce or by private petition. If the species is proposed for listing, the secretary must publish a notice to that effect in the Federal Register, notify relevant state and local governments and scientific organizations, and hold a public hearing if requested. The secretary then has one year to collect additional information and to determine the final listing, whether endangered, threatened, or not in need of protection (Bean 1983a:336–338).

The difficulty of determining listing status has both generated direct controversy over FWS decisions and magnified the impact of this controversy by expanding the scope of bureaucratic discretion. Listings depend on taxonomic distinctions between species and subspecies, estimates of population size, and evaluation of the threats to the species, all of which are highly uncertain and open to conflicting interpretations of scarce data. Oversight hearings in 1979 described the problem as follows:

> The simple fact is that there may never be sufficient personnel within the Service to expeditiously review the status of all the plants and animals that may be candidates for the list. In addition to the over 700 species now on the list, another 158 animals and 1850 plants have been formally proposed for listing. Hundreds of other species have been preliminarily identified as potential candidates for the list . . . the Service developed no less than six priority systems through fiscal year 1978. Nevertheless, none of these systems had ever been implemented because Service officials could not agree on the scope, comprehensiveness, criteria, definitions, and other components which should be included in the system. (Committee on Merchant Marine and Fisheries 1980)

On the one hand, the difficulties create endless delays in species listing and subject the service to pressure from interested legislators, from environmental interest groups, and from economic interests protesting the uncertain status of their projects. On the other,

scientific and technical uncertainty has been used by affected interests to serve their own purposes; subsequent controversy and litigation have served to delay action further (Yaffee 1982:chapters 4 and
5).

The gray wolf. Controversy over the gray wolf listing exemplifies
the expansion of conflict following implementation of the ESA.
The gray wolf was listed as endangered in 1967 and gained legal
protection under the 1973 act, which listed as endangered four
subspecies: the eastern timber wolf, gray wolf, northern Rocky
Mountain wolf, and Mexican wolf. The FWS was immediately subjected to pressure from the state of Minnesota, which had a long
history of wolf predation control and which requested that its population of eastern timber wolves be downlisted to threatened status
to allow continued predator control and hunting. In 1978, the secretary of the interior reclassified the wolves by combining all four
subspecies into a single gray wolf species, with the Minnesota
wolves as a threatened population. This classification allowed continued predator control, but the FWS continued to reject the state's
demands that hunting be allowed. Meanwhile, the Minnesota Department of Natural Resources refused to cooperate in a management plan until both predator control and hunting were permitted.
In 1981, after Secretary of the Interior James Watt entered office,
the service agreed to the state's management plan. The plan was
finalized in 1983 but was immediately challenged in the courts by
environmental groups. In 1985, the decision was overturned in
Sierra Club v. Clark (Yaffee 1982:77; Goldman-Carter 1983:68–72, 87–
92; Shea 1977:12; Endangered Species Act Amendments of 1988:12;
Anonymous 1983:11; Davis 1989:708).

The wolf case also demonstrates the expansion of political conflict
over agency decisions regarding conservation and recovery plans.
The Sierra Club decision sparked substantial congressional conflict
over its implications for other areas. As part of its wolf recovery
plan, the FWS proposed its reintroduction in Yellowstone National
Park and restoration in Montana and Idaho. The fears of ranchers
in those areas that wolves, as well as the grizzly bears that already
inhabit Yellowstone, would threaten their livestock were magnified
by the prohibition on hunting implied by the 1985 ruling. Senators

from Idaho, Minnesota, Montana, and especially Wyoming pushed for amendments to the ESA that would allow hunting and trapping, and threats by Senator Alan K. Simpson of Wyoming to introduce such an amendment helped keep ESA reauthorization bills off the Senate floor in 1987 and 1988. In May 1990, studies demonstrating that the wolf would pose no significant threat to livestock or to the park's wildlife prompted Senator James A. McClure of Idaho to introduce a bill urging reintroduction, with the condition that wolf populations elsewhere (that is, Idaho) be downlisted to permit sport hunting and predator control. The debate is still continuing (Anonymous 1983:11; Davis 1989:708; Committee on Merchant Marine and Fisheries 1987; Suro 1990b).

Incidental take. Another area of controversy concerns the taking of endangered species. The original act defined taking broadly, including to harass, harm, pursue, hunt, shoot, wound, kill, trap, capture, or collect, or to attempt to engage in any such conduct (Committee on Merchant Marine and Fisheries 1988:4). The term was interpreted to apply to a wide range of activities such as forestry or fishing that caused incidental mortality or harm, but since even incidental take was subject to criminal prosecution, the FWS typically responded to such cases either by failing to enforce the provision or by modifying listings. Thus, three species of sea turtles, threatened by incidental capture in shrimp trawls and already listed as endangered by CITES, were initially classified as threatened, and two others were not listed until 1978 (Bean 1983a:353; Yaffee 1982:67, 88–89).

In 1982, however, the ESA Amendments authorized the secretary of the interior to permit such takings "if they are incidental to, and not the purpose of, the carrying out of an otherwise lawful activity" (Bean 1983a:353; Committee on Merchant Marine and Fisheries 1988:31). A permit is required for such takings, and its granting is contingent on the submission of a conservation plan to mitigate incidental take and the determination that the number of such takings is not sufficiently high to threaten the survival and recovery prospects of the species. The provision gives greater flexibility to the FWS to limit such takings and creates incentives for cooperation in mitigation measures (Bean 1983a:353–354).

In some cases, these measures have proven effective in managing conflict. Mitigation measures negotiated between the Interior Department's Minerals Management Service and the NMFS established permitting requirements for the use of explosives in Outer Continental Shelf (OCS) waters to remove oil and gas structures, and the measures have been demonstrated to reduce related sea turtle mortality (Klima et al. 1988:33–42). A more controversial issue has concerned the use of TEDs, or turtle excluder devices. Following consultation with shrimpers and environmental organizations, in June 1987 the NMFS issued regulations requiring shrimp trawlers in the Gulf of Mexico and parts of the Atlantic to use the devices. The state of Louisiana and Concerned Shrimpers of Louisiana attempted to block the regulations in the courts, arguing that TEDs reduced the shrimp catch. Continued resistance, especially by Texas fishermen who blockaded shipping channels in the summer of 1988, led the commerce secretary to suspend enforcement. Pressure from interests in Texas, Louisiana, and North Carolina led to amendments of the ESA in 1988 to delay the effective dates of the regulations, to May 1989 for offshore areas and May 1990 for inshore. Further delays occurred because of continued litigation, but in September 1989 environmental groups succeeded in obtaining a court order demanding enforcement by the commerce secretary (Anonymous 1987:88; Anonymous 1988a:61; Anonymous 1989; Committee on Merchant Marine and Fisheries 1987; Endangered Species Act Amendments of 1988:2309–2310). In both the gray wolf and sea turtle cases, FWS and NMFS's willingness to accommodate economic interests was influenced by their conflicting organizational mandates. The FWS has historically been allied with state fish and game agencies and has long been responsible for aiding in predator control programs. Furthermore, the Interior Department, in which it is situated, has typically seen its purpose as making available resources for development (see Clark and McCool 1985, chapter 3, for a history of the agency). Similarly, the NMFS is charged primarily with promoting U.S. fisheries and is therefore sympathetic to appeals by threatened commercial interests (Yaffee 1982:chapter 7). However, even in cases where the services have assumed greater vigilance, they have often been thwarted by congressional intervention or cowed by public pressure.

Section 7 and the 1978 amendments. The latter is true of the designation of critical habitat in large part because such designations bring into play the now-famous section 7 of the act, which prohibits any federal action likely to destroy or adversely modify habitat necessary to the conservation or recovery of endangered species. While this provision received little attention at the time of the act's passage, it subsequently proved the most controversial of the act's requirements (Rohlf 1989:137–138; Bean 1983a:361–363). The most well known case is the Tennessee Valley Authority's (TVA) Tellico Dam project, which was halted because of the discovery that the area to be modified included most of the known habitat of a small fish, the snail darter. When challenged in the courts, the TVA defense argued that the project was exempt from the provisions of section 7 because the project was begun before the discovery of snail darter populations. The Supreme Court ruled in 1978, however, that the closing of the dam's gates would clearly represent a federal action harmful to the continued existence of the species and was therefore unlawful (Bean 1983a:361–363; Rohlf 1989:137–138; Witt 1978:1616).

Section 7 had generated several other conflicts as well, as environmental groups and private citizens obtained court action to delay the Meramec Dam in Missouri, which threatened the Indiana bat; the Dickey-Lincoln Dam, which threatened the furbish lousewort; and the Gray Rocks Dam in Wyoming, which threatened whooping crane habitat. But it was largely the Tellico controversy that sparked intense congressional battles over the application of section 7 and demands for amendment of the act. The battle for amendment was led, not surprisingly, by representatives from Tennessee and their allies among development interests, and the act was defended by environmentalists seeking to preserve it intact, although even some environmentalists believed the law might need to be altered (Light 1978b:3269–3272; Reed and Drabelle 1984:90–95).

Ultimately, the act was amended in 1978 to allow for exceptions to section 7. A seven-member Endangered Species Committee was established to decide on such exceptions, with projects first required to demonstrate the absence of reasonable alternatives, benefits that exceeded the costs of species loss, and national or regional significance. Petitions for exemption could only be submitted by the state governor, the federal agency, or the holder of a federal permit or license. Ironically, the committee refused to exempt Tellico, and Congress was forced to do so legislatively by attaching a rider to an unrelated bill (Light 1982a:3045–3046; Bean 1983a:365).

The 1978 Amendments also altered the process for habitat designation. The original act had specified that critical habitat be designated at the time a species was listed; however, a clear definition of critical habitat was not made until 1975, and the secretary of the interior had designated critical habitat for only thirty-three species by 1978. The potential economic impact of the designations and the conflicts of the late 1970s contributed greatly to FWS conservatism. In fact, the first proposal for habitat designation was made for the Mississippi sandhill crane as a result of litigation over the building of Interstate 10, and the first designation to be finalized was that of the snail darter, in response to litigation over the Tellico Dam project. Furthermore, as reported in the oversight hearings of 1979, FWS had failed to act on petitions for listing in order to avoid political controversy over habitat of economic importance and instead had focused inordinate time and resources on less controversial species. In other cases, habitat designations were continuously scaled down in size, as for the Houston toad, or were never finalized, as for the extensive range of the grizzly bear, protection of which would threaten western ranchers and development interests (Yaffee 1982:61–66, 92–97; Committee on Merchant Marine and Fisheries 1980:5–6).

The 1982 amendments. The 1978 amendments required not only that critical habitat be specified at the time of listing but also that economic considerations be taken into account in the designation. That requirement further complicated and delayed the listing procedure, and virtually assured that economic costs would be taken into account in listing as well as habitat designation. As a result of the amendment, the two thousand species already proposed for listing in 1978 were withdrawn pending consideration of the new requirements, and listings thereafter slowed to a trickle. The slowdown was considerably aggravated during the first years of the Reagan administration, which drastically cut agency funding and personnel and subjected FWS to its drive for regulatory relief; no new species were listed during the administration's first year, and only four had been listed by the time of the 1982 amendments. Congress therefore faced intense pressure in the 1982 reauthorization process from conservationists, who demanded that listings be made more quickly and solely on the basis of biological data. Congress responded by stressing that only biological criteria were to be taken into account in listings and by providing for delays in habitat designation if such habitat was indeterminable or if emergency listing procedures were required (Rohlf 1989:25–28; Bean 1983a:334–336; Chandler 1982:15; Campbell 1982:10, 13–14; Angle 1982:1107).

Affected interests, on the other hand, had continued to protest against listings already made or under consideration. Western development interests recommended that invertebrates and plants be removed from ESA protected lists, the Pet Industry Joint Advisory Council advocated formal hearings to prevent unwarranted listings, and Safari Club International petitioned for downlisting of several African species to allow their trophies to enter the United States (Campbell 1982:41; Committee on Environment and Public Works 1982:31, 589). An especially noteworthy case for delisting concerned the bobcat. The bobcat had been listed as threatened under CITES in 1976 because of its similarity in appearance to a number of endangered furbearers; its listing was intended to aid in protection of those species and to prevent overexploitation of the bobcat as other species were depleted. Although it was listed under CITES, it had not been added to ESA protected lists, and in 1977 Defenders of Wildlife submitted a petition to the Interior Department for a status review. When exports were found not to threaten the species, state agencies and the International Association of Fish and Wildlife Agencies (IAFWA) pressured the federal government to propose removal of the bobcat from CITES lists, since listing represented federal interference with state management of a species not considered to be threatened domestically and a drain on resources to meet requirements for status monitoring and the development of management plans (Tober 1989:85–94; Ryden 1982:26–29).

The CITES delisting proposal was defeated, largely through the efforts of U.S. environmental organizations. Defenders obtained a court injunction barring further export of bobcat pelts; the court found that CITES requirements for export permits demanded reliable population estimates, of which there were none. During the 1982 reauthorization hearings, Congress was petitioned by the IAFWA, the American Fur Resources Institute, and the American Fur Industry, Inc., to impose a legislative solution. The act was duly amended to provide that population estimates, if unavailable, would not be required for CITES export permits (Tober 1989:88–97; Campbell 1982:40; Ryden 1982:28–29; Committee on Environment and Public Works 1982; Davis 1982a:1403; Davis 1982b:2385).

Interestingly, the bobcat controversy in the 1982 reauthorization process was linked to sea turtle protection under CITES. In 1978, the Interior and Commerce Departments had prohibited imports of green turtle products, including those from Cayman Turtle Farm (CTF), which could not meet stringent CITES requirements. CTF challenged in the courts, but was rebuffed by conservationists represented by the Environmental Defense Fund. In 1982, CTF and the Cayman government lobbied Congress to repeal the ban, and the Cayman government was represented in the 1982 reauthorization hearings. Congressional interest in the case was stimulated by strong British support for the CTF cause: it was hoped that the U.S. case for relaxing CITES restrictions on farming operations could be used to enlist British aid in relaxing delisting procedures to allow bobcat exports (Bean 1983b:17–19; Committee on Environment and Public Works 1982:447). Both efforts eventually failed.

The 1982 reauthorization process also saw continued conflict over the application of section 7. The coalition of more than thirty conservation and scientific organizations defending the act pointed out that the average interagency consultation on habitat modification lasted only seventy-eight days, and of the 9,868 consultations taking place between 1978 and 1982, only 185 were considered to pose a threat to a species, and only 15 of them were unable to proceed. However, industrial interests such as the American Mining Congress, the National Forest Products Association, the Western Regional Council, the National Agricultural Chemicals Association, the Union Camp Corporation, the Weyerhauser Company, and the Wickes Forest Industries pressed for the weakening of habitat protection provisions, arguing that they interfered with economic projects, created costly delays, threatened jobs, and imposed unreasonable requirements for project alterations. They also argued that the exemption process was too complicated to provide relief. Development interests in the western states strengthened their complaints against section 7 by arguing that the ESA protections conflicted with existing water allocation formulas by requiring stable water flows to protect fish and other species. Represented by the Western States Water Council, these interests demanded that the act be amended to restore state control over water resources. Congress therefore balanced the relaxation of habitat designation procedures with measures encouraging interagency consultation prior to project start-up and streamlining the exemption process. The amendments also required that federal agencies consider state water rights in developing programs to protect species (Campbell 1982:10–13; Committee on Environment and Public Works 1981; Angle 1982:1107–1108; Koch 1982:43–44; Committee on Merchant Marine and Fisheries 1988:2).

The 1988 amendments and beyond. The 1982 amendments reauthorized the ESA for three years; continued controversy, however, prevented passage of another reauthorization until 1988, and the endangered species program had to be funded by yearly appropriations until then. Fifteen years after the act's passage, the conflicts were much the same as those witnessed in earlier reauthorization battles. In 1985 and 1986, for example, Senate action was delayed at the request of Senator Lloyd Bentsen of Texas, who opposed FWS proposals to list the Concho water snake that inhabits an area to be inundated by the proposed Stacy Dam. In 1987 and 1988, both House and Senate were besieged by shrimping interests opposed to TED regulations and by the IAFWA and western ranchers opposed to restrictions on wolf and grizzly hunting, and Senate action was again blocked. Western senators proposed the inclusion of economic criteria in the development of recovery plans, and continued efforts were made to give added protection to state water rights. And an Oklahoma representative attempted to obtain an amendment delisting the leopard darter minnow threatened by the proposed Lukfata Dam (Davis 1989; Davis 1987:3138; Anonymous

1986:41; Fitzgerald and Feeney 1988:39–40; Committee on Merchant Marine and Fisheries 1987:313; Stern 1988:2113).

Despite those conflicts, the 1988 amendments strengthened rather than weakened the act: they stiffened penalties for violations, authorized substantial increases in the FWS endangered species budget, provided new protections for endangered plants, and provided for FWS monitoring and protection of both candidate species and recovered species. Furthermore, while the National Marine Fisheries Service's TED deadlines were extended, the wolf lobby failed to offer an amendment (Anonymous 1988b:4; Endangered Species Act Amendments of 1988:2306–2309; Stern 1988:2113; Fitzgerald and Feeney 1988:39–40).

Although the demands of economic interests were largely defeated in 1988, the endangered species conflict shows no signs of abating. Yellowstone wolf recovery plans remain stalled, forestry concerns and environmentalists oppose each other over cutting restrictions in southern forests to protect the red-cockaded woodpecker, and FWS consideration of downlisting the bald eagle has raised protests among conservationists (Feeney 1990b:4; Feeney 1990c:4; Feeney 1989c:4; Anonymous 1990:B8). Congress has again been drawn into endangered species battles, this time over the spotted owl, which inhabits old-growth forests in the Pacific Northwest, and which is threatened by logging. Environmentalists petitioned FWS for listing in 1987, but their petition was rejected on what a 1989 General Accounting Office (GAO) report determined to be political and economic grounds. A court finding that the FWS decision had been made on the basis of insufficient information spurred FWS to publish a listing proposal in mid-1989; while FWS considered the final listing, temporary court injunctions blocked logging in owl habitat. In early 1990, Oregon and Washington delegations in the House and Senate obtained legislation overriding the court injunctions and authorizing record timber sales on federal lands to compensate for the depressed sales of 1989. The final listing has not yet been made; in the meantime, timber interests claim that the owls are actually quite numerous, while environmental groups such as the Wilderness Society, Sierra Club, Defenders, Audubon, and local organizations press for the preservation of old-growth forests as well as owls (Feeney 1989b:4; Hager 1989:2306–2309; Feeney 1990a:5–6).

Because of the tens of thousands of jobs potentially threatened by listing, the spotted owl controversy may also represent the greatest threat thus far to the unity of the environmental movement. While the preceding discussion has focused on battles between environmental and development interests, conflicts within the environmental community have also arisen: for example, strategic considerations led the National Wildlife Federation (NWF) to break ranks on the issue of the 1978 amendments, supporting the amendments as the only means of mitigating the harm done to the cause of wildlife conservation. Like the NWF, Defenders became somewhat of an outcast in the environmental community following its strong defense of bobcat protection, which was considered by other groups to threaten the act itself through the controversy it generated. The support of the Audubon Society for FWS recovery plans for the California condor, which entailed the capture of all remaining wild birds, subjected the society to intense criticism from the Sierra Club and Friends of the Earth, which were also involved in conservation efforts. In both the spotted owl case and the Tellico controversy, charges have been made that by using the endangered species issue to halt development conservationists with other agendas have threatened the ESA itself (Yaffee 1982:136–137; Tober 1989:chapters 3 and 4; Disilvestro 1989:chapter 8; Light 1978b:3270; Feeney 1990a:5–6). While such conflicts have been relatively rare, they have added to the uncertainty facing service officials and, in some cases, have strengthened the influence of economic interests in pressing for amendments. And as the spotted owl controversy suggests, intensifying competition over a shrinking resource base is likely to generate even greater divisions in the future.

Conclusion: The Implications of ESA Implementation

One means of evaluating endangered species policy involves the familiar standard of efficiency versus representation, generally understood to pose the fundamental dilemma for democratic systems. The standard of efficiency clearly demands that the stated goals of the act be achieved within the time and resource constraints set by the policy. This standard has not been, and probably cannot be, met for the ESA. The FWS and NMFS are not only unable to cope with the enormous tasks involved in implementation but have repeatedly been hindered by external pressure to weaken the protection mandated by the act. When they have not responded to the pressure, Congress has intervened directly. A few species have been saved: the bald eagle, the American alligator, the whooping crane. But, in the meantime, the number of species known to be threatened or endangered has exploded. As of the 1988 reauthorizations, for example, some four thousand species were awaiting action, and Congress was pressed to direct FWS to monitor their status to prevent them from becoming extinct in the interim. Moreover, a 1989 GAO report found that recovery plans had been prepared for only slightly more than half of the five hundred U.S. species listed, and the plans were seldom being fully effected. The status of a third of listed species was declining, while the status of only a sixth was improving (Rohlf 1989:43–48; Feeney 1989a:5–6).

The standard of representation may be more easily met. The scope of public participation has continuously expanded, partly as a result of periodic legislative revisions, for example, provisions for public participation in recovery plan formation mandated by the 1988 amendments (Endangered Species Act Amendments of 1988:2307). Environmentalists, for their part, would argue that commercial, development, and other affected interests have been more than adequately taken into account. But this standard offers little in the way of evaluation, for if many sides have been heard, none has been satisfied. Advocates of preservation are dismayed to witness the decline of one species after another, while those espousing different values continue to pay the costs of conservation efforts.

Alternative standards of evaluation are offered by various conceptions of social learning. Yaffee, for example, is hopeful that continual muddling and experimentation represent a learning curve that will gradually result in the development of more efficient methods of accommodating the values represented in the conflict (1982:157–158). A broader definition, one that incorporates representation as well, is offered by Stone: "The phrase, social learning, is an effort to say that good policymaking involves more than an effort to adopt policy initiatives to the capacities of implementing agents in a political environment. *Social* learning is also more than an improved institutional memory; it represents an effort to increase public understanding of social policy and the problems against which policy is directed" (1985:495).

The second definition offers the most helpful way of viewing the issues involved in ESA implementation, and environmental policy in general. Efficiency is a standard for small problems in which the goals and values of those involved are reasonably consistent; the goals of environmental or species protection, however, stand in stark conflict with societal norms of economic growth, and no amount of policy adjustment will bring the two into harmony. As Downing concludes in his analysis of the Environmental Protection Agency's (EPA) water pollution control, "The problem of environmental externality control generates costs to some and benefits to others. Government action is required to accomplish control; therefore, environmental quality improvement is a political issue. Changing institutional forms will not make it less political" (1983:584). And politics is inefficient.

Nor does social learning in the sense suggested by Yaffee offer much encouragement. Ironing out procedural kinks in order to resolve value conflicts more smoothly may have been effective in 1978, or in 1982, but it offers no permanent achievements. Administration of the ESA is conflictual in large part because the problems, the interests affected, and thus the effective means of conflict resolution are continually changing. This fact was made abundantly clear by the 1988 reauthorization process, which included not only old contradictions but also a host of new problems. The backlog of candidate species noted earlier is only one of them. Just as troublesome is the need to continuously monitor and protect recovered species, such as the bald eagle and whooping crane, from new threats (Suro 1990a:B7; Luoma 1989:19; Anonymous 1990:B8). Put somewhat differently, there is no such thing as *a* problem or *a* policy: both are continually redefined through action. This process essentially explains the lack of separation between policy making and implementation, or between politics and administration. In the context of the ESA, it explains why administering the act has been so much more political than its passage. Until the policy is applied, no decision must be made as to the amount of economic value that society is willing to sacrifice for the sake of a given (or uncertain) quantity of environmental value. Moreover, since the wider context of this choice is never the same, the choice must be made repeatedly. While that is true of almost any policy, it is most extreme for environmental issues because of the number and magnitude of the choices and because of the rapidity with which the scientific and technical contexts of the decision change. The politics of ESA implementation is therefore the politics of continual social learning, in which society defines and redefines both the problem and its willingness to address it.

References

Angle, Martha. 1982. "House, Senate panels Approve Bills on Endangered Species." *Congressional Quarterly Weekly Report* 40(20):1107.

Anonymous. 1983. "Defenders Contests Wolf Killing Plans." *Defenders* 58(5):11.

———. 1986. "Endangered Law Still Is Awaiting Action by Senate." *Defenders* 61(3):41.

———. 1987. "Turtle Saving Rules for Shrimp Boats Are Phased in This Year." *Marine Fisheries Review* 49(3):88.

———. 1988a. "Court Okays Sea Turtle Safety Rules." *Marine Fisheries Review* 50(3).

———. 1988b. "Endangered Law Passes Congresses." *Defenders* 63(6).

———. 1989. "U.S. Orders Shrimpers to Provide Escape Door to Aid Rare Turtles." *New York Times,* 6 September.

———. 1990. "U.S. Seeking to Drop Bald Eagle from a Danger List." *New York Times,* 6 March, p. B8.

Bean, Michael J. 1983a. *The Evolution of National Wildlife Law.* New York: Praeger.

———. 1983b. "Turtle Trouble on Grand Cayman." *Defenders* 58(1):17–19.

Bryner, Gary C. 1987. *Bureaucratic Discretion: Law and Policy in Federal Regulatory Agencies.* New York: Pergamon Press.

Campbell, Faith Thompson. 1982. "The Endangered Species Act: Facing Extinction?" *Environment* 24(5):10, 13–14.

Chandler, William J. 1982. "Up for Review: The Endangered Species Act." *The Nature Conservancy News* 32(1):15.

Clark, Jean Nienaber, and Daniel McCool. 1985. *Staking Out the Terrain: Power Differentials Among Natural Resource Management Agencies.* Albany, N.Y.: State University of New York Press.

Committee on Environment and Public Works. United States Senate. 1981. *Endangered Species Act Oversight Hearings.* Washington, D.C.: U.S. Government Printing Office.

———. 1982. *Hearings on Endangered Species Act Amendments of 1982.* Washington, D.C.: U.S. Government Printing Office.

Committee on Merchant Marine and Fisheries. House of Representatives. 1980. *Oversight Report on the Administration of the Endangered Species Act and the Convention on International Trade in Endangered Species.* Washington, D.C.: U.S. Government Printing Office.

———. 1987. *Endangered Species Act Reauthorization Hearing.* Washington, D.C.: U.S. Government Printing Office.

———. 1988. *Endangered Species Act of 1973 As Amended Through the 100th Congress.* Washington, D.C.: U.S. Government Printing Office.

Davis, Joseph A. 1982a. "House, Senate Panels Approve Bills On Endangered Species." *Congressional Quarterly Weekly Report* 40(24):1403.

———. 1982b. "Final Action Near on Endangered Species Bill." *Congressional Quarterly Weekly Report* 40(39):2385.

———. 1987. "Bill Would Reauthorize Endangered Species Act." *Congressional Quarterly Weekly Report* 45(51):3138.

———. 1989. "Ranchers Want Right to Hunt Wolves, Bears." *Congressional Quarterly Weekly Report* 46(12):707–708.

Disilvestro, Roger L. 1989. *The Endangered Kingdom: The Struggle to Save America's Wildlife.* New York: John Wiley & Sons.

Downing, Paul B. 1983. "Bargaining in Pollution Control." *Policy Studies Journal* 11(4):577–586.

Endangered Species Act Amendments of 1988. Public Law 100–478, Stat. 2306–2323, 7 October 1988.

Feeney, Andy. 1989a. "Recovery Plans Not Followed, Says GAO." *Defenders* 64(2):5–6.

———. 1989b. "Agency Proposes Spotted Owl Listing." *Defenders* 64(4):4.

———. 1989c. "Yellowstone Wolf Bill Introduced." *Defenders* 64(4):4–5.

———. 1990a. "Congress Overrides Courts On Owls." *Defenders* 65(1):5–6.

———. 1990b. "FWS Considers Eagle Downlisting." *Defenders* 65(1):4.

———. 1990c. "Red-Cockaded Rules Upheld." Defenders 65(1):4–5.

Fitzgerald, John M., and Andy Feeney. 1988. "Endangered Species: The Senate Acts." *Defenders* 63(5):39–40.

Goldman-Carter, Janice. 1983. "Federal Conservation of Threatened Species: By Administrative Discretion or by Legislative Standard?" *Boston College Environmental Affairs Law Review* II(1):63–104.

Hager, George. 1989. "Small Owl Incites Big Battle Over Environment, Jobs." *Congressional Quarterly Weekly Report* 47(36):2306–2309.

Hardin, Charles M. 1974. "Observations on Environmental Politics." Pp. 183–186 in Stuart S. Nagel, ed., *Environmental Politics*. New York: Praeger.

Jones, Charles O. 1974. "Speculative Augmentation in Federal Air Pollution Policy-Making." *The Journal of Politics* 36:438–464.

Klima, Edward F., Gregg R. Gitschlag, and Maurice L. Renaud. 1988. "Impacts of the Explosive Removal of Offshore Petroleum Platforms on Sea Turtles and Dolphins." *Marine Fisheries Review* 50(3):33–42.

Koch, Kathy. 1982. "Controversy Looms Again on Endangered Species Act." *Congressional Quarterly Weekly Report* 40(2):43–44.

Light, Larry. 1978a. "Congress Clears Legislation Allowing Some Exemptions to Endangered Species Act." *Congressional Quarterly Weekly Report* 36(42):3045–3046.

————. 1978b. "Endangered Species Law Itself Is Endangered." *Congressional Quarterly Weekly Report* 36(45):3269–3272.

Lowi, Theodore J. 1964. "American Business, Public Policy, Case Studies, and Political Theory." *World Politics* 16(4):677–715.

Luoma, Jon R. 1989. "Logging of Old Trees in Alaska Is Found to Threaten Eagles." *New York Times*, 7 November, p. 19.

Mann, Dean E., ed. 1982. *Environmental Policy Implementation: Planning and Management Options and Their Consequences*. Lexington, Mass.: Lexington Books.

Maynard-Moody, Steven. 1989. "Beyond Implementation: Developing an Institutional Theory of Administrative Policy Making." *Public Administration Review* 49(2):137–142.

Reagan, Michael D. 1987. *Regulation: The Politics of Policy*. Boston: Little, Brown.

Reed, Nathaniel P., and Dennis Drabelle. 1984. *The United States Fish and Wildlife Service*. Boulder, Colo.: Westview Press.

Ripley, Randall B., and Grace A. Franklin. 1976. *Congress, the Bureaucracy and Public Policy*. Homewood, Ill.: Dorsey Press.

————. 1982. *Bureaucracy and Policy Implementation*. Homewood, Ill.: Dorsey Press.

Rohlf, Daniel J. 1989. *The Endangered Species Act: A Guide to Its Protections and Implementation*. Stanford, Calif.: Stanford Environmental Law Society.

Ryden, Hope. 1982. "Will the Bobcat Join the Vanished?" *Defenders* 57(1):26–29.

Sabatier, Paul, and Daniel Mazmanian. 1980. "The Implementation of Public Policy: A Framework for Analysis." *Policy Studies Journal* 8(4):538–560.

Shea, Kevin. 1977. "The Endangered Species Act." *Environment* 19(7):6–15.

Stern, Amy. 1988. "Senate Votes for Shrimpers over Sea Turtles." *Congressional Quarterly Weekly Report* 46(31):2113.

Stone, Clarence N. 1985. "Efficiency Versus Social Learning: A Reconsideration of the Implementation Process." *Policy Studies Review* 4(3):484–495.

Suro, Roberto. 1990a. "Whooping Cranes Coming Back, But Nearby Barges Pose a Threat." *New York Times*, 13 February, p. B7.

———. 1990b. "Wolves at Park's Door Set a Test for Wildlife." *New York Times*, 29 May, p. B6.

Tober, James A. 1989. *Wildlife and the Public Interest: Nonprofit Organizations and Federal Wildlife Policy*. New York: Praeger.

Witt, Elder. 1978. "Supreme Court Blocks TVA Operation of Dam Threatening Snail Darter." *Congressional Quarterly Weekly Report* 36(25):1616.

Yaffee, Steven L. 1982. *Prohibitive Policy: Implementing the Federal Endangered Species Act*. Cambridge, Mass.: MIT Press.

PART 3
ECONOMIC ISSUES
IN WILDLIFE POLICY

6

Pursuing a New Paradigm in Funding State Fish and Wildlife Programs

Cliff Hamilton

The Funding Problem

Insufficient funding is a problem common to most governmental programs. All levels from local school boards to large federal agencies are engaged in this common struggle. Fish and wildlife departments are no exception. Most find themselves unable to meet diverse constituent demands or effectively answer threats to the resource. Consequently, many are engaged in a search for additional revenue. For many fish and wildlife agencies, meeting the crunch of budget shortfalls has replaced managing the programs, the personnel, and the resource as the dominant activity of top administrators.

The dominant paradigm for funding agency programs—those policies, beliefs, and rules for success that make up "knowing how to do it"—has long been one of getting money through traditional sources and spending it within tightly controlled budgets set by legislation. The "funding" quest within this paradigm has been one of seeking new sources of money or ways to increase present sources. Efforts to accomplish the quest are confined to traditional strategies like getting constituent and legislative approval for the new source or increase. Most of the agency's program-funding energy is focused on that system. Managers are selected and promoted, in large part, for their ability to carry on the traditional paradigm. Those with the most knowledge, experience, and training in the present system rise to decision-making levels, and the established paradigm continues despite the mounting stack of problems that the current system cannot solve.

Most potential new sources of money have no direct link to fish and wildlife. Funds from the proposed source are not derived from those who stand to directly benefit from the program or those whose activities threaten resource viability. Thus, there are few compelling reasons for legislators or voters to seriously consider such new sources for fish and wildlife needs. While many citizens may be sympathetic, other social needs regularly place well ahead of fish and wildlife in the funding olympics. It seems clear that with very few exceptions developing major new money sources strictly for fish and wildlife programs in any state is so remote a possibility that it hardly justifies serious consideration.

Most agency managers still see the funding problem as one of inadequate money, as if getting money were the end of the job rather than only one means to the real end. Agency solutions to the problem thus continue to mirror traditional approaches. Most agency lists of new items to tax are long and detailed. Success in capturing any of them for fish and wildlife programs is another matter. To date, that success has been poor to nonexistent. Future prospects appear no better. In the face of funding demands for other social needs like drug problems, crime, abused children, the homeless, or education, it seems almost arrogant for fish and wildlife interests to assume they can capture any major new money source totally for themselves. And so the traditional agency quest for money continues as testimony to the power of an entrenched paradigm.

Barriers in Our Minds

Many writers have focused on paradigms in looking at problem solving and change. They offer their own definitions. All recognize the complexity of the concept. In *Discovering the Future, The Business of Paradigms*, Joel Arthur Barker offers one of the simpler definitions. He defines a paradigm as "a set of rules and regulations that 1) defines boundaries; and 2) tells you what to do to be successful within those boundaries" (1989:6). In *Powers of the Mind*, Adam Smith notes, "When we are in the middle of a paradigm, it is hard to imagine any other paradigm" (1975:20).

An established paradigm or mind-set is a powerful thing, especially one developed early in life. In "Between Trapezes," Larry Wilson (1987:53) points out that schools are based on a system of "known" answers. Schools train students to find *the* right answer. They produce people who continue to do as they learned. Few learn to look beyond established methods, especially if those methods have proven successful or useful in the past. Wilson points out that in times of change and uncertainty "knowledge is the enemy of learning." We believe we "know" how to do things, based on our past successes. That prevents us from seeking new solutions or learning new ways. Thus, as Wilson notes, "nothing fails like success." Those with the most expertise and training in the current paradigm are often least able to find creative or new solutions, even when the situation grows critical.

Roger von Oech (1983) says much the same in *A Whack on the Side of the Head*. Like Wilson, von Oech discusses our school-induced mind-set of seeking *one* right answer when, in fact, there may be many workable solutions. He notes that the third or fourth solution to a problem is often the most creative. Learning how to learn new ways of doing things is the solution to thriving in times of great change offered by Alvin Toffler (1970) in the classic book *Future Shock*. Although now two decades old, Toffler's book is still relevant because it describes how to cope in a time of unpredictable, accelerating change. Few can deny that it is an accurate description of our society today.

Wilson, Von Oech, and Toffler offer good reasons to reconsider much of what we "know" from past successes in funding fish and wildlife agency programs. This is particularly true where getting *money* is apparently the singular purpose of the funding quest. For many administrators, getting money is viewed almost as an end in itself rather than only a means to an end.

Getting the job done is the real end. The pursuit of money often obscures that true purpose. Money is only one of many means available. Some parts of the job cannot be accomplished with money at all. The committed "product champion" who struggles against peer pressure or supervisor opinion to create a management break-through and the enthusiastic support of volunteers who have been "let in" to work closely with agency personnel provide a benefit not bought with money. Genuine cooperative relationships with other agencies, organizations, or businesses and the benefits that go with them are also things money cannot buy. In fact, those relationships often emerge only as a result of money shortfalls.

The New Funding Paradigm

Conventional policies and well-worn procedures are of little use when upheavals of public attitude have altered the rules for success. In times of change, a new "map" and a new direction are often necessary to succeed. To do this we may need to change our whole mind-set about where we are headed and our approach to the journey. When traditional methods, no matter how successful in the past, leave many problems unsolved, a truly new approach—a new paradigm—may be the only hope for a sustainable future. It involves a whole change in mind-set and the rules for success. For fish and wildlife agencies, the new funding paradigm or the new way of "knowing how to do it" must focus, not on getting money, but on the real objective of *getting the job done.* In this approach, money and budgets become just one of many ways to accomplish the task. Agencies must develop new funding mechanisms that until now have largely been ignored or not taken seriously.

In the new paradigm, getting the job done will focus on volunteers, partnerships, joint ventures, shared personnel, donated funds, and other resources, in addition to traditional money sources. Funding from traditional money sources like licenses, stamps, and tags will continue to provide a base level of operation. Alternative sources and mechanisms will fill the remaining needs. The secret of the new paradigm is identifying the job to be done and looking equally at all possible ways to accomplish it. In many situations, a job will require packaging certain portions so each can be accomplished through the most appropriate funding mechanism.

We should not expect transition to the new funding system to be a smooth one. Practitioners of an established paradigm often have a heavy personal, professional, and emotional investment in it. They seldom give up without a struggle. Just questioning an established paradigm can generate conflict. In their book *In Search of Excellence,* Peters and Waterman (1982) discuss early attempts to pinpoint and reverse causes for the decline in American business superiority. Some of those efforts questioned the basis of existing business logic and rationality. That challenge was not seen by the business community as an examination of past narrow thinking. Rather, it was regarded as an attack on the "businessman's intellect and soul" and was accompanied by finger pointing, charges, and counter charges. As the authors note, the old rationality does not give up easily.

Efforts to simplify complex agency rules and policies in order to stimulate creative innovation are seldom welcomed by an entrenched bureaucracy. Rules and policies form the basis of the current paradigm and establish power and control. They are readily applied as a defense against any threat to established norms. Government tends to be strong on control and short on tolerance for creativity and innovation. Many an agency employee's attempts to get the job done by nontraditional means have run into paradigm boundaries guarded by fiscal officers, administrators, and legislators. Excellence in management, as Peters and Waterman (1982) remind us, is characterized by a preference for creativity, innovation, and action. Poor or failing management systems are long on control and short on flexibility. In these times of change and unstable agency funding, a new policy paradigm supporting tolerance and flexibility in getting the job done seems most likely to be successful. That policy shift will not come easily.

The Paradigm Shift

The real Renaissance of the late Middle Ages was not an explosion of art, music, literature, and scientific discovery. They were only by-products. The Renaissance was what Thomas Kuhn (1970), in *The Structure of Scientific Revolutions*, calls a paradigm shift: a change in the set of fundamental attitudes, beliefs, and philosophy about how things are or should be. The paradigm of the Dark Ages was one of protecting and repelling. Thick walls protected cities and people from invading armies. Inquisitions and dungeons repelled invasion of new ideas that did not agree with what was "known" at the time. That paradigm served for a time but eventually prevented the resolution of more problems than it solved.

Policies and rules based on getting money for agency programs have served well for a time but are now falling behind in their ability to resolve many new funding problems. Like the emergence from the Dark Ages, the shift to a new agency funding paradigm must involve a kind of renaissance of its own. It requires a change in mind-set and a fundamental shift in attitudes, beliefs, and assumptions about how to get the fish and wildlife management job done.

Kuhn (1970) notes that once a paradigm shift begins, things move fast. The speedy change is supported by a flood of new information and experimental successes. Few events illustrate such a shift more graphically than the recent, widespread upheaval of communist governments and their replacement with ones more closely aligned with basic human values. In any shift, conditions ultimately stabilize, and the old paradigm is replaced by one that is better and more useful. The process, however, is often filled with tension, anger, and perhaps violence. Events in changing or attempting to change the paradigm of communist rule in China, Romania, and the Soviet Union are excellent examples.

A paradigm shift also represents the death of an old way of

thinking and acting. Anger is often an early reaction of people who learn they are dying. Anger about the impending death of one's life-style or belief system is consistent with this finding. Thus, for agency administrators to adopt a new funding policy paradigm, even in the face of declining traditional money sources, requires admitting the existing system may be facing its demise. Angry reactions from administrators and legislators are natural and predictable. The paradigm shift is seldom an orderly process.

A Change in Agency Life-style

The new funding paradigm, focused on getting the job done, carries many implications about how agencies will operate in the future. Less certain "support" from any one source is the likely norm. Agency life-style will thus demand more flexible, less certain, and less controlled budgets. Agencies will also need to employ a wide range of methods to get the job done. These will require more flexible approaches to personnel as well as funding.

Where money is involved, new, flexible vehicles will be required for handling nontraditional and less reliable money sources. Less certain income from new sources will require less constricting legislative control of agency budgets and more open and trusting relationships between agency professionals and lawmakers. Partnerships or joint ventures with other agencies and private organizations will increase as more and more conservation interests find no one has enough funding to "go it alone." The use of incentives such as challenge grants to "leverage" public and private dollars will become an accepted practice. Staff sharing between public and private agencies will reduce duplication of personnel, especially those with special skills and training. The new funding paradigm will also make much greater use of unpaid staff or volunteers.

As the new paradigm becomes fully implemented, no single funding source will dominate in the way hunting and fishing licenses and tags have in the past. The new system will involve a more diversified approach than the current one. Money will be only one of many means to achieve the desired end. Just as nature has practiced for aeons and financial investors have done for decades, agencies that gain diversified funding sources will insure minimal impact on the system from reduction or loss of any one part.

With diversity, whether in human or biological systems, interrelationships develop among components. Synergy becomes possible through these supportive interrelationships. In a synergistic system, the productive capability exceeds what the parts could produce operating independently. A diverse, integrated funding system for fish and wildlife programs provides the same opportunities. Some examples have already been observed:

- Volunteers develop money sources to support their own projects.
- Visibility for corporate sponsors of current programs attracts inquiries from others.
- Consumer sales items that support a program also advertise the program to other people.
- Ease of handling money through a flexible vehicle such as a trust fund encourages others to seek funds for their own program needs.
- Volunteers recruit others in the process of sharing their own experiences.
- Donors who would not give to an agency contribute to a foundation even though the money is still used on agency projects.
- Recognition events attract media publicity, provide program visibility, and end up attracting additional support.

Diverse systems can more readily adapt to change in response to different opportunities or demands. This promotes a kind of dynamic stability in the system. A funding policy based on "getting the job done" uses principles of diversity and the enhanced ability to adapt that goes with those principles. That flexibility is essential in times of uncertainty and change.

In *Thriving on Chaos*, Thomas Peters (1987) explains that flexibility is a critical component for survival in times of change. He notes that the means to quickly exploit opportunity, shift the program, and develop new "niches" are essential if the organization is to prosper under changing conditions. Fish and wildlife agencies have typically been confined to a bureaucratic funding system of set budgets, fixed time intervals, and restricted options. This system simply will not function at an adequate level in uncertain times.

With a funding paradigm focused on getting the job done, many of the rigid budgets disappear. They are replaced by a more flexible system of matching needs against a range of ways to meet them. Administrators, commissioners, and legislators will still set the priorities. Agency managers will operate the system by selecting the funding method(s) most suitable for any given project. Many of the methods will be earmarked for specific projects only. Money will accomplish some tasks, volunteers will do others, and cooperative efforts among agencies or organizations will complete still others. In the same way that agencies developed flexible working hours and benefits for changing life-styles of their employees, they will need to develop flexible budget systems and new policies to accomplish a changing funding environment as well.

John Naisbitt (1982) reminds us in *Megatrends* that future leaders must be "facilitators and not order-givers." To operate the new, flexible funding systems, managers will need facilitative skills to bring the right project together with the best means for accomplishing it. Legislators, commissioners, and top agency administrators will establish general guidelines and priorities for management programs rather than tightly controlled policies and budgets as they currently do. Much greater authority for spending and action must also be placed at the field level as Peters (1987) describes.

A new system will also require flexible vehicles for handling a variety of funding mechanisms. Examples of this are already beginning to appear. Some states have or are developing revolving accounts, unanticipated revenue funds, unknown-source budget limitations, foundations, and trust funds. As the new paradigm develops, there will be a proliferation of these and other vehicles. They will permit readily taking in contributions, sales proceeds, grants, and money from other nontraditional sources and matching them with projects through a system of guidelines and priorities.

Recent efforts by several states to broaden the funding base and constituency reveal that many potential sources of money or other support simply do not trust traditional agencies to act on their behalf (Arrandale 1990). Citizens have grown wary of approving any funds, especially new ones, without clear directions for their use. Thus, any new money sources will likely be earmarked for specific activities. Those who provide the money will also want to see timely results. New vehicles and policies to allow receipt and expenditure of funds without a lot of bureaucratic delays will become even more essential.

The new paradigm must also bring a greater level of trust and diversified spending authority. Peters (1987) emphasizes this and recommends simplified systems that place much higher spending and action authority out at the front line. Accomplishing this requires adopting a facilitative attitude rather than one of traditional order giving by those in power positions. Legislators must relax their tight grip on agency budgets. Top agency administrators must also give field managers increased autonomy and freedom to make decisions. In doing so, traditional power holders pass some of their authority on to lower levels. The benefit of giving up this power comes in the greater power of having managers and field staff who have a real involvement and ownership in the total process.

Peters and Waterman (1982) identify employee commitment as a key factor separating excellent performances in the workplace from average ones. The sharing of power leads to ownership and commitment. Doyle and Strause (1976) also identify the value of giving up power to get more power as an important concept in problemsolving. Clearly, when power, spending authority, policy setting and decision making are held at and disbursed from the top, the probability of getting the job done at a high level of excellence is diminished.

Adversarial relationships often found between legislators and agencies must be replaced by an attitude of partnership and cooperation focused on serving the public and resource needs. Too often, issues of power and control dominate the relationship between lawmakers and agencies. Public interests and the resource are forgotten in the struggle. Since politics is about the holding and disbursing of power, there will be much less "playing politics" under the new paradigm. A system of diverse funding mechanisms, including flexible money sources, volunteers, and cooperative projects, simply does not lend itself to tight administrative control.

Getting the job done will require trust, shared power, flexibility, cooperation, easy access to information, and general openness.

The interrelated nature of resource management today creates many areas of overlapping responsibility among agencies. These "edges" provide opportunities to accomplish jobs that no single agency or organization could do alone. Under the new paradigm, state, federal, and private interests will undertake joint ventures in increasing numbers, motivated by a common goal of getting the job done. There will be more programs like Project WILD and Responsive Management in which many agencies pool resources to develop what no one could afford to do independently. For agencies in need of a new or an improved image, the negative side of partnerships and joint ventures is a loss of visibility through sharing of recognition for the new accomplishment. Each partner must weigh this "new image" loss against the cost savings of cooperative efforts and the need to get the job done.

The concept of joint ventures can be extended to sharing personnel as well. The Intergovernmental Personnel Act (IPA), for example, provides for exchanging staff between state and federal agencies. The program offers an effective approach under the current paradigm, and its benefits are already apparent. Combining administrative staffs into departments of natural resources, use of special services from a central pool, and positions funded jointly by state and federal agencies are other examples of cooperative efforts. Like other joint ventures, something will be lost as well as gained in staff sharing. Peters and Waterman (1982) verify the cost of duplication and the resulting increase in performance stimulated by competition. This subtle value seems unlikely to be recognized or to escape government belt-tightening and downsizing that will occur as traditional money-based funding systems continue to fail.

The use of unpaid staff—volunteers—will increase substantially under the new paradigm. Today, agencies are beginning to recognize volunteers as an important source of new funding. In the early years of resource management, volunteers were an essential part of many agency programs. They helped stock fish, developed habitat areas, transplanted wildlife, and assisted in other ways. In those years before fish and wildlife management was a recognized profession, agencies simply lacked the means to do the job. Citizen help was vital. Then, user numbers began to climb, money for programs increased, and college graduates began to dominate agency ranks. Fish and wildlife staffs went professional. Citizens' money was welcome, but their presence on the job was often viewed as more hindrance than help. Now the boom in user numbers and budgets is over. Agencies again lack the resources to do the job alone and citizens are being asked to help in increasing numbers.

Programs like hunter education have long relied on an organized, trained, and certified corps of volunteer instructors. With similar organization and coordination, few activities within existing agency jobs cannot be done by volunteers. Unfortunately, volunteer activities to date have often been one-shot weekend projects of nontechnical, low-skill nature. Employment of volunteers in the new paradigm will involve a more organized, comprehensive, and integrated approach and tasks requiring high levels of skill and training.

Volunteers have a high, positive, cost/benefit ratio, but they are not free. It takes time and resources to select, train, nurture, evaluate, and motivate volunteers. Good volunteer management can provide an important and cost-effective way to get the job done. As an added benefit, volunteers get acquainted with the agency and become strong program supporters. Fortunately, just when volunteers are being recognized as a valuable resource, volunteer service is enjoying a nationwide surge in popularity.

Fish and wildlife agency personnel have long prided themselves on being professionals in their field. Employment of volunteers, sharing staff, partnerships, and sponsorships in the new paradigm will test that perception. Many agency employees draw much of their job satisfaction from the life-style or job style the work offers. Sharing with other agencies, organizations, or volunteers will alter the very nature of many fish and wildlife jobs. Many agency professionals will spend much less time afield "doing the job" and more in the office and the meeting room coordinating and facilitating its completion. This means a major decrease in doing the "fun stuff" and probably giving some of it up entirely. The professionalism test comes as managers attempt to sort out their real personal motivations between doing the job personally and seeing that it gets done.

The practice of "leverage," or putting up a limited amount of money in order to control or stimulate a larger sum, is well known to the financial and business community. The concept has applications in getting the job done in fish and wildlife programs as well. Use of incentive or challenge grants is already beginning in some agencies as a way of multiplying the effectiveness of limited program dollars. Sponsorships, joint ventures, and volunteer programs all represent the concept of getting a bigger job done with less of the agency's own money. Leveraging is also a fundamental principle underlying much of the new funding paradigm.

Volunteers, partnerships, and shared staffs offer the benefits of a more balanced and diversified funding approach. In the same way, every successful financial investor recognizes the value of a diversified portfolio to counter the ups and downs of any one category. Diverse natural systems have long been recognized as more stable than those of low diversity. Developing an agency support system under the new paradigm will follow many of the natural principles of diversity and reap many of the stabilizing benefits. A range of ways to get the management job done counters the vagaries of social change, legislative whims, effects of a bad winter, and economic conditions.

Few businesses, for example, want to be caught with only one source of supply for critical parts or raw materials. Agencies can learn the same lesson of diversity. Consumptive users have virtually been a sole source of fish and wildlife agency program funding. The dependence on a specific source represents a lack of diversification that now has agencies scrambling for new "suppliers." Many are sliding into a "line down" situation with more and more programs being threatened by cuts as limited funding sources become less reliable or actually decrease. Under the new paradigm, diversified funding systems will offer a form of dynamic stability and adaptability to change in the overall program mix. No single source will dominate funding the way consumptive user fees have for decades.

A New Level of Organization

In his book *Evolution, The Grand Synthesis,* Ervin Laszlo (1987) points out that systems of all kinds, whether simple organisms, biological communities, or human societies, evolve in much the same way. They proceed from simple to complex and then become simple again as their evolution moves to successively higher levels of organization. Laszlo's synthesis concludes that when forces change in a dynamic system that is out of equilibrium the system enters an evolutionary transition marked by uncertainty and chaos. He notes that evolution is not a smooth process but one of "leaps and bursts" with times of both stability and chaos. This parallels much of Kuhn's (1970) thinking concerning characteristics of a paradigm shift.

Agency fiscal managers may pale at the thought of tracking a more complex set of fund sources, especially many earmarked for specific programs. When viewed in traditional ways, a system of volunteers, cooperative projects, shared staffs, and dedicated funding sources looks like an unwieldy structure. That might be true under the current system of rigid and inflexible budgets, centralized spending authority, and tight legislative controls. The new funding paradigm, however, represents a new level of organizational structure. Under it, many destabilizing forces operating on a money-only system are removed. The result is a more simplified rather than a complex approach.

Few can escape the reality that forces on traditional fish and wildlife agencies have changed or that current funding systems are growing unstable. Many agencies today are operating in a dynamic system of managed chaos. Parallels between agency funding situations and Laszlo's (1987) description of evolutionary processes seem obvious. Thus, Laszlo's grand synthesis model offers strong evidence that evolution is occurring and hints about its direction. Periods of chaos, stability, and uncertainty can be found in most fish and wildlife agency funding situations in recent years. Laszlo indicates that in the evolutionary process, any one of a number of new steady-state or stable situations may emerge when the current burst of evolutionary activity finally settles down. That implies that no single or predictable mix of funding approaches will emerge for any one agency. It is also consistent with a report by the Oregon Department of Fish and Wildlife (1987) that concludes that there is probably no one "right" combination of alternative funding sources for the agency.

Obviously, different agencies are at different places in the evolutionary shift of their funding system. Many are still struggling just to understand the real basis of their problems. Even at this early stage, the foundation for a policy change and a shift in traditional approaches is strong. Achieving the large potential of the new paradigm will require some *glasnost,* or openness, on the part of agencies. They must open their doors and invite their publics in. They must welcome and encourage the public to become part of what they do—as partners, supporters, volunteers, and providers.

Developing an open approach means letting go of some of the mystique about fish and wildlife professionals, which has been maintained for too long. It means sharing visibility and public recognition of accomplishments with citizen groups, businesses, other agencies, and individuals. It also means sharing decision making about the direction of management programs and their results. A lot of private individuals, businesses, and organizations want and are willing to help with specific programs or parts of programs. They are not willing, however, to become more public "support" through mandatory new taxes and fees over which they have little control.

Fish and wildlife are an attractive resource to millions of Americans. Allowing those citizens to be involved and to select an appropriate level of support for this resource is what the new paradigm is all about. Essentially, citizens, businesses, and organizations "vote" directly with their checkbook and volunteer time for those fish and wildlife programs they feel are worthy. This is counter to traditional policies of mandatory money sources governed by appointed or elected officials. It risks citizens' and agency managers' choosing different priorities but offers the power of broad-based public support as well.

Even under the new paradigm, traditional licenses and excise taxes will continue to provide a base level of funding for fish and wildlife agencies far into the future. Offering services and programs above that basic level will require new policies and some new ways of viewing funding in the face of voter and legislative resistance to new money sources. Focusing on getting the job done rather than on finding money offers a compelling new approach. It is already beginning to operate in some states, and a flourish of activity in this area can be expected. The happy paradox of it all may be that with extensive citizen involvement in fish and wildlife programs, helped by emerging new environmental concerns, approval of a major new money source may be possible some years in the future. The unhappy part is things will get a lot worse in many states before the real benefits of policy changes and a new funding paradigm become clear.

Conclusion

Traditional funding support for fish and wildlife programs has come almost exclusively from user fees and taxes. Those who pay the fees and taxes are becoming less able or willing to meet the needs. New support for management activities must come from a new funding paradigm focused on getting the job done instead of just getting money. Support for the conceptual base of the new approach is found in the research and the writings of many authors and from diverse disciplines. Its beginnings are already evidenced in new programs and practices now emerging across the nation. There is a remarkable consistency in and reinforcement of the new paradigm in this evidence. However, while the need is great and the evidence of change is strong, it will take a number of years to produce a confirmed reality.

Unlike a natural organism, a government agency is unlikely to become extinct. Thus, in times of instability and change, evolution to a new form via merger, reorganization, or restructuring is the probable course. While a new set of attitudes, beliefs, policies, and rules can unlock new and creative funding applications, the process will likely be one of paced evolution rather than fast revolution or mutation. Until a new and more stable funding situation is achieved, agencies must accept what they cannot change of the current problem, change what they can as fast as their culture will allow, and have the wisdom to know the difference as they move toward a new funding paradigm.

References

Arrandale, Tom. 1990. "Can Game Departments Cash in on That Warm and Fuzzy Feeling?" *Governing* (July):48–52.

Barker, Joel Arthur. 1989. *Discovering the Future, The Business of Paradigms.* St. Paul, Minn.: ILI Press.

Doyle, Michael, and David Strauss. 1976. *How to Make Meetings Work.* New York: PBJ Books.

Kuhn, Thomas. 1970. *The Structure of Scientific Revolutions.* Chicago: University of Chicago Press.

Laszlo, Ervin. 1987. *Evolution, The Grand Synthesis.* Boston: Shambhala Publications.

Naisbitt, John. 1982. *Megatrends.* New York: Warner Books.

Oregon Department of Fish and Wildlife. 1987. "Tomorrow's Dollars, The Report of the Diversified Funding Task Force." Unpublished internal report.

Peters, Thomas J. 1987. *Thriving on Chaos, Handbook for a Management Revolution.* New York: Alfred A. Knopf.

Peters, Thomas, and Robert Waterman. 1982. *In Search of Excellence.* New York: Warner Books.

Smith, Adam. 1975. *Powers of the Mind.* New York: Random House.

Toffler, Alvin. 1970. *Future Shock.* New York: Random House.

von Oech, Roger. 1983. *A Whack on the Side of the Head.* New York: Warner Books.

Wilson, Larry. 1987. "Between Trapezes." *Windstar Journal* (Winter):50–54.

7

THE USE OF ECONOMICS IN FEDERAL AND STATE FISHERY ALLOCATION DECISIONS: CASE OF THE GULF RED DRUM

Trellis G. Green

Tale of Cajun Recipes, Overfishing, and Jobs

Paul Prudhomme, the famous Louisiana Cajun chef, catapulted his "blackened redfish" recipe into a nationwide culinary craze in 1983. At that time, he could not comprehend the impact his seafood creation would have on issues as far removed from the kitchen as scientific management goals of conserving and allocating threatened species. The red drum (redfish) problem reached beyond pure management science to encompass interagency jurisdictional conflicts, overlapping government regulation, and self-interested politics. Economic science played a moderating role throughout by providing managers with values of the red drum resource in its different uses and by conveying a precedent for allocating fishery resources in the future.

Table 7.1 indicates how commercial red drum harvest increased drastically after 1983 to supply the new market demand for blackened redfish. However, there was no fishery management plan

(FMP) being considered for red drum either by the Gulf Council, responsible for managing offshore federal waters (Exclusive Economic Zone [EEZ]), or by state agencies with jurisdiction over inshore, territorial waters.[1] It seemed the world was caught off guard by a yuppie fad requiring exploitation of a single fish.

Prior to 1983, red drum had been a low-profile, unglamorous fish, most popular among estuarine recreational anglers. As a result, commercial fishing effort for red drum had been nondirected, and the nature of the harvest was largely by-catch. Because there was little scientific information about sustained harvest or economic value, federal officials became concerned about the prospect of overfishing the stock and contemplated conservation alternatives.

Meanwhile, as market demand escalated in 1984, commercial fishing effort quickly shifted from gill nets, targeting inshore juvenile stock, toward purse seine technology in the offshore EEZ that targeted the larger, five-to-twenty-five-year-old breeder stock. So concentrated were these offshore red drum that they were affectionately referred to as *mother lodes*. By that time purse seine capacity had already surpassed eight million pounds of Gulf red drum annually (Green 1989). In defense, commercial advocates embraced the "frontier theory" that marine stocks were too vast to overfish. This position held that fish mortality is subject to natural biological cycles, meaning that the biomass could withstand enormous human exploitation on a sustained basis without protection (Ingrassia 1991:A5).

Given the lack of good scientific information about the implications of potential harvest capacity and the known fragility of the red drum's biological juvenile-breeder interdependence, in 1984 the secretary of commerce requested that the Gulf Council draft an FMP for red drum in the EEZ. The Gulf Council responded that an FMP was inappropriate. In the meantime, during 1985, a separate "gamefish" conflict erupted in Florida. There, the anticipated FMP-induced loss of commercial fishery jobs was again the burning issue, but the Florida debate had shifted to the red drum's comparative economic value in recreational versus commercial use. Arguments raged about how to measure economic value scientifically, letting the economic genie out of the bottle.

Table 7.1. Patterns of Recreational and Commercial Red Drum Landings in the Gulf of Mexico: 1979–1988

| | Recreational Fishery | | | | | Commercial Fishery | |
| | Total Gulf Landings | | Average Weight | Percent Landings in EEZ | | Total Gulf Landings | Percent in EEZ |
Year	Number (Thousands)	Pounds (Thousands)	(Per Fish)	Number (Thousands)	Pounds (Thousands)	Pounds (Thousands)	
1979	4080	8562	2.10	0.3	0.4	2771	2.9
1980	3404	8185	2.41	3.7	15.7	2729	1.8
1981	2442	5889	2.42	4.8	5.2	2748	1.1
1982	5105	10412	2.04	1.6	5.1	2425	3.2
1983	3627	7535	2.08	10.6	26.5	3087	6.7
1984	2782	6705	2.41	8.2	21.3	4335	22.8
1985	2271	6798	2.99	2.6	5.3	6343	54.5
1986	2738	6814	2.49	2.7	3.2	14020	61.6
1987	1623	4869	3.00	10.2	27.2	4890	0.6
1988	na	na	na	na	na	291	1.0

Source: Adapted from information in Goodyear (1989).

Research Implications for the Gulf Council's
Red Drum FMP

The Secretarial Plan and Gulf Research Conclusions

Believing that the Gulf Council had abdicated its regional conservation obligation in 1986, the secretary of commerce exercised federal authority under section 304(c) of the Magnuson Act by imposing an emergency closure of the Gulf EEZ red drum fishery (U.S. Department of Commerce 1986). To assist the Gulf Council in drafting final FMP amendments, the Secretarial Plan included a cursory economic impact statement (EIS), as well as preliminary biological and environmental information. A more complete economic analysis was needed for future research, one that utilized accepted value techniques to augment ongoing biological studies. The *State-Federal Cooperative Program for Red Drum Research in the Gulf of Mexico* (SFCPRDR) was then established as an umbrella of universities and Gulf states. It was funded primarily by the National Marine Fisheries Service (NMFS) to provide the Gulf Council with necessary scientific information.[2] The SFCPRDR funneled interdisciplinary expertise into the *Red Drum Scientific Assessment Group* (RDSAG), which was appointed by the Gulf Council to interpret research findings and make FMP recommendations.

Research studies under the SFCPRDR pointed to four important conclusions, summarized in RDSAG (1989).[3] First, Goodyear (1989) confirmed the many biological studies that indicated the red drum spawning stock biomass per recruit (SSR) in federal waters had fallen below the critical 20 percent equilibrium rate. It was concluded that the SSR must be restored in order to preserve and sustain the species. Second, state and federal jurisdictions were found to be intertwined for conservation policy. Biologically, this is because 30 percent of juvenile stocks must escape from state waters to join breeder stocks in the EEZ in order to attain a 20 percent SSR. This stock adjustment would involve indeterminate time lags. Third, these conservation goals required the following FMP: (1) *allowable biological catch* (ABC) must be zero harvest in federal waters (EEZ), and (2) states must implement cooperative bag and size reductions to increase juvenile offshore escapement rates, while submitting annual escapement reports.

Fourth, policy to achieve *optimum allocation* was investigated in an economic study by Green (1989), which corroborated the previous three conclusions.[4] This economic analysis went a bit further to suggest that the optimal use of the Gulf red drum fishery would be a gradual reallocation of red drum stock from the commercial to the recreational sector, especially for instate estuarine waters. With the ABC constraint in the FMP, movement toward the optimum could still be achieved by initially lowering recreational allocations in state waters below the historical norm and then gradually increasing them as the SSR rises. In any event, there should be a commitment to develop an economically feasible aquacultured stock to meet market demand.

In 1988, the Gulf Council embraced the thrust of these four RDSAG recommendations in a formal FMP (Amendment 2, 1988). By then most Gulf states had implemented or were considering cooperative conservation measures. Optimum allocation, however, was not expressed as formal policy in the FMP amendment, although the Gulf Council did acknowledge a need to utilize more social science research in future allocation decisions. A permanent red drum advisory group that included economists and social scientists was established in 1991 by the Gulf Council. The South Atlantic Council adopted a similar FMP in 1990.

Background to Economic Optimum Allocation Findings

Optimum allocation is an efficiency-based standard, which means that the greatest possible societal well-being (benefits) can be enjoyed over time by the largest number of individuals in society. Benefits to individuals may be gained directly by commercial or recreational use and consumption, and indirectly without use and consumption (Bishop 1987). To develop a true measure of benefit in terms of human well-being, costs incurred by society (expenditures) to enjoy or use the fishery, for whatever purpose, must be subtracted from gross benefits enjoyed from that use. This leaves as a residual the *net benefit*, which is the only way to value fish in a truly optimum manner among different users. Economists specialize in measuring these net benefits (Smith 1990), which will be discussed in detail later, and Green (1989) applied the concept to the theory of optimum allocation to reach his conclusion about red drum. A similar conclusion was reached by Leeworthy (1990) for mackerel.

Essentially, the basic idea behind the theory of optimum allocation is quite simple. That is, to achieve the optimal fishery state, fish must be allocated to those who receive the most net benefit, within the limits of the biomass constraint. Consistent with the Magnuson Act, the total dollar amount of national benefits to all, or economic value, that results when fish are allocated optimally is known as the *optimum yield value* (OY).[5] Any other allocation is inefficient and will result in an economic value less than OY, although it may be more equitable to particular groups who would otherwise lose jobs and income.

Many have trouble understanding these economic concepts, especially net benefit, and become confused when economic jargon appears to send conflicting messages. One purpose of this discussion is to clarify these economic concepts in broad terms that are easy to understand and apply. In treating the topics, emphasis will be placed on demonstrating how maximizing income and expenditure impact does not maximize net benefit and how net benefit can actually be used in the red drum case.

Economics in Red Drum Territorial Debates and Institutions of State Fisheries Management

Emergence of Economics in State Fisheries Management

Economics came to the forefront of red drum allocation conflicts in two Gulf states, before and during the preparation of the federal EIS required in the Secretarial FMP by the Magnuson Act (Sec 303[b]6, Sec 301[a]). The issue was not just whether economics should be used, but whether and how it would be used in regard to measuring the relative worth of commercial versus recreational value. To comprehend the use and misunderstanding of economics, one must grasp the many dimensions of the red drum debacle as it evolved through the existing political, institutional, and legal structure of state fisheries management. Instead of a few well-defined government bodies, management authority in the United States is fractured into a maze of disparate state, interstate, federal, and state-federal jurisdictions, each interlocked with the others. Agencies are not commensurately endowed with staffs of biologists and social scientists who actively interact with each other. The judicial role varies widely by state.

Agencies have historically tended to deemphasize economics and the social sciences in regulatory actions, although that is now changing. Perhaps part of the reason for this is a failure of marine science education, but biology naturally elicits priority in fisheries management because it is the ultimate physical constraint within which economic and social values can be derived. Biology, as well as economics, clashed with institutional politics and vested industry alignments as the red drum issue unfolded after 1983, but in the end it was the OY allocational implication from economics that fishery managers had the most trouble accepting.

The science of economics is new to the allocation game. Therefore, acceptance comes slowly because *efficiency* implications may radically alter historical allocation patterns in a way perceived as detrimental and unfair to established users and their way of life. This is the troublesome equity problem, addressed specifically in the National Standards of the Magnuson Act, along with efficiency concerns.

In general, most regulatory mandates at the state level do require some consideration of equity, but the policy *trade-off* between equity and efficiency is not well understood. Equity itself is a subjective, ethical concept. Decision makers can be reluctant to come to grips with the hard choices that must be made when changing allocation policy along the trade-off. People and their livelihoods may be hurt, while others may be rewarded. Managers sometimes lack basic knowledge about the use of economic and human dimensions sciences in this regard and are skeptical when they are used to assess the fishery allocation issue.

As a result, on a political and emotional level, decision makers sometimes emphasize short-run equity concerns or postpone efficiency moves to unspecified future dates. This was true of the Gulf Council during the early stages of the red drum conflict. As in other conflicts, court appeals were often used in the red drum case to extract equity for commercial fishermen at the expense of societal efficiency. Sociologists and anthropologists were summoned to address sociocultural impacts, such as the displacement of fishing communities (Lampl 1986), which were at odds with economic or biological findings. Economics had little to offer as a policy guide for equity issues like income redistribution. In this regard, red drum was not very different from other allocational conflicts (Huppert 1988), except that commercial fishing was not directed historically toward red drum to the extent that it had been in other conflicts, for example, salmon on the West Coast.

State Red Drum Conflicts: Texas and Florida

The red drum conflict actually originated during 1882 (Heffernan and Kemp 1980), long before blackened redfish, when Texas bay anglers and conservationists first complained that commercial fishermen overharvested red drum spawning stock. The Texas legislature initially restricted the use of small mesh nets in 1887, beginning a long-standing series of increasingly stringent conservation regulations dealing with quotas, bag limits, mesh size/type, legal zones, and season. Policy was usually based upon sketchy biological data.

As in many states, fisheries management in Texas is ultimately the responsibility of the governor and legislature, rather than an independent commission.[6] Following the Uniform Wildlife Regulatory Act of 1967, which gave counties the option to manage through the Texas Parks and Wildlife Department (TPWD), the Red Drum Conservation Act of 1977 placed all Texas counties under the *partial* authority of the Texas Parks and Wildlife Commission (TPWC). The TPWC was subject to final review by the executive branch.

The TPWC moved quickly in the 1970s to upgrade the quality of scientific input, soliciting the expertise of both biological and human dimensions scientists through TPWD. In 1975 the TPWD launched a program of independent, standardized, recreational fishery sampling. This program provided a reliable data base of harvest and socioeconomic information to expand upon existing data from Texas seafood dealers and NMFS commercial landings surveys.[7]

The commercial sector, clinging to the frontier theory and income loss, voiced opposition to each TPWC red drum regulation and once resorted to a court injunction, although that move failed. The growing recreational lobby in Texas remained steadfast in its contention that commercial interference and overharvest were not being contained, and intensified pressure on the TPWC and the legislature. Although there was little scientific data to substantiate the position of the recreationists prior to the 1970s, results of the TPWD survey program supported the recreational case on economic and biological grounds. Escalation of an increasingly violent red drum "bay war," culminating in actual gunfire between commercial fishermen and recreational anglers, elevated red drum to top priority within TPWD and its commission.

After several bills were circulated through various committees of the Texas legislature (Matlock 1982), H.B. 1000 was signed into law by the governor on May 19, 1981. The bill banned commercial fishing for red drum and granted the species *gamefish* status with a reduced ABC. In August 1981, commercial lobbyists challenged the constitutionality of H.B. 1000 in the federal district court, contending that TPWD data was statistically unreliable. Judge James De Anda refused the temporary injunction, ruling that TPWD data and analyses, including economics, constituted a rational legislative basis for allocation.

An *economic impact* study by Matlock (1981) was central to the passage of H.B. 1000. It showed that recreational fishing was worth over $300 million in expenditures, compared to only $5 million of expanded wholesale commercial landings. Subtracting these two totals was purported to give an estimate of net impact, which was positive in favor of the recreational sector. The logic was intuitive: the sector with the greatest positive impact value was more valuable to society and should receive a larger share to achieve efficiency.

In Florida, the use of economic science in the red drum allocation debate mirrored the institutional fabric of fisheries management in that state. Regulatory power rested in the semi-independent Florida Marine Fisheries Commission (FMFC), a group of experts appointed by the governor. FMFC rules are subject to preliminary review by an internal state administrative court before final approval by the governor and full cabinet. The cabinet, however, is composed of bureaucrats who are not fishery experts. Administrative court rulings can be appealed to the federal district court.

In February 1986, after reviewing the Texas gamefish program and a computer model of the Florida fishery, the FMFC expressed a need for red drum conservation in Florida waters. One scenario indicated that a gamefish rule with stricter size limits would allocate 58 percent more fish to recreational anglers. A policy options paper was then issued to assess red drum strategy in accordance with the FMFC mandate to allocate fish on the basis of *optimum sustained benefit* with equity, but benefit was not defined clearly in the mandate.

The options paper, however, expanded the mandate to specifically include economics as a valid measure of *positive* net impact (benefit) in order to justify reallocation from one sector to another. The jargon was confusing and inconsistent, and the parties could not agree on the exact meaning of net impact. Nevertheless, the debate clearly shifted from a sole consideration of biological conservation to the inclusion of economic aspects of allocation. There was a growing sense that given whatever economic value with which the experts could agree was appropriate—benefit, impact, positive, net, or gross—gamefish might be a justifiable conservation tool if recreational economic value was considerably greater than the corresponding commercial value.

On March 6, 1986, the FMFC voted five to two to designate red drum a gamefish. Before the vote, the Sport Fishing Institute, on behalf of recreational interests, presented an economic impact analysis similar to the one used in Texas to show gamefish would generate over $25 million of retail sales in Florida, while imposing only $3.2 million in commercial revenue loss. Commercial advocates were not prepared for the economic analysis and presented facts about income from commercial shellfish landings.

In July 1986, the FMFC held a public hearing in lieu of the final ruling. The Gulf and South Atlantic Fisheries Development Foundation, Organized Fishermen of Florida, and Minority and Small Business Council were among the commercial advocates who failed to discredit the economic impact analysis. The Florida Conservation Association strengthened the gamefish case by updating the economic impact analysis with net benefit values, deemed more appropriate by economic experts: consumer's surplus (sportfishing use value) and producer's surplus (commercial rent). These were crudely estimated net benefit figures, which were confusing to some because they involved more than just income and spending. Nevertheless, the final FMFC vote was six to zero in favor of gamefish.

Commercial advocates subsequently challenged the FMFC ruling in the Florida administrative court before it went to the governor. Commercial economists joined the economic debate, contending that gamefish benefits would not be positive because 58 percent more recreational catch would raise angling activity by only 6.7 percent, not enough gain to offset the commercial unemployment loss. This result, dubbed the "Green coefficient," was taken from statistical parameters estimated in an economic study of tourist sportfishing value by Green (1985). The finding received a tremendous amount of press coverage, as the media smelled a hot news story. Technically, economists refer to this parameter as *catch elasticity*, the relative percent change in fishing effort in response to a relative percent change in catch rate.

Correctly applied, catch elasticity is a key factor in allocation decisions "at the margin" because it isolates any additional impacts that can be ascribed *ex post* to a given policy change (gamefish), rather than comparing aggregate levels of values that already exist, for example, the Texas study. The problem was that the elasticity considered did not pertain to red drum or to Florida resident anglers, and the coefficient contained a statistical bias.[8] To make matters worse, the coefficient was misinterpreted by applying the wrong units of measure to the wrong target population (Green and Nissan 1987). Nevertheless, the administrative hearing officer was convinced by the "Green coefficient" in a political atmosphere. He killed the FMFC gamefish rule, finding it arbitrary and capricious, as well as a violation of the FMFC equity mandate.[9] As a result, the FMFC appealed the decision to the First District Court of Appeals, which promptly overturned the administrative court ruling and cleared the way for final passage.

On April 2, 1987, Governor Martinez and his cabinet considered the final ruling in a highly charged, emotional hearing that attracted a national television audience. The recreational side was armed with economic facts and fancy biological models. In a review of economic impact analyses, anglers called upon the author of the "Green coefficient" to demonstrate how it was technically misapplied. With the governor's cabinet visibly on display in front of TV cameras, the commercial advocates skillfully abandoned all bioeconomic rationale, choosing instead to pack the hearing room and adjoining streets with tearful, sign-toting wives and family to focus entirely on fairness and equity. The bait-and-switch tactic worked because the final decision was to close the fishery to all users until a rule could be found to "distribute the pain equally." The commercial side claimed victory, although everyone lost. Economic and biological facts were replaced by political expediency, which is too often the ultimate decision maker (Huppert 1988).

Under Florida's sunset provision, the red drum gamefish rule came back before the governor and cabinet in another even more heated hearing during December 1988. The same arguments were presented, but this time the meeting hall was packed disproportionately with recreational constituents and their sign-toting families. Gamefish was passed, reducing bag limits to one red drum per day for either sector and prohibiting all commercial sale.

Critique of Economic Impact Analysis and the Desirability of Economic Net Benefit Measures for Allocating Fish

Problems with Economic Impact Analysis

Economic impact studies emphasize the industry effects of fishing in terms of spending, income, and jobs. It was the primary allocation methodology used throughout the red drum conflict in the Gulf of Mexico. Allocating fish optimally to generate OY value is only one managerial goal prescribed in the Magnuson Act (National Standards, Sec 301[a]), along with social, cultural, and ecological factors. However, the use of economic impact analysis as a means to attain optimum allocation can be problematic, and that fact is well documented in the literature (Bishop 1987).

Economic impact analyses do not consider both sides of the benefit-cost equation of fishery use in a true net benefit sense (see Research Implications for the Gulf Council's Red Drum FMP). Rather, economic impact analysis looks at each side of the equation in only one gross sense: the cost side for recreational consumption (gross spending) and the production side for commercial landings and wholesale/retail sales (gross revenue). *Net economic impact* is merely the difference between these two gross sales values.

That type of net impact fails to consider the real value of scarce resources (labor and capital) in their best alternative uses if they were not used for fishing, that is, opportunity cost. The reason is recreational benefits and commercial market rents (profit) are ignored. Therefore, economic impact is only a partial value measure rather than the full measure of well-being recognized in NMFS value guidelines (Huppert 1983). Moreover, the impact goal itself is inconsistent. For example, Leeworthy (1990) has shown empirically that maximizing sales impact is not always consistent with maximizing employment. Green and Nissan (1987) have shown theoretically that maximizing sales and employment does not guarantee optimal allocation.

Neither commercial nor recreational economic impact can fully account for the benefits enjoyed by ultimate seafood lovers and recreational anglers, and both values depend erroneously upon current market price. Thus, if events or policies change the quantity of activity or product that can be enjoyed (making the activity or product more or less available), economic impact cannot reveal in money value the true implications of the changed circumstance. For example, if Desert Storm had permanently raised the market price of gasoline, by definition the expenditures incurred for a fishing trip would necessarily increase. Obviously, this would not mean that anglers necessarily receive a proportionate change in the benefits enjoyed from greater or lesser fishing satisfaction simply because they are spending more on gasoline.

Economic impact values are direct and indirect benefits only to specific private business sectors rather than society at large. If fish reallocation causes one business sector to gain the same amount of income and jobs that another sector loses, society as a whole has not incurred a net loss, just a change in the composition of those gains and losses. This free substitution is the very nature of a market economy, and such changes in supply and demand occur all the time. For example, if consumers stop buying fish at the market because allocation policy restricts harvest, they will shift their expenditures (impacts) to something else and other sectors will gain. Likewise, if anglers are restricted in their fishing activity by species/season/site, they will respond by transferring expenditures to other species/seasons/sites, or they will spend money on other activities.[10] However, even if the angler spends the same money on other items, the angler's well-being is likely to be diminished after the allocation restriction, and the loss of well-being is the essence of the value problem in allocating fish.

Illustration of Net Benefit Value in Fisheries Allocation

The fact remains that it is not the income and spending impacts per se that are permanently lost to society when policy restricts fishery harvest or activity. Rather, what society loses in a real sense—called "deadweight" by economists—is those net benefits that could be enjoyed before the policy change regarding fish consumption and angling activity but cannot be recaptured afterward when money is spent elsewhere on other things. Well-being may lessen, even if the same money is spent. On the commercial side, if fishing is the highest valued occupation in which a fisherman can be employed, that operator may lose profit (fishery rent) if his or her resources are transferred to some other less highly valued occupation.

We now illustrate this basic principle for the case in which policy decreases fish allocation. Assume that red drum angling is banned totally. Suppose an angler, who would rather fish for red drum than hunt, spent sixty dollars per trip to catch red drum before the ban. The angler will not gain or lose any spending from the ban because he or she will choose to spend it, say, on hunting or something else. The economy does not lose the sixty dollars of income and spending because, after market adjustments, the hunting industry expands by sixty dollars to offset the sixty-dollar loss in the angling industry. Of course, the losses suffered by the angling industry are, nonetheless, a temporary equity problem until losses can be absorbed and displaced resources employed elsewhere in the economy, as supply and demand adjust (see note 10). Some displaced resources may elect to gain employment and income in the expanded hunting industry.

After the dust settles, however, the permanent, deadweight loss to people from the ban, which remains unabated on the recreational side, is the value to the angler of those unique enjoyments from fishing that cannot be recaptured from other activities. Hunting is not the same as fishing. Moreover, the loss of well-being in money terms can be greater than the sixty dollars of spending, depending upon how much the angler is *willing to pay* to avoid the fishing ban. Such is true whether or not the angler is able to avoid a ban. This is another way of asking how much recreational fishing is really worth to the angler.

On the commercial side, vessel operators, wholesale dealers, and retail businesses stand to lose net benefits (profits or fishery rent), as earnings fall and costs rise, which commercial resources had previously earned from red drum production. The extent of commercial net benefit loss depends upon the availability of substitute species and resource inputs, in addition to the nature of the production process (Wohlgenant 1988). Seafood consumers would be deprived of benefits from eating red drum and must search for substitutes.

Of course, the same value logic applies in reverse if policy increases fish allocation. In the case of higher allocation on the recreational side, net benefit gain is the new benefits, net of expenditures, enjoyed purely as a result of the expanded angling effort and catch prospects not capturable before. On the commercial side, the net benefit gain is the additional income net of expenses that is earned from the additional allowable harvest.

If net benefit is the correct measure, why do economists employ economic impact analysis? There are three basic reasons. First, data and methods to derive net benefit are scarce and expensive, with results that can be similar to economic impact analysis (Rockland 1983). Second, the economic impact rationale is more palatable to decision makers, who understand the political reality that expenditures generate income and jobs. Third, vague guidelines for acceptable benefit standards, such as in the Magnuson Act, have led to loose interpretations equating economic impact to benefit. To some managers, net benefit is an abstract concept of little use (Bell 1988).

Measurement of Net Benefit for Fishery Allocation

Net benefit, as applied to allocation decisions, is the difference between the gross benefit and the gross cost to users (or nonusers) from a change in the distribution of fish stocks. Economists refer to net benefit value in many ways: welfare value, surplus value (consumer's or producer's), use value, rent, and economic value. All mean essentially the same thing, net benefit. Gross benefit is always derived from some sort of demand relationship, market or nonmarket, and gross cost corresponds to the direct economic impact.

There are separate net benefits for commercial and recreational sectors, just as there are separate economic impacts. Summing the net benefits in both sectors gives the total pie of economic fishery value to society, that is, well-being or national benefit. The amount by which net benefit changes for either sector when its allocation changes is called the *marginal net benefit*. The marginal amount gives the incremental change in the pie of total economic value resulting from the reallocation. Allocation decisions are made "at the margin," so to speak.

Recreational Net Benefit

Specifically, in the recreational sector, net benefit is the gross benefit, computed as the dollar value of demand for recreational fishing trips minus actual fishing related costs, including time (Bockstael et al. 1987). Recreational demand is mostly nonmarket because anglers do not usually fish to sell catch. Net benefit is measured empirically with data by calculating the *consumer's surplus* (Willig 1976; Hanemann 1985) from demand functions established statistically with nonmarket demand techniques (Smith 1990). Marginal net benefit from reallocation is the difference in the money value of consumer's surplus before and after the allocation change.

Many want to understand how economists actually calculate nonmarket demand and net benefit in the recreational sector. It is rather complex. Since the idea of Hotelling (1947), the economic literature has abounded with technical advancements in nonmarket demand and consumer's surplus measurement. However, the profession has failed miserably to effectively communicate those developments in a nontechnical way to the noneconomist community. The reader is referred to Smith (1990) and Davis and Lim (1987) for a more complete, somewhat nontechnical discussion.

Briefly, there are two broad categories of methods that are used to measure nonmarket net benefit. The first category is the *cash* method, which offers actual money payment to anglers to establish value by auctioning fishing rights de facto. The second category includes *survey* methods, which simulate a fishing rights auction by applying statistical models, some highly sophisticated, to survey data collected from anglers. Cash methods are obviously the most accurate but are too expensive to use in practice, although Bishop and coauthors (1983) used it to establish duck-hunting net benefit.

Survey methods to compute net benefit are classified as either *indirect* or *direct* models. The oldest application by Clawson (1959) is the indirect approach known as the *travel cost model* (TCM). The TCM is the most flexible and widely used technique (Ward and Loomis 1986). The TCM assumes that correctly defined trip costs to a site can approximate the price per trip needed to estimate recreational fishing demand. From the demand, consumer's surplus is calculated mathematically as willingness to pay (or sell) to acquire (give up) fishing access rights or fishing quality (Hausman 1981). A newer TCM variation, called the *random utility model* (RUM), attempts to avoid overestimating net benefit from recreational demand by accounting for multiple site substitution (Hanemann 1985). That is, if access is denied or quality is lower at one site, net benefit may not be lost entirely if visits can be made to similar sites elsewhere. In many instances RUMs provide greater accuracy on a sound theoretical basis, but they require expensive data collection and are very difficult to estimate and interpret (Hanemann et al. 1987).

The direct survey method includes several variants of the *contingent valuation model* (CVM), which utilizes primary data from face-to-face interviews. With regard to site access rights or changes in fishing quality (catch), anglers are asked to openly state how much they would be willing to pay to acquire/retain (or sell/give up) said rights or quality. As such, CVM is in the spirit of the cash method, but it has been criticized because of the hypothetical nature of questions that do not require actual payment or receipt of money. That is, it is difficult to know whether anglers give honest answers when money does not change hands. More recent CVMs try to overcome that criticism by using referendum data (given a random payment, indicate "yes" if willing to pay and "no" otherwise) with advanced statistical techniques (Cameron 1988).

Commercial Net Benefit

For the commercial sector, net benefit is gross sales earnings (benefit) from market seafood demand, minus operating costs. This is commonly referred to as fishery *rent*, or *producer's surplus*. Producer's surplus can be calculated numerically from empirically estimated market demand and supply curves. A simpler method is to compute net income from cost and earnings studies, if demand and supply are not available. Just and Heuth (1979) give conditions under which net benefit at the ex-vessel harvest level incorporates all net benefits incurred up and down the wholesale-retail chain. In many cases the difference is insignificant, but economists are working to provide standardized methods to deal with the problem (Easley and Smith 1988).

However, Mishan (1968) argues that producer's surplus is only relevant to commercial net benefit when it can measure a positive rent to production inputs: that is, profits are not *dissipated* by over-capitalization in an open access fishery (Scott 1955). When profits are at or below zero, the only net benefit measure that might be of relevance is the consumer's surplus for the commercial fishery. This consumer's surplus is the willingness of consumers to pay in excess of prevailing market price to enjoy seafood. In overcapitalized fisheries, such as red drum and mackerel, market consumer's surplus is probably the best measure of commercial net benefit, rather than producer's surplus.

If the fishery is not overfished and profits are positive, commercial marginal net benefit from reallocation policy is the change in producer's surplus (rents) before and after the allocation change. If rents are close to zero, commercial reallocation net benefit is the change in consumer's surplus from commercial seafood demand caused by changes in ex-vessel allowable harvest, or fish supply (Leeworthy 1990).

Evolution of Allocation Goal and Economic Approach

Pre-Magnuson Years: Law of the Sea

Before 1976 the international Law of the Sea sustained an open-access, laissez-faire tradition of fish allocation in U.S. waters, dating back to English common law. The United States claimed jurisdiction only out to twelve miles, although bilateral and multilateral conservation agreements were occasionally made between the United States and other nations. Commercial fishermen and recreational anglers had virtually coequal rights to the fishery, and allocations were primarily made among commercial gear types. There were a few exceptions, such as the Texas red drum conflict, but they were not common.

Early fishery management literature tended to dismiss recreational sector conflict with commercial fisheries by assuming (1) the recreational sector was economically unimportant and (2) the fishery was not biologically stressed from nonmarket use. Adequate harvest and foreign fishing, rather than domestic overfishing, were major policy concerns in the nineteenth and early twentieth centuries.

Conservation regulations were aimed at allocating commercial gear types to elicit maximum sustainable market yield and employment, not optimally allocating a stock between market and nonmarket users within a conservation target. Regulations focused on conserving the biomass to maximize yield and income of a single user sector. Thus, there was no clear distinction between the goals of conservation and allocation. It is no wonder that the concept of fishery benefit was associated with commercial income and employment. As a result, the economic value of one domestic sector relative to the other was not so important to early management objectives.

Without a private market or sole owner to limit access, commercial fishermen will compete for fish by expanding capacity until marginal cost equals average revenue (not marginal) and resource rents (net benefit) become zero or negative. This is the classic over-capitalization problem discussed by Scott (1955) and Crutchfield (1956). Inefficiency results because the same harvest could be achieved profitably with much less effort and overfishing leads to stock depletion. The existence of a nonmarket recreational fishery only compounds the open access problem, particularly for species like red drum exploited by both sectors. The combination of increased domestic/foreign capitalization and recreational fishing popularity in the latter stages of the twentieth century justified government regulation beyond twelve miles on efficiency grounds.

The Magnuson Act

The Magnuson Fisheries Conservation and Management Act of 1976 replaced the Law of the Sea with formal governmental regulation of fisheries in U.S. federal waters, specifically the Exclusive Economic Zone. Federal jurisdiction was extended to two hundred miles, and management was vested in seven regional councils under the Department of Commerce hierarchy. The Magnuson Act gives economics a formal role for defining "optimum physical yield" as a conservation objective to achieve "maximum national benefit" (see note 5). It corresponds to the efficiency notion of OY, and acknowledges a distinction between the goals of conservation (biological) and optimum allocation (socioeconomic).

The Magnuson Act, however, is less clear about which economic benefit standards to use in order to achieve the efficiency goal, although quantitative measures are known. To complicate matters, specific standards of social, cultural, and ecological values to address the equity goal, which is to be achieved simultaneously, are not given either. As for efficiency, the national standards in section 301(a) characterize "efficiency in utilization of fishery resources" as a FMP allocation criterion, but Executive Order 12291 stipulates that economic impact be utilized. Yet it has been shown that economic impact, as used by economists, is not a barometer of efficiency because it measures cost rather than national benefit.

There was little economic and behavioral research on fishing during the early days. At that time, the rule for allocating fish resources was purely biological (Ditton 1980). However, increasing population, coastal development, health concerns, and leisure lifestyles intensified commercial and recreational demands upon the fishery. Demand ultimately reached the point that allocation among competing human users, within the biomass constraint, evolved into a distinct objective, no less important than conservation of the biomass itself. In this spirit, the Magnuson Act acknowledges that allocation must include economics and social science, the *people* sciences.

Principles of Optimum Fishery Allocation

Dynamic Economic Theory

The dynamic theory of optimum fishery allocation between commercial and recreational users has been discussed by Easley and Smith (1988), Bishop and Samples (1980), and McConnell and Sutinen (1979). Optimum allocation maximizes the economic pie of all net benefits realized in the present and in the future by people in all sectors using or enjoying the fishery. The total dollar value of net benefits in the pie, when fish are allocated optimally, is the OY value. Future net benefits must, of course, be discounted back to the present, requiring some notion of social time preference. Thus, at the optimum allocation the sum of net benefits in both sectors—consumer's surplus for recreational fisheries and producer's surplus for commercial fisheries—would be as large as it could be in each time period.

The methodology of dynamic fish and effort allocation is the optimal control method. Optimal control is a complex mathematical tool that regulates the intertemporal flow of net benefits in both sectors, at an appropriate discount rate, with a system of taxes and user fees. However, there are several problems with the dynamic approach.

One problem is that optimal control must account for *stock effects*, which arise from joint competition for fixed stocks in each time period. First, the access effect causes increased effort by one sector to reduce fish available to the other. Second, congestion can occur at sites where both sectors are fishing. Third, the harvest effect causes one year's catch to affect future years' effort and catch.

Another problem is the technical fact that optimal control is very complex and requires bioeconomic data that are unavailable. On a more practical front, the dynamic theory would be difficult to implement because the Magnuson Act itself prohibits fees levied in excess of administrative costs. Other problems concern the selection of the proper discount rate (Bell 1988).

Allocation in Empirical Practice: The Balance Scale Analogy

In practice, a static benefit-cost rule is employed to obtain optimum allocation for one time period, as discussed by Edwards (1991). The static allocation rule is based on the *compensation principle*, which means that a change in allocation is optimal if those who are made better off would be able to compensate those who are made worse off (Bishop 1987).[11] The main difference is that the static rule does not consider stock effects and maximizes net benefits at a single point in time. For static allocation, we ignore where the extra fish come from, although a more dynamic model would incorporate such stock effects.

With the static rule, a change in allocation is justified (a move toward OY) so long as the additional (marginal) net benefit to the sector receiving extra fish exceeds the additional (marginal) net benefit that would accrue if the other sector were to receive the same extra fish. Reallocation would continue until the marginal net benefit from the same extra fish share is the same amount in either sector.

To illustrate this principle, figure 7.1 makes an analogy with a balance scale. Each side of the scale measures the additional dollars of marginal net benefit, which results from a given physical share of extra fish being added to the commercial sector and to the recreational sector. The resulting total money value of economic net benefits is shown by the circular pie below the balance scale. At optimum allocation in figure 7.2, the scale is balanced and the volume of the economic value below is maximum.

A change in allocation is assessed by physically placing the given share of extra fish on each side and weighing the resulting money value of marginal net benefits associated with that extra share on both sides of the scale. To be optimum, the extra harvest is first allocated to the sector with the heavier economic value, the marginal net benefit value. Next, that economic value is taken off the scale and added to the economic value pie below. Now the scale is cleared and ready to measure the marginal net benefit value of the next additional fish allocation. Because of the economic law of *diminishing marginal utility,* the weight of net benefit value declines as allocation proceeds.

If the scale remains unbalanced, extra fish should continue to be added to the heavier side, possessing the larger marginal net benefit, until the scale balances at optimum yield value (OY) in figure 7.2, and the economic value to society below the scale is maximized. Notice that the relative money share in the maximum economic value pie does not have to balance because one sector may place a higher worth on fish.

Figure 7.1. Suboptimum allocation.

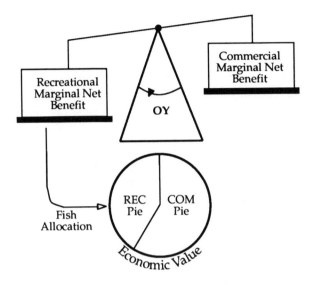

Figure 7.2. Optimum allocation.

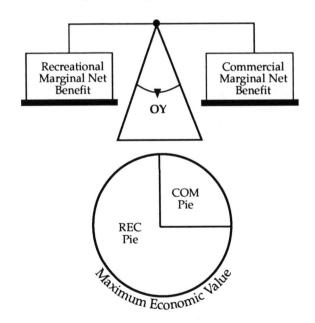

Application to Optimum Gulf Red Drum Allocation

The optimum allocation rule is applied in table 7.2 to six red drum allocation policies using marginal net benefit estimates for both commercial and recreational sectors. For simplicity, think of columns (3) and (6) as the two sides of the allocation balance scale, except they reflect the change from the original base allocation rather than the change from the previous change.[12] In all cases, marginal net benefits (losses) associated with a given allocation increase (or decrease) are greater for the recreational sector than for the commercial sector.[13] Thus, results support a general pattern of red drum reallocation to sportfishermen.[14]

To obtain these results, recreational data for variables on effort, catch, and trip cost are taken from the 1986 Marine Recreational Fisheries Statistics Intercept Survey (MRFSIS), conducted by NMFS, and the 1981 Socioeconomic Survey (SES) in Hiett and coauthors (1983). The MRFSIS contains 13,741 usable angler interviews by mode, site, and season, and a subsample of 2,348 anglers, who targeted red drum specifically. The 1981 SES, which contains detailed cost and socioeconomic data from a telephone follow-up, is used to adjust trip cost for on-site fees and fishing expenses. Commercial figures are based on price and landings data obtained from Goodyear (1989), NMFS (1986), and other landings data from the NMFS Southeast Regional Office. Data are applied to the methodology in Leeworthy (1990).

To compute recreational net benefit in column (3), an indirect survey, random utility model is used. The RUM is applied to variables on trips, travel cost, average expected red drum catch, catch of other estuarine species, and interaction between red drum and other catch. The result is an estimate of individual trip demands (nonmarket). A detailed explanation of catch definitions can be found in Green (1989:17). Trip cost includes on-site fees and expenses, as well as time costs (McConnell and Strand 1981).

The RUM assumes the angler has some probability of choosing among alternative sites based on different travel costs, attributes, and catch rate expectations. Multinomial logit regression of trips to sites in four Gulf states is applied to travel cost and catch variables.

Table 7.2. Optimum Allocation: Net Benefits from Red Drum Allocation Policy (1986)

| | Allocation Policy[a] | Marginal Net Benefits When Fish Are Allocated to the Recreational or Commercial Fishing Sector (in millions of dollars) | | | |
| | | Recreational Sector[b] | | Commercial Sector[c] | |
Recreational Perspective: Per Trip Change in Expected Physical Nonmarket Catch (percent per trip) (1)	Commercial Perspective: Annual Change in Physical Market Harvest, Equivalent on a Yearly Basis to per Trip Recreational Change (thousands of pounds) (2)	Low Participation (3)	High Participation (4)	Marginal Gross Benefit (5)	Marginal Net Benefit (6)
+10	+668.3	10.34	17.57	.42	.27
+25	+1670.8	24.06	40.89	1.40	.74
+50	+3341.8	43.32	73.60	2.12	1.72
−10	−668.3	−11.42	−19.40	−.42	−.27
−25	−1670.8	−30.75	−52.24	−1.10	−.74
−50	−3341.5	−73.68	−125.19	−2.12	−1.72

Note: In terms of the allocation balance scale, the reader should focus on net benefits in columns (3) and (6).

[a]Figures in columns (1) and (2) represent equivalent changes in fish physically available for each sector to exploit.

[b]Recreational net benefit is based on percent changes in catch from column (1), applied to regression coefficients estimated with the random utility model (Green 1989:93) and the formula of Hanemann (1985). Texas's participation is aggregated into the MRFSIS Gulf total with an expansion factor provided by the Southeast Regional Office of NMFS.

Low participation is a widely quoted, conservative estimate of 7.9 percent of Gulf trips, used by Centaur (1977). The 7.9 percent rate is consistent with the red drum first preference participation rate computed from the 1986 MRFSIS and 1981 SES samples. High participation is 17 percent and is advocated by Matlock (1986). The high rate is consistent with a broader definition in the 1986 MRFSIS for anglers choosing red drum as their first or second preference.

[c]Marginal gross benefit is the extra total revenue from increased commercial landings, valued at the weighted average 1986 ex-vessel price per pound. Marginal net benefit corresponds to the ex-vessel *consumer's surplus* methodology of Leeworthy (1990), detailed in note 15. Producer's surplus is not used because data is unavailable and rents are likely to be dissipated (Bell 1978; Ingrassia 1991).

Nonmarket demand shifts for each state, as indicated by regression coefficients on red drum catch (Green 1989:93), are used to compute per trip, weighted net benefits attributable directly to marginal increases (decreases) in allocation with consumer's surplus formulas in Hanemann (1985). Individual net benefits (Green 1989:102) are then aggregated for the Gulf region across all anglers, assuming two participation rates (Matlock 1986) in columns (3) and (4). These are explained in table 7.2. Net benefit, based on the low participation rate in column (3), is used to keep recreational values as low as possible.

Commercial marginal net benefit in column (6) is computed with consumer's surplus from red drum market demand by adapting the methodology of Leeworthy (1990).[15] Producer's surplus cannot be estimated directly because there are no applicable cost and earnings studies, and commercial rents are dissipated for all practical purposes in the overcapitalized Gulf fishery (Bell 1978). Marginal gross benefit from reallocation, the commercial economic impact, is given in column (5) for comparison.

Implications for Fisheries Management Policy

Economic analysis of net benefit, as applied to the optimum fish allocation rule, supports the hypothesis that reallocating wild red drum in the Gulf of Mexico from the commercial to the recreational sector will increase the economic value of the fishery toward the theoretical optimum yield. The OY is the highest economic value that can be obtained from any allocation of fish harvest. Therefore, the analysis supports de facto the Gulf Fishery Management Council's policy contained in its 1988 FMP amendments, but this support is based on economic efficiency grounds rather than a biological foundation. It is shown that the benefit-maximizing OY goal is in the spirit of the Magnuson Act and that stock allocation in fishery management has evolved into a goal that is somewhat distinct from biological conservation.

Lack of data, however, to conduct more comprehensive bioeconomic and human dimensions studies precludes a more precise determination of the extent to which red drum reallocation should proceed now, or how it might be adjusted in the future. Only the direction in which reallocation should proceed is indicated. However, it is not a problem in the short run because the Gulf Council's FMP (Amendment 2) constrains allocation within strict ABC guidelines.

Social sciences must be integrated with biology to consider the best use of the marine fishery. Biology and economics can be used to engineer an optimum allocation target that promotes a conservation goal, even as efficiency is achieved. Sociology and other human dimensions sciences can address the equity problem by modifying and fine-tuning the short-run, redistributional aspects of optimum allocation. The extent of equity redress depends upon how much efficiency society is willing to sacrifice for fairness, as well as the nature of the biomass constraint. Social scientists need to cooperate to find a more consistent basis for comparing methodology and jargon across disciplines so that managers can better apply research findings to actual decision making (Green 1992).

The confusion of efficiency and equity as allocation criteria is complicated by federal and state regulatory mandates, which disregard the policy trade-off between efficiency and equity goals. Mandates, including the Magnuson Act, require the application of conflicting efficiency and equity criteria simultaneously. However, the mandates do not suggest any general standard for determining how much efficiency for gaining sectors should be sacrificed in exchange for fairer treatment in the short run. This assumes that different people can agree on what is fair. Many of the judicial and interagency conflicts during the red drum conflict were fueled by this mixed signal, allowing one side to pick a single goal without accounting for the sacrifice of the other. The situation fosters an emphasis on short-run management, bordering on chauvinism, in which equity is used to ascribe to one fishery sector a set of unique, preeminent rights. Such a myopic view wrongly emphasizes costs, rather than net benefits, and seeks to preserve jobs in one sector by postponing and compromising the necessary moves toward efficient use in a more highly valued sector.

A preoccupation with equity over the course of time ignores the waste and depletion of resources that inefficient allocation inevitably transfers to future generations, who might decide allocation differently in their own behalf. It is ironic that a policy overemphasizing equity can be unfair in the long term if maximizing sales, income, and jobs maintains unsafe harvest patterns used in the past. A self-interest equity policy that seems so fair to a way of life for human resource exploiters may well threaten the perpetuation of the very biomass upon which their occupation and others' enjoyment depends. The hypothesis that—for renewable common property fisheries—exploiters, who live in an inefficient fishery environment, have policed themselves to protect the resource has yet to be supported by the evidence (Ingrassia 1991).

Efficient allocation, based on optimality principles within sound conservation constraints, guarantees species sustainability that offers the opportunity for business and society to exploit the fishery in a way that gives people the most well-being. It does not mean that seafood will be unavailable at the market, nor does it mean anglers or commercial operators will always have exclusive rights, except in the most clear-cut cases (Green and Nissan 1987). Optimum allocation policy must be monitored by providing support to multidisciplinary research, which can detect changes in society's tastes and preference ordering, relative economic valuation, and biomass condition.

Important to the industrial development of the region is the long-run efficiency implication of allocating marine resources in an optimal manner to their highest valued use. That is, in order to sustain a viable market seafood supply, wild stocks might need to be augmented through the development of a privatized, commercial, red drum aquaculture sector. The feasibility of such an approach is presently undetermined.

The modern generation of outdoor recreationists who are exploiting, consuming, and otherwise enjoying the fruits of a productive, though stressed, fishery are already expressing the concept of economic efficiency and optimality in ways they might not even realize. For example, anglers today talk about catch and release. Industry and angler associations are discussing angler ethics and environmental awareness. Even Chef Prudhomme has unveiled a new menu that features "blackened chicken" and "blackened catfish."

Notes

1. Texas was an exception, banning commercial red drum sale in 1982. Alabama followed suit in 1984 without controversy.

2. Most federal dollars were channeled through the Marine Fisheries Initiative Program (MARFIN).

3. Environmental quality became a fifth strand in the red drum web of intrigue. In July 1989, the RDSAG discussed ominous implications in Goodyear (1989:21) that red drum offshore recruitment was failing as far back as the mid-1970s, long before Prudhommes's Cajun craze. Declining water quality (pollution) and vanishing wetlands (development) were cited as possible explanations, in addition to long-run biological cycles. This does not diminish the need for a FMP, but it questions overharvest as the sole culprit and an FMP as the only solution. Increased natural mortality and loss of maturing recruits could be an early warning signal of the collapse of a spawning stock, whose gametes support estuarine fisheries across the northern Gulf.

4. This study provoked criticism and allegations of scientific bias. Some fishery officials questioned the use of economics and social sciences in general, and Edwards (1991) outlines cases of misuse.

5. The Magnuson Act defines "optimum physical yield" as the fish quantity (in pounds) that maximizes dollar "national benefit," with emphasis on use value of food production and recreational activity.

6. Mississippi and North Carolina are the only two states, within the red drum's range, that delegate sole fishery management authority to an independent commission.

7. Today the TPWD data program has evolved into an innovative research support infrastructure that strives to be on the cutting edge of developments in biological, economic and other human dimensions sciences. In 1979, NMFS began its annual *Marine Recreational Fisheries Statistics Survey* series, which included Texas counties only until 1986. There has been much discussion about ways to improve the NMFS survey so it can be more useful in socioeconomic research.

8. The bias is downward in this case, which means the catch elasticity

estimated from data is lower than the true catch elasticity. Therefore, anglers in the real world would likely be more responsive to actual catch changes. The statistical cause is known technically as "sample self-selection bias." This problem occurs when estimates made from a subsample (red drum anglers) exclude information about the general population (all anglers and marine recreationists).

9. This is a typical scenario that occurs when highly technical matters, which involve statistical and complex social science issues, are submitted to a court body, especially one with a state administrative jurisdiction. Often the court does not have adequate legal precedent or the specialized knowledge required to adjudicate the merits of opposing technical arguments.

10. This reasoning does not belie the equity question of income redistribution in the transition costs borne by the losing sectors. In fact, this issue is a focal point of social impact assessment methods (SIA), discussed in Vanderpool (1987).

11. Rockland (1983) formalizes static allocation in a seven-equation model, which Leeworthy (1990:11) shows will reduce to two equations: one for recreational net benefit and another for commercial net benefit.

12. If allocation changes in columns (1) and (2) were shown in even increments (10, 20, 30 percent) and net benefits in column (3) were subsequently computed by subtracting the current from previous allocation change (24.06–10.34), figures in column (3) would decrease in magnitude. Each extra allocation would generate less extra net benefit (diminishing marginal utility).

13. Recreational figures do not include *nonuse* values, and commercial figures are not subjected to equity adjustments. Nonuse values, discussed in Bishop (1987), include existence value and option price. Existence value captures intrinsic gratification to people for knowing the fishery exists in a viable state. Option price is the value to people today of the availability of the fishery for future use. Commercial equity adjustments can utilize quality of life indices from Social Impact Assessment or subjective ethics considerations from philosophy. Given the magnitude of value difference, it is not likely that these could change the empirical results.

14. Perhaps recreational net benefits are overestimates to some extent, despite efforts to be conservative, because of methodological and data limitations inherent in the MRFSIS design. However, such errors could not be as great as the twenty to sixty orders of magnitude necessary to reverse allocation findings. Another potential source of error is commercial net benefit underestimation caused by omission of wholesale and retail derived demand. This is only a problem if the market conditions of Just and Heuth (1979) do not hold for red drum, and even then the upward adjustment would not be twenty to sixty orders of magnitude. In fact, Easley and Smith

(1988) report that ex-vessel estimates in many cases might be sufficiently close as to be indistinguishable from wholesale/retail estimates.

15. To compute commercial consumer's surplus for red drum, we need the ex-vessel demand for seafood, given by the following function,

(1) $Q = a - bP$,

where Q = annual landings in pounds, P = price per pound, and "a" and "b" represent red drum market parameters. Parameter "b" is the change in pounds demanded by consumers in response to a change in market price.

Commercial consumer's surplus from Leeworthy (1990) is

(2) $CS = Q^2 / 2b$,

and price elasticity η is obtained as

(3) $\eta = b \times (\bar{P}/\bar{Q})$,

where $\bar{P}$ the mean annual price and $\bar{Q}$ the mean annual pounds landed. Price elasticity is the percentage change in pounds demanded by consumers in response to a percentage change in price. Manipulating (3) obtains formula (4), which is used to approximate the b_r parameter applicable to red drum for computing consumer's surplus in (2),

(4) $b_r = \eta_r \bar{Q}_r / \bar{P}_r = 11.6211621$ million.

In (4) η_r is the assumed red drum price elasticity of 2, $\bar{Q}_r$ is the mean annual pounds of ex-vessel red drum landings in table 7.1 from 1979 through 1988 (4.3 million pounds per year), and $\bar{P}_r$ is the prevailing price per pound of red drum obtained from the NMFS Southeast Regional Office ($.74/lb). Parameter b_r means that an increase of 10 cents in ex-vessel red drum price will reduce pounds demanded per year by about 1.2 million pounds.

To compute commercial consumer's surplus from allocation policy (ΔQ_r), where $Q_o = \bar{Q}_r$ is the original allocation and $Q_1 = (\bar{Q}_r + \Delta Q_r)$ is the new allocation, substitute into the following formula,

(5) Net Benefit = $[Q_1^2 / 2b_r - Q_o^2 / 2b_r]$,

where $2b_r = 23,243,242$ and $Q_o = \bar{Q}_r = 4,300,000$. The net benefit in (5) is an overestimate to the extent of a "correction factor" given in Bockstael and Strand (1987). We ignore this error in order to be conservative and because b_r is approximated by (4). Moveover, evidence in Bell (1978) and Leeworthy (1990) suggests an elasticity higher than 2, which would further reduce commercial net benefit.

References

Amendment 2 of the Fishery Management Plan for the Red Drum Fishery of the Gulf of Mexico. 1988. Tampa, Fla.: Gulf of Mexico Fishery Management Council.

Bell, F. W. 1978. *Food from the Sea: The Economics and Politics of Ocean Fisheries.* Boulder: Westview.

———. 1988. "Economic Theory and Efficient Allocation of Fishery Resources." Pp. 12–17 in J. Walter Milon, ed., *Marine Fishery Allocations and Economic Analysis.* Tampa, Fla.: Southern Natural Resource Economics Committee.

Bishop, R. C. 1987. "Economic Values Defined." Pp. 24–33 in D. J. Decker and G. R. Goff, eds., *Valuing Wildlife: Economic and Social Perspectives.* Boulder: Westview.

Bishop, R. C., T. A. Heberlein, and M. J. Kealy. 1983. "Contingent Valuation of Environmental Assets: Comparisons with a Simulated Market." *Natural Resources Journal* 23:619–633.

Bishop, R. C., and K. C. Samples. 1980. "Sports and Commercial Conflicts: A Theoretical Analysis." *Journal of Environmental Economics and Management* 7:220–223.

Bockstael, N. E., I. E. Strand, and W. M. Hanemann. 1987. "Time and the Recreational Demand Model." *American Journal of Agricultural Economics* 69:294–302.

Cameron, T. A. 1988. "A New Paradigm for Valuing Non-Market Goods Using Referendum Data: Maximum Likelihood Estimation by Censored Logistic Regression." *Journal of Environmental Economics and Management* 15:355–379.

Centaur Management Consultants. 1977. "Economic Activity Associated with Marine Recreational Fishing." Final report. NOAA 6–35195. National Marine Fisheries Service.

Clawson, M. 1959. "Methods of Measuring the Demand for and Value of Outdoor Recreation." Reprint no. 10. Resources for the Future. Washington, D.C.

Crutchfield, J. A. 1956. "Common Property Resources and Factor Allocation." *Canadian Journal of Economics and Political Science* 22:292–300.

Davis, R. K., and D. Lim. 1987. "On Measuring the Value of Wildlife." Pp.65–75 in D. J. Decker and G. R. Goff, eds., *Valuing Wildlife: Economic and Social Perspectives.* Boulder, Colo.: Westview.

Ditton, R. B. 1980. "Recreational Striped Bass Fishing: A Social and Economic Perspective. Pp. 63–75 in *Marine Recreational Fisheries* 5. Washington, D. C.: Sport Fishing Institute.

Easley, J., and V. K. Smith. 1988. "Uses and Abuses of Economics in Fishery Allocation Analysis." Pp. 24–40 in J. Walter Milon, ed., *Marine Fishery Allocations and Economic Analysis.* Tampa, Fla.: Southern Natural Resource Economics Committee.

Edwards, F. E. 1991. "A Critique of Three 'Economics' Arguments Commonly Used to Influence Fishery Allocations." *North American Journal of Fisheries Management* 11:121–130.

Goodyear, C. P. 1989. "Status of the Red Drum Stocks of the Gulf of Mexico." CRD 88/89–14. Miami, Fla.: Southeast Fisheries Center, Coastal Resources Division.

Green, T. G. 1985. "Compensating and Equivalent Variation of the Florida Saltwater Tourist Fishery." 45–9–A. Ann Arbor: University Microfilms International.

————. 1989. "The Economic Value and Policy Implications of Recreational Red Drum Success Rate in the Gulf of Mexico." National Marine Fisheries Service. Grant No. NA87WC–H–06146. Hattiesburg: Department of Economics and International Business, University of Southern Mississippi.

————. 1992. "Importance of Fish Consumption to Sport Fishermen: An Economic Analysis." *Fisheries* 16(6):13–19.

Green, T. G., and E. Nissan. 1987. "Economic Analysis for Resolving Disputes Between Commercial and Recreational Fisheries." Pp. 205–221 in M. Casey Jarman and F. C. Whitrock, eds., *Proceedings of the Conference on Gulf and South Atlantic Fisheries: Law and Policy.* MASGP–87–013. Oxford: Coastal and Marine Law Research Program, University of Mississippi.

Hanemann, W. M. 1985. "Applied Welfare Analysis with Qualitative Response Models." Working Paper No. 241. Berkeley: California Agricultural Experiment Station, University of California.

Hanemann, W. M., R. T. Carson, R. Gum, and R. Mitchell. 1987. "Executive Summary and Results." Chaps. 5–9 in T. Wegge, project manager, *Southcentral Alaska Sport Fishing Economic Study.* Alaska State Contract No. 86–0413. Sacramento, Calif.: Jones and Stokes Associates.

Hausman, J. A. 1981. "Exact Consumer's Surplus and Deadweight Loss." *American Economic Review* 71:662–676.

Heffernan, T. L., and R. J. Kemp. 1980. "Management of Red Drum in Texas." Pp. 71–80 in *Proceedings Colloquium on Biology and Management of Red Drum and Seatrout.* Ocean Springs, Miss.: Gulf States Marine Fisheries Commission 5.

Hiett, R. L., K. A. Chandler, A. K. Reniere, and R. A. Bolstein. 1983. "Socioeconomic Aspects of Marine Recreational Fishing." NMFS No. 80–ABC–00152. Alexandria, Va.: KCA Research.

Hotelling, H. 1947. "An Economic Study of the Monetary Evaluation of Recreation in the National Parks." Letter to the National Park Service. Washington, D.C.: U.S. Department of the Interior, National Park Service and Recreational Planning Division.

Huppert, D. D. 1983. *NMFS Guidelines on Economic Valuation of Marine Recreational Fishing.* NOAA–TMNMFS–SWFC–32. National Marine Fisheries Services, La Jolla, Calif: Southwest Fisheries Center.

————. 1988. "Marine Fishery Regulation in the U.S. and the Role of

Economic Analysis." Pp. 1–9 in J. Walter Milon, ed., *Marine Fishery Allocations and Economic Analysis*. Tampa, Fla.: Southern Natural Resource Economics Committee.

Ingrassia, L. 1991. "Dead in the Water: Overfishing Threatens to Wipe Out Species and Crush Industry." *Wall Street Journal*, 16 July, pp. A1,A5.

Just, R. E., and D. L. Heuth. 1979. "Welfare Measures in a Multimarket Framework." *American Economic Review* 69:947–954.

Lampl, L. L. 1986. "Feeding the People From Generation to Generation: An Ethnology of the Pine Island Fishermen." Unpublished manuscript. University of Florida, Gainesville.

Leeworthy, V. R. 1990. "An Economic Allocation of Fishery Stock." Ann Arbor: University Micro Films International.

Matlock, G. C. 1981. *Economic Impact Statement for H.B. 1000*. Submitted to the Texas House of Representatives as required by Art. 54291, V.A.R.C.S., Texas Parks and Wildlife Department.

———. 1982. "The Conflict Between User Groups of Red Drum and Spotted Seatrout in Texas." Pp. 101–108 in Richard H. Stroud, ed., *Marine Recreational Fisheries 7*. Washington, D.C.: Sport Fishing Institute.

———. 1986. "Estimates of the Number of Red Drum Anglers in Texas." *North American Journal of Fisheries Management* 6:292–294.

McConnell, K. E., and I. E. Stand. 1981. "Measuring the Cost of Time in Recreation Demand Analysis: An Application to Sport Fishing." *American Journal of Agricultural Economics* 63:153–156.

McConnell, K. E., and J. G. Sutinen. 1979. "Bioeconomic Models of Marine Recreational Fishing." *Journal of Environmental Economics and Management* 63:153–156.

Mishan, E. J. 1968. *Cost-Benefit Analysis*. New York: Praeger. National Marine Fisheries Service. 1986. Current Fisheries Statistics. Annual Gulf Landings. Washington, D.C.

Red Drum Scientific Assessment Group. 1989. "Report of the Second Red Drum Scientific Assessment Group Meeting." Tampa, Fla.: Gulf of Mexico Fisheries Management Council.

Rockland, D. B. 1983. "An Economic Analysis of Delaware's Recreational/Commercial Fisheries Conflict." Ph.D. dissertation, University of Delaware, Newark.

Scott, A. D. 1955. "The Fishery: The Objectives of Sole Ownership." *Journal of Political Economy* 63(2):116–124.

Smith, V. K. 1990. "Can We Measure the Economic Value of Environmental Amenities?" *Southern Economic Journal* 56(4):865–879.

U.S. Department of Commerce. 1986. *The Fishery Management Plan for the Red Drum Fishery of the Gulf of Mexico*. St. Petersburg, Fla: National Marine Fisheries Service, Southeast Regional Office, National Oceanic and Atmospheric Administration.

Vanderpool, C. K. 1987. "Sociology Theory and Methods: Social Impact Asessment and Fisheries." *Transactions of the American Fisheries Society* 116:479–485.

Ward, F. A., and J. B. Loomis. 1986. "The Travel Cost Demand Model as an Environmental Policy Assessment Tool: A Review of Literature." *Western Journal of Agricultural Economics* 11:164–178.

Willig, R. 1976. "Consumer's Surplus Without Apology." *American Economic Review* 66:589–597.

Wohlgenant, M. K. 1988. "Retail to Farm Linkage of a Complete Demand System of Food Commodities." United States Department of Agriculture Technical Bulletin. Washington, D.C.

PART 4
HUMAN DIMENSIONS
AND WILDLIFE POLICY

8

Nonconsumptive Wildlife-Associated Recreation in the United States: Identity and Dimension

Jean C. Mangun
Joseph T. O'Leary • William R. Mangun

Introduction

Empirical support for the popular theory that the nature of wildlife-related recreation was changing first became available from national survey data in the late 1970s. The magnitude of public interest in nonconsumptive recreational use of wildlife (recreational activities not associated with the taking or harvesting of a species) was confirmed.

Results of the 1975 National Survey of Fishing, Hunting, and Wildlife-Associated Recreation (USDI 1977) and the 1977 National Outdoor Recreation Survey (USDI 1978) reflected widespread participation in wildlife-oriented activities other than hunting or sport fishing. Although direct comparisons were hampered by different definitions of nonconsumptive resource use, a combined estimate indicated that a range of 30–50 percent of the U.S. population participated in these activities (Hay and McConnell 1979). The comprehensive 1980 National Survey of Fishing, Hunting, and Wildlife-

Associated Recreation (USDI 1982) estimated that 55 percent of the nation's population sixteen years and older in 1980 participated in some form of nonconsumptive activity (Shaw and Mangun 1984). More recently, results of the 1985 National Survey of Fishing, Hunting, and Wildlife-Associated Recreation (USDI 1988) reported that 74 percent of the U.S. population sixteen years and older participated in nonconsumptive wildlife use. Reported activities included observing, identifying, photographing, and feeding wild animals. More in-depth analysis of the 1980 National Survey (FHWAR) found differential nonconsumptive participation rates among the different Bureau of the Census geographic regions (Shaw and Mangun 1984). The East North Central Census Geographic Region had the highest participation rate with 60 percent of the regional population involved in activities whose primary purpose was wildlife-related (USDI 1982).

This documented public interest in nonconsumptive wildlife recreation has significant implications not only for resource allocation decisions but also for development of management policies and programs that incorporate nongame species (Hay and McConnell 1979; Lyons 1982; Hay 1988). Shaw and King's (1980:219) statement that "today . . . hunters are no longer the only major interest group concerned with wildlife" still holds true. The progressive management agency of the future will have to recognize the needs and characteristics of all wildlife resource user groups in order to both represent and respond to its entire constituency (Geis 1979; Behrens-Tepper 1986).

Historically, monies used for wildlife management programs in the United States came almost exclusively from sport license sales or excise taxes levied on hunting and fishing equipment (Loomis and Mangun 1987; Kallman et al. 1987; Mangun and Mangun 1991). Few provisions existed for using sportsmen-generated dollars on anything other than management of game species (IDNR 1986). This skewed management policy forced nongame enthusiasts and nonconsumptive users to channel their conservation efforts primarily through private wildlife organizations rather than through government agencies (Shaw and King 1980; Tober 1989).

Most states have initiated ambitious programs for management of nongame and endangered species (Mangun 1986). The federal Endangered Species Act of 1978 and the Fish and Wildlife Conservation Act of 1980 either provided planning funds or the promise of additional funds if the states adopted such programs. The future of these and similar state programs is uncertain unless management agencies learn how to tap the human and financial resources of the nonconsumptive wildlife recreationists (Jackson 1982; Loomis and Mangun 1987; Hall and O'Leary forthcoming; Mangun and Shaw 1984).

An important component in the mobilization of support for nongame conservation programs is a better understanding of just what public is being targeted. That effort will be unable to achieve necessary levels of support until nonconsumptive use of the wildlife resource is considered to be an activity rather than a personality (Lyons 1982). The activity of nonconsumptive use is pursued by a variety of wildlife enthusiasts whose involvement in the activity ranges from marginal to avid (Behrens-Tepper 1986). In addition, virtually every source available suggests that public interest and involvement in nongame wildlife conservation will continue to increase (Duffus and Dearden 1990). As significant rates of nonconsumptive participation have been found (USDI 1982, Shaw and Mangun 1984; USDI 1988), further research aimed at increasing knowledge about nonconsumptive users and social characteristics is important (Duffus and Dearden 1990). Identifying the heterogeneity of interest and commitment to nonconsumptive use of the wildlife resource becomes a basis for locating program support, anticipating conflict, and creating consumer-oriented development opportunities in both the private and public sectors (O'Leary and Behrens-Tepper 1985; Behrens-Tepper 1986; Mangun et al. 1991). This chapter presents some of the latest information on the sheer magnitude of involvement in nonconsumptive wildlife-related recreation and its application in wildlife policy formulation and program planning.

A Review of the Nonconsumptive Wildlife Use Literature

As a profession not previously noted for rapid response to social trends, wildlife management is showing a burgeoning concern with nongame wildlife and nonconsumptive use of all wildlife that is nothing short of remarkable. The large numbers of Americans interested in nonhunting, recreational encounters with wildlife (Shaw and Mangun 1984; Kellert 1985; Hay 1988) have necessitated a major reevaluation of the profession's priorities in terms of resource and clientele.

Since pivotal speeches of the early 1970s (Barske 1970; Chambers 1971; Allen 1972), the body of literature that addresses aspects of the nongame issue has appeared to grow exponentially. The timely nature of this issue is evidenced by the fact that studies conducted as recently as 1976 are characterized as "early." Three general categories of interest emerge upon review of the literature: (1) justification and status of nongame conservation programs; (2) identification of nonconsumptive user groups; and (3) economic analyses of alternative funding mechanisms for nongame programs. The first two categories are considered in this chapter.

Management of Nongame Wildlife

Evolution of the nongame funding issue began with the framing of arguments for provision of management programs for nongame wildlife conservation. The Committee on North American Wildlife Policy reported (Allen 1973) that several societal factors were contributing to a continued shift in use of the wildlife resource from a consumptive to nonconsumptive mode. Other early writers (Crawford 1976; Graul et al. 1976; Wright 1976; Martyr 1978) argued for adoption of an ecosystem management approach in which nongame species were essential components. Additional rationale for nongame management was provided by Pister (1976) who illustrated projected demand for wildlife-oriented recreation and consumable resource supply as diverging curves. He proposed that the public's increased demand for wildlife-oriented recreation could only be met by management of the total wildlife resource, game and nongame species alike. Lime (1976) stressed the importance of the encounter for its own sake—the role of wildlife in enhancing a nonconsumptive recreational experience regardless of the encountered species' game status. By the end of the seventies, wildlife professionals were approaching a consensus on the role and importance of nongame wildlife in an integrated approach to resource planning and management (Bury et al. 1980).

Results of a 1980 survey (Zwank et al. 1980) indicated that forty-nine states had initiated at least some type of nongame program. Despite their growing legitimacy, however, state-level programs in 1980 remained underfunded (NWF 1980; USDI/IAFWA 1983). The Fish and Wildlife Conservation Act of 1980 provided for federal assistance to those states developing management plans that incorporated nongame species (Odom 1981; Loomis and Mangun 1987). That specification was an incentive to state agencies to implement or expand their programs for nongame wildlife conservation. Numerous writers (Madson and Kozicky 1972; Callison 1974; Talbot 1974; Bury 1975; Messersmith 1976; Ryan et al. 1978; Janecek 1980; Newcombe 1980) outlined the essential components of successful plans from a private organization, state, or federal perspective. The common denominator in the plans was the call for state game departments to broaden their outlook and see wildlife as more than "game" (Scheffer 1980). Each state, however, represented a unique set of species and personalities around which its nongame program was built. In the early 1980s, many states like Illinois, Indiana, Michigan, Ohio, and Wisconsin held public workshops to set priorities for their individual state nongame programs.

Survival of these and similar state programs depends on continued public input and identification of new sources of financial support (Applegate and Trout 1984; Mangun 1986). The status of nongame and endangered species programs throughout the United States is reviewed by Thompson (1987). Numerous recent studies examine the linkages between support for nongame programs and nonconsumptive user groups (Brown et al. 1986; Manfredo and Haight 1986; Moss et al. 1986; Behrens-Tepper et al. 1988). The state of Florida has successfully blended the needs of both consumptive and nonconsumptive users into a broad-base of support for its nongame program based on an innovative funding mechanism (Klay and McElveen 1991).

Nonconsumptive Use of the Wildlife Resource

Although several authors have proposed that there is but one resource and one public (Weeden 1976; Wilkes 1977; Brocke 1979), wildlife recreationists traditionally have been categorized on the basis of which activity they do or do not pursue. The traditional emphasis placed by managers on game species and consumptive users has caused other types of wildlife enthusiasts to become disillusioned with the management process (Witter and Shaw 1979; Shaw and King 1980; Langenau 1982). A first step in the remedy of this situation would be to dispel the misconception that nongame, nonhunting, and nonconsumptive use are synonymous terms (Lyons 1982). For example, game species of wildlife often enhance nonconsumptive recreational experiences of persons who in other situations may also participate in consumptive activities (Lime 1976; Lyons 1982, Brown et al. 1984). Jackson (1982) argued that state agencies most successful in enlisting public support for nongame and endangered wildlife programs would be those who welcomed nongame enthusiasts and nonconsumptive wildlife users into the management fold; Minnesota and Colorado provide examples of states that have endeavored to do so. Understanding more about the diverse attitudes and behavior of those who engage in nonconsumptive wildlife recreation will assist state agencies in the identification of new sources of funding for their nongame programs. Many of the funding mechanisms suggested for the federal Fish and Wildlife Conservation Act were identified out of their relationship to behavior patterns of nonconsumptive users (Loomis and Mangun 1987).

It has remained difficult to draw conclusions about trends in nonconsumptive wildlife use because of lack of uniformity among existing national survey data (Hay and McConnell 1979). However, considerable evidence has been presented that demonstrates a real shift in popular sentiment and behavior toward wildlife (Kellert 1979, 1980, 1985; Scheffer 1980).

The first major studies that sought to characterize nonconsumptive users of wildlife and their activities concentrated on expenditures and participation rates (More 1979). The oft-cited DeGraaf and

Payne study (1975) estimated that $500 million was spent in 1974 by those recreationists intent on encountering, identifying, and photographing nongame species of birds. Fazio and Belli (1977) turned their attention to differential species preferences expressed by a state sample of nonconsumptive users. Pomerantz (1977) investigated childhood attitudes that would predispose a person toward nonconsumptive wildlife activities. After reviewing the available literature on demand for nonconsumptive recreational opportunities, More (1979:14) concluded that the wildlife profession was only "beginning to appreciate the scope of the interest."

The 1980 National Survey of Fishing, Hunting, and Wildlife-Associated Recreation provided the first nationwide data base dealing with characteristics of nonconsumptive users, types of activities, wildlife involved, and potential sources of funding for nongame programs (Shaw and Mangun 1984). These data have proved useful (Shaw et al. 1985) in identifying the range of outdoor environments in which nonconsumptive wildlife recreation occurs. Brown and coauthors (1984) used the same data set to characterize the "dual user"—those persons who participate in consumptive as well as nonconsumptive wildlife-related activities.

Data from the 1980 National Survey of Fishing, Hunting, and Wildlife-Associated Recreation have also been used to develop an activity scale or index of nonconsumptive wildlife users (Behrens-Tepper 1986). This study concluded that "there is not just one type of nonconsumptive user but rather a range of individuals acting along an array of nonconsumptive activity involvement" (Behrens-Tepper 1986:4). A recent more qualitative study by Duffus and Dearden (1990) described a conceptual framework of the roles and interactions among components of nonconsumptive wildlife use. Both studies proposed that a better understanding of the relationships between behavior and attitudes of nonconsumptive wildlife users can make any nongame management effort more effective.

National Surveys of Nonconsumptive Wildlife Use

The 1980 National Survey of Fishing, Hunting, and Wildlife-Associated Recreation developed by the U.S. Fish and Wildlife

Service and conducted by the U.S. Bureau of the Census included sections that composed the first detailed national survey of nonconsumptive use of wildlife (USDI 1982). The 1980 FHWAR provided the first opportunity to analyze a nationwide data set on wildlife resource-based recreation other than traditional sports afield. The 1985 FHWAR provided the first opportunity for an appreciation of the direction in which nonconsumptive wildlife-related activities were headed and for anticipation of future trends (USDI 1988). Berryman (1987:6) observed that such broad surveys and their subsequent analysis "provide clear, strong, and scientifically valid evidence of the economic importance of and public interest in wildlife resources and their uses."

The rest of this chapter is devoted to an examination of apparent changes in nonconsumptive participation reported between the 1980 and 1985 national surveys. The information presented concentrates on patterns of primary residential and nonresidential participation since these activities represent specific or direct involvement in observing, photographing, or feeding wildlife rather than peripheral, incidental, or unplanned purpose.

Survey Methodology

With the exception of sample size, the nonconsumptive portions of the 1980 and 1985 FHWAR Surveys were highly similar (USDI 1988). Statistically reliable information on nonconsumptive participants, days of participation, and expenditures had been reported at the regional level in 1980 but were reported at the state level in 1985 (Fisher and Grambsch 1989). The increased reliability was achieved by increasing designated sample size from almost seven thousand in 1980 to approximately thirty thousand in 1985 (USDI 1982, 1988). In order to reduce survey costs, the nonconsumptive questionnaire used in 1980 for in-person interviewing was adapted for computer-assisted telephone interviewing (CATI) in 1985. Approximately one-third of the 1985 nonconsumptive sample was interviewed by telephone (USDI 1988; Fisher and Grambsch 1989).

Fisher and Grambsch (1989) noted that adapting the questionnaire for telephone interviews led to shorter species lists and fewer questions about trip destinations. With the exception of expenditures, all questions whose results are presented in this chapter were the same in both 1980 and 1985.

Each survey was conducted in two phases: an initial random screen of households to identify participants in wildlife-related activities and a detailed follow-up interview with participants in selected households. The initial screening phase of both surveys successfully contacted over one hundred thousand households randomly selected from expired Current Population Survey (CPS) samples (USDI 1982, 1988). The detailed nonconsumptive user subsamples were selected from the screening sample of households containing at least one nonconsumptive participant. One-half of each nonconsumptive user subsample was selected from the sample of households also containing sportsmen. The other half of the nonconsumptive user subsamples was selected from the sample of households containing nonconsumptive participants only (USDI 1982, 1988). The manner in which the participant households in each of the two groups were further sorted differs slightly between the 1980 and 1985 surveys. In 1980, the nonconsumptive user households were sorted by triptaker and nontriptaker. In 1985, the nonconsumptive user households were sorted by type of participation: primary residential, secondary residential, primary nonresidential, and secondary nonresidential. More detailed explanations of how nonconsumptive participant households were designated for interviewing purposes was reported in the appendices of each national survey report. Although these slight differences in subsample designation may not contribute to differences in results, the reader should be aware when subsequent comparisons are made.

Direct comparability of results between National Surveys of Fishing, Hunting, and Wildlife-Associated Recreation remains a problem. The problem will be compounded with the advent of the results of the 1991 national survey because of the modified methodology involving sampling. Because of recall bias concerns, the Bureau of the Census will conduct interviews at three different times throughout the year beginning with the 1991 national survey. Regardless of direct comparability problems, national recreation surveys remain valuable tools for input into policy formulation and program planning (O'Leary et al. 1990).

Categories of Nonconsumptive Wildlife-Associated Recreation

In an attempt to make the terminology in the national survey report as clear as possible, authors of the 1980 survey developed the nonconsumptive questionnaire based on a framework with two key criteria: (1) whether involvement with wildlife was the primary purpose of the activity or secondary to some other purpose and (2) whether the activity was residential (in the immediate vicinity of home) or nonresidential (more than one mile from home).

The two criteria result in four combinations: (1) *primary nonresidential*—trips or outings of at least one mile for the primary purpose of observing, photographing, or feeding wildlife (trips to zoos, circuses, aquariums, and museums and trips to fish or hunt are not included); (2) *primary residential*—activities around the home whose primary purpose is wildlife related, including (*a*) closely observing or trying to identify birds or other wildlife, (*b*) photographing wildlife, (*c*) feeding birds or other wildlife on a regular basis, (*d*) maintaining natural areas of at least one-fourth acre for which benefit to wildlife is an important concern, (*e*) maintaining plantings, (shrubs, agricultural crops) for which benefit to wildlife is an important concern, and (*f*) visiting public parks within one mile of home for the purpose of observing, photographing, or feeding wildlife; (3) *secondary nonresidential*—enjoyment from seeing or hearing wildlife while on a trip or outing of at least one mile that is taken for another purpose, such as camping, driving for pleasure, or boating; (4) *secondary residential*—enjoyment from unplanned opportunities to see or hear wildlife while pursuing other activities around the home, for example, enjoying birds while doing yardwork (USDI 1982:30).

Results Reported in National Surveys

The nonconsumptive paradigm categorizes participation into primary and secondary, residential and nonresidential (Shaw et al.

Table 8.1. 1985 Participation by Persons 16 Years of Age or Older
in Nonconsumptive Wildlife-Related Activities
(numbers in thousands)

	1985	(%)	1980	(%)
U.S. Population	181,095	100	169,942	100.0
Total no. of participants	134,700	74	93,250	54.9
Total no. of primary participants	109,597	61	83,173	48.9
Primary residential	105,286	58	79,670	46.9
Primary nonresidential	29,347	16	28,822	17.0
Total no. of secondary participants	127,427	70	88,805	52.3
Secondary residential	117,411	65	80,475	47.4
Secondary nonresidential	89,532	49	73,773	43.4

1985). Table 8.1 presents a direct comparison of the changes reported between the 1980 and 1985 national surveys based on those categories of participation.

In 1980, the overall number of participants in wildlife-related nonconsumptive activities was approximately ninety-three million (or 54.9 percent of the total U.S. population sixteen years of age and older). The 1980 national survey report (USDI 1982) stated that the standard error of the estimated number of nonconsumptive users is 1,684,000; the 95 percent confidence interval for the number of 1980 nonconsumptive users was calculated at 89,882,000 to 96,618,000. In 1985, the overall number of participants in wildlife-related nonconsumptive activities was over 134 million (or 74 percent of the total U.S. population sixteen years of age and older). The 1985 national survey report (USDI 1988) stated that the standard error of the estimated number of nonconsumptive participants is 840,000; the 95 percent confidence interval for the number of 1985 nonconsumptive participants was listed as 133,018,000 to 136,376,000. Consideration of these error ranges allows us to be reasonably certain that significant increases in nonconsumptive participation have been reported between 1980 and 1985.

Although standard errors of 1980 expenditures are not readily available, the 1980 survey reported that primary nonconsumptive enthusiasts spent over $10 billion in pursuit of their activities. In 1985, primary nonconsumptive participants spent $14.2 billion with a 95 percent confidence interval from $11 to $17.5 billion. Again, it appears that a real increase has occurred.

Comparison with Consumptive Activities

In order to put the nonconsumptive numbers in perspective, it was useful to examine participation in fishing and hunting during 1985. The total number of anglers was more than forty-six million (26 percent of U.S. 16+) and hunters almost seventeen million (9 percent of U.S. 16+) who spent over $41 billion and $10 billion, respectively. The trends charted in these populations showed a substantial increase in the number of anglers including rate of participation and a substantial decrease in the number of hunters including participation rate.

Changes in Nonconsumptive Numbers

The 1985 survey enabled us to identify increases or decreases in numbers of participants in nonconsumptive use of wildlife from 1980 to 1985 for those categories of information where participation figures were reported at the regional or national level. Between 1980 and 1985 there was a substantial growth in the absolute number of nonconsumptive wildlife users as well as the percentage of the U.S. population they represent. There was a major increase of 19 percent in the overall proportion of nonconsumptive wildlife users and 12 percent in the proportion of primary nonconsumptive enthusiasts between 1980 and 1985 (table 8.1). Closer examination revealed that the largest growth occurred in both the primary and secondary residential activity areas. This would suggest that wildlife managers should consider placing greater emphasis on urban wildlife programs involving interpretation and technical assistance to homeowners.

The percentages of nonresidential participation add additional support to the idea that urban wildlife programs should be given greater emphasis. In contrast to the high growth in residential use, nonresidential participation leveled off between 1980 and 1985. Although secondary nonresidential use increased 6 percent, primary nonresidential participation involving trips taken chiefly for the purpose of observing, feeding, or photographing decreased by 1 percent.

Demographic Differences

Age

Nonconsumptive wildlife use patterns appeared to be highly related to the behavior of "baby boomers," those persons born between 1946 and 1961. In 1980, this cohort was aged nineteen to thirty-four; in 1985 it was aged twenty-four to thirty-nine. The survey age categories that correspond to the age range of the baby boomers exhibited the largest percentages of primary nonconsumptive participants in both 1980 and 1985 (table 8.2). That relationship is important if the baby boomer cohort is the primary support base for nonconsumptive wildlife. As baby boomers become older and wealthier, they will acquire more political clout to demand additional wildlife-related recreational opportunities. The popularity among baby boomers of "cocooning" (that is, sticking close to home for leisure activities) may partially explain the sudden increase in residential nonconsumptive behavior. The next largest participation group is the over-fifty-five cohort. This age group is also politically efficacious, possessing considerable discretionary time necessary to stimulate policy changes concerning wildlife programs. The United States is in a time of demographic transition laden with potential policy implications. Both observations illustrate that wildlife managers should pay particular attention to these two age groups.

Shaw and Mangun (1984) noted that the data from the 1980 FHWAR survey on primary nonconsumptive participation showed that wildlife was enjoyed purposefully by people of all age groups. That observation can be made again for 1985, with increased

Table 8.2. Age Distributions for U.S. Population of Participants in
Nonconsumptive Wildlife-Associated Activity in 1980 and 1985
(numbers in thousands)

Age Group	Number		% of Group Involved		% of Activity Participants	
	1985	1980	1985	1980	1985	1980
Primary Nonresidential						
16–17	1,307	1,383	17	16.1	4	4.2
18–24	4,217	5,960	17	20.9	14	20.7
25–34	9,231	9,236	23	24.5	31	32.0
35–44	7,216	4,796	21	18.4	25	16.6
45–54	3,077	3,340	13	14.8	10	11.6
55–64	2,519	2,482	11	11.4	9	8.6
>64	1,779	1,625	6	6.6	6	5.6
TOTAL	29,347	28,822				
Primary Residential						
16–17	3,811	3,229	50	37.5	4	4.1
18–24	12,034	10,967	47	38.4	11	13.0
25–34	22,851	20,154	58	53.4	22	25.3
35–44	21,317	13,172	63	58.4	20	16.5
45–54	14,189	10,575	59	46.9	13	13.3
55–64	14,440	10,663	63	49.1	14	13.4
>64	16,644	10,909	59	44.3	16	13.7
TOTAL	105,286	79,670				

involvement for all age groups in primary residential activities (table 8.2). The pattern differed slightly for primary nonresidential activities, showing slight decline in those younger than thirty-four, a small increase for those thirty-five years through fifty-four years, and the same involvement level between 1980 and 1985 for those fifty-five years and above.

Sex

In 1980, the number of female participants in primary residential activities was slightly larger than male involvement in terms of absolute numbers, but the percent of those involved was virtually the same (table 8.3). This pattern was similar in 1985, although

Table 8.3. Participants by Gender for Persons 16 Years of Age and Older in Primary Nonresident and Residential Activities in the U.S.: 1980 and 1985 (numbers in thousands)

Gender	Number		% of Group Involved		% of Activity Participants	
	1985	1980	1985	1980	1985	1980
Primary Nonresidential						
Male	14,421	14,911	17	18.5	49	51.7
Female	14,926	13,912	16	15.6	51	48.3
TOTAL	29,347	28,823	16	17.0		
Primary Residential						
Male	47,930	37,012	56	45.8	46	46.5
Female	57,356	42,657	60	47.8	54	53.5
TOTAL	105,286	79,670	58	46.9		

there was a slightly higher proportion of women involved than in 1980.

Education

Nonconsumptive participation was strongly related to education level in both primary residential and primary nonresidential activities (table 8.4). Higher proportions of people with some college background participated in both primary activities; their numbers remained relatively stable in regard to nonresidential activities, the area of otherwise general decline between 1980 and 1985.

Race

Nonconsumptive participation in primary residential activities went up in terms of absolute numbers for both whites and blacks from 1980 to 1985 (table 8.5). The finding in 1980 that whites were about twice as inclined to be involved in these types of activities continued to hold in 1985. Residential participation went up for all race categories in 1985, including the "Other" category.

Table 8.4. Participants by Educational Background in Primary
Nonresidential and Residential Activities in the U.S.: 1980 and 1985
(numbers in thousands)

Years Education	Number		% of Group Involved		% of Activity Participants	
	1985	1980	1985	1980	1985	1980
Primary Nonresidential						
< 8 yrs.	820	1,621	5	6.4	3	5.6
9–11 yrs.	3,115	3,543	12	12.4	11	12.3
12 yrs.	9,829	10,580	14	16.9	33	36.7
1–3 coll.	7,428	6,100	22	23.2	25	21.2
4 coll.	4,102	3,359	24	24.1	14	12.4
5 coll.						
TOTAL	29,347	28,822				
Primary Residential						
< 8 yrs.	8,545	7,968	47	31.4	8	10.0
9–11 yrs.	14,478	11,672	54	40.9	14	14.7
12 yrs.	40,015	29,455	57	47.1	38	37.0
1–3 coll.	21,837	14,437	64	55.0	21	18.1
4 coll.	10,606	7,856	62	56.4	10	9.9
5 coll.	9,806	8,281	64	62.0	9	10.4
TOTAL	105,286	79,670				

Table 8.5. Participants by Race for Persons 16 Years of Age and Older
in Primary Nonresidential and Residential Activities in the U.S.:
1980 and 1985 (numbers in thousands)

Race	Number		% of Group Involved		% of Activity Participants	
	1985	1980	1985	1980	1985	1980
Primary Nonresidential						
White	28,065	27,347	18	18.6	96	94.9
Black	810	961	4	5.3	3	3.3
Other	472	514	7	10.8	2	1.8
TOTAL	29,347	28,822				
Primary Residential						
White	96,867	73,926	62	50.3	92	92.8
Black	6,460	4,511	35	24.8	6	5.7
Other	1,960	1,233	30	25.9	2	1.5
TOTAL	105,286	79,670				

**Table 8.6. Participants by Income Background in Primary
Nonresidential and Residential Activities in the U.S.: 1980 and 1985
(numbers in thousands)**

Income	Number		% of Group Involved		% of Activity Participants	
	1985	1980	1985	1980	1985	1980
Primary Nonresidential						
< 10,000	2,544	3,832	9	10.6	9	13.3
10–20,000	5,579	7,249	14	17.9	19	25.2
20–25,000	3,254	4,999	20	22.8	11	17.3
25–30,000	4,385	3,572	17	21.8	15	12.4
30–50,000	8,646	4,312	21	22.1	29	15.0
50–75,000	2,501	1,171	18	20.0	9	4.1
> 75,000	1,487	1,171	20	20.0	5	4.1
NR	950		10			
TOTAL	29,347	28,822				
Primary Residential						
< 10,000	13,792	13,711	50	38.1	13	17.2
10–20,000	21,785	19,185	53	48.0	21	24.1
20–25,000	9,819	12,412	60	56.5	9	15.6
25–30,000	14,460	8,641	57	52.8	14	10.8
30–50,000	27,436	11,069	68	56.9	26	13.9
50–75,000	8,432	3,014	61	51.3	8	3.8
> 75,000	4,530	3,014	60	51.3	4	3.8
NR	5,034				5	
TOTAL	105,286	79,670				

Income

In both the 1980 and the 1985 data, there was a consistent relationship in nonresidential participation with rising income (table
8.6). Of the participants in nonresidential activities, those in the
highest income categories showed the largest percent and absolute
changes in participation from 1980. However, primary residential
activities stood out in terms of their overall increase in participation
at the national level. From 1980 to 1985 there were not only sharp
increases in the higher income categories for those participating at
home but also dramatic increases in the lower income groups. A
residential wildlife experience is normally a pleasant, inexpensive

activity for lower income groups. It would be ideal if managers were prepared to respond to that interest with provision of appropriate urban wildlife programs; however, fiscal constraints and jurisdictional issues often hamper efforts in this direction.

Census Geographic Regional Comparisons

In comparing primary participation at the regional level, few regions show significant changes between the 1980 and 1985 numbers of participants and percentages of participation (table 8.7). Where differences exist, they are so small as to be almost insignificant. Primary residential participation, on the other hand, grew dramatically in every region. The proportion of persons participating in any specific region ranges from a high of 68 percent in the North Central—West region to a "low" of 50 percent in the Pacific region. Southern regions experienced the greatest changes during the five-year period.

State Comparisons

The 1985 FHWAR provided the first national survey with statistically reliable state-level data on nonconsumptive wildlife use. Because of the uniformly consistent methodology, the 1985 FHWAR made it possible to make accurate comparisons among states. Because of their large populations, California, New York, and Texas had the largest numbers of participants overall in nonconsumptive wildlife-related activities in 1985. However, the state with the highest participation rate was Wyoming with 96 percent of its population indicating some form of nonconsumptive wildlife-related activity. North Dakota and Oklahoma followed closely at 92 percent. When primacy is taken into consideration, Oklahoma ranked first with 80 percent of its residents indicating that they were primary nonconsumptive enthusiasts; Ohio ranked second with 77 percent. With regard to secondary nonconsumptive participation rates, 95 percent of Wyoming citizens aged sixteen and over indicated that they

Table 8.7. Geographic Distribution of Nonconsumptive Population 16 Years Old or Older and Selected Populations of Primary Nonresidential and Residential Participants in Nonconsumptive Wildlife-Associated Activities in 1980 and 1985 (numbers in thousands)

Census Geographic Region	Number		% of Group Involved		% of Activity Participants	
	1985	1980	1985	1980	1985	1980
Primary Nonresidential						
New England	1,736	1,657	18	17.7	6	5.7
Middle Atlantic	4,445	4,111	15	14.8	15	14.3
North Central						
—East	5,601	6,099	18	19.8	19	21.2
—West	2,802	3,000	21	23.5	10	10.4
South Atlantic	4,406	3,739	14	13.3	15	13.0
South Central						
—East	1,258	1,173	11	10.9	4	4.1
—West	1,549	1,842	13	10.5	9	6.4
Mountain	2,119	2,125	22	25.2	7	7.4
Pacific	4,431	5,076	17	20.9	15	17.6
TOTAL	29,347	28,822				
Primary Residential						
New England	6,016	4,952	61	52.9	6	6.2
Middle Atlantic	15,678	11,872	54	42.6	15	14.9
North Central						
—East	20,482	17,936	66	58.3	19	22.5
—West	8,923	6,783	68	53.1	8	8.5
South Atlantic	17,943	11,270	58	40.2	17	14.1
South Central						
—East	6,589	4,117	58	38.2	6	5.2
—West	10,757	6,837	55	39.0	10	8.6
Mountain	5,668	4,133	60	49.1	5	5.2
Pacific	13,228	11,770	50	48.4	13	14.8
TOTAL	105,286	79,670				

enjoyed seeing or hearing wildlife while they were participating in some other activity. Ninety-one percent of North Dakota residents and 89 percent of Idaho and Oklahoma residents participated similarly. The rural nature of these states may enhance the opportunity for a secondary nonconsumptive experience.

It is interesting to note that the state of Hawaii, where native wildlife populations have been depleted, reported the lowest over-all nonconsumptive participation rate in the nation, 58 percent. New York and California, two other states with highly urbanized populations, reported similarly low participation rates: New York (61 percent) and California (65 percent). However, urbanization alone does not preclude participation in nonconsumptive activities. The lower participation rates may be symptomatic of the inade-quacy or unavailability of urban wildlife programs.

With regard to expenditures, California residents spent the great-est amount of money to participate in nonconsumptive wildlife-related activities. Californians spent over $1.7 billion for equipment and travel-related expenditures. Certainly the high cost of living in California, combined with its large population, contributes to these numbers. Texas, however, which is neither the next most populous state nor the wealthiest, ranks second with $1.4 billion in noncon-sumptive-related expenditures.

Summary and Conclusions

The magnitude of participation in nonconsumptive wildlife-re-lated activities reflected in recent national surveys demonstrates that nonconsumptive use of wildlife in America is an idea whose time has come. The popularity of wildlife-associated recreation as-sumedly has never been at higher levels. People are highly inter-ested and care what happens to wildlife. Their concern is exhibited through high levels of participation in observing, feeding, and pho-tographing wildlife (nonconsumptive use) often surpassing partici-pation rates in the traditional activities of fishing and hunting wild-life (consumptive use).

The sharp increases in residential participation tend to indicate that programs oriented toward urban wildlife have raised the con-sciousness of the urban audience. Now that the extent of participa-tion in nonconsumptive activities has been demonstrated at the national level, the question to be asked is, Where do these activities go from here? What second-generation programs and activities will influence both the wildlife and the urban audience? How will the new activities be accommodated with fiscal and physical resource constraints? The answer to these questions must be addressed in the short run since many of those most involved represent influential economic and political groups in American society. It would be unfortunate to fail to take advantage of that extensive interest.

An important question that emerges from these data is, Why hasn't primary nonresidential participation followed the patterns of growth found in the other nonconsumptive areas? In many of the studies of recreational trends an argument has been made that a variety of social phenomena will limit participation in some activities. Examples include the rise of the dual-income family, single-parent families, more working women, holiday and vacation scheduling problems, and a general perception that time is a scarce resource influencing the way in which people organize their travel. Each of the examples could represent a basis for developing a plausible explanation for stable, nonresidential participation trends, but the data tend to show a more pervasive stability. Additional study here would certainly assist in helping to understand the dynamic and its implication for wildlife management activities throughout the nation. A similar argument could be made for investigating secondary residential and nonresidential participation to better clarify what types of activities are being done in these areas.

These data represent an important benchmark in our ability to make comparisons within one of the largest bodies of recreational activities and interests in the nation. For effective wildlife planning and policy formulation to occur in the United States, the U.S. Fish and Wildlife Service and the respective state fish and wildlife agencies must make a continuing commitment to monitoring wildlife-related activities and how they are changing in this country.

References

Allen, Durward L. 1972. "The Need for a New North American Wildlife Policy." *Transactions of the Thirty-seventh North American Wildlife and Natural Resources Conference* 37:46–54.

———. 1973. "Report of the Committee on North American Wildlife Policy." *Transactions of the Thirty-eighth North American Wildlife and Natural Resources Conference* 38:152–181.

Applegate, James R., and James R. Trout. 1984. "Factors Related to Revenue Yield in State Tax Checkoffs." *Transactions of the Forth-ninth North American Wildlife and Natural Resources Conference* 49:199–204.

Barske, P. 1970. "Changing Ideas and Concepts of a Wildlifer's Responsibilities." *Transactions of the Forty-ninth North American Wildlife and Natural Resources Conference* 49:199–204.

Behrens-Tepper (now Mangun), Jean C. 1986. *An Analysis of Wildlife-Associated Nonconsumptive Users and Their Support for Nongame Wildlife Programs in the Upper Midwest (East North Central Region).* Final Report for the 1985–1986 Environmental Conservation Fellowship of the National Wildlife Federation. West Lafayette, Ind.: School of Forestry and Natural Resources, Purdue University.

Behrens-Tepper, Jean C., Joseph T. O'Leary, and Robert D. Feldt. 1988. "Differing Public Perceptions of Nongame Wildlife Issues." Paper presented at the Joint Technical Meeting of the Indiana Chapters of American Fisheries Society and The Wildlife Society, Nashville, Ind., March.

Berryman, Jack H. 1987. "Socioeconomic Values of the Wildlife Resource: Are We Really Serious?" Pp. 5–11 in Daniel J. Decker and Gary R. Goff, eds., *Valuing Wildlife: Economic and Social Perspectives.* Boulder, Colo.: Westview Press.

Brocke, Rainer H. 1979. "The Name of the Nongame." *Wildlife Society Bulletin* 7(4):279–289.

Brown, Tommy L., Nancy A. Connelly, and Daniel J. Decker. 1984. *An Analysis of the Overlap in Participation of Consumptive and Nonconsumptive Wildlife Users.* Ithaca, New York: Outdoor Recreation Research Unit, Cornell University.

———. 1986. "First Year Results of New York's 'Return a Gift to Wildlife' Tax Checkoff." *Wildlife Society Bulletin* 14:115–120.

Bury, R. B. 1975. "Conservation of Non-game Wildlife in California: A Model Program." *Biological Conservation* 7(3):199–210.

Bury, R. B., H. W. Campbell, and N. J. Scott, Jr. 1980. "Role and Importance of Nongame Wildlife." *Transactions of the Forty-fifth North American Wildlife and Natural Resources Conference* 45:197–207.

Callison, C. H. 1974. "Nongame Wildlife Programs of Private Organizations." *Transactions of the Thirty-ninth North American Wildlife and Natural Resources Conference* 39:87–104.

Chambers, R. E. 1971. "Status of Nongame Wildlife Programs: Our Responsibility." *Transactions of the Twenty-eighth Northeast Fish and Wildlife Conference* 28:1–7.

Crawford, J. A. 1976. "Nongame Wildlife—The Role of the University." *Wildlife Society Bulletin* 4(3):116–119.

DeGraaf, R., and B. Payne. 1975. "Economic Values of Nongame Birds and Some Urban Wildlife Research Needs." *Transactions of the Fortieth North American Wildlife and Natural Resources Conference* 40:281–287.

Duffus, David A., and Philip Dearden. 1990. "Non-Consumptive Wildlife-Oriented Recreation: A Conceptual Framework." *Biological Conservation* 27:213–231.

Fazio, J. R., and L. A. Belli. 1977. "Characteristics of Nonconsumptive Wildlife Users in Idaho." *Transactions of the Forty-second North American Wildlife and Natural Resources Conference* 42:116–128.

Fisher, Warren L., and Anne E. Grambsch. 1989. "Development, Use, and Future of the National Survey of Fishing, Hunting, and Wildlife-Associated Recreation." *Wildlife Society Bulletin* 17(4):538–543.

Geis, Al D. 1979. "Management and Research Needs for Urban Wildlife." Pp.40–45 in M. H. Markley, ed., *Proceedings of the Sixty-eighth Convention of the International Association of Fish and Wildlife Agencies (IAFWA).* Washington, D.C.

Graul, W. D., J. Torres, and R. Denney. 1976. "A Species-Ecosystem Approach for Nongame Programs." *Wildlife Society Bulletin* 4(2):79–80.

Hall, Dale A., and Joseph T. O'Leary. Forthcoming. "Analysis of Trends in Birding from the 1980 and 1985 National Surveys of Nonconsumptive Wildlife-Associated Recreation."

Hay, Michael J. 1988. *Net Economic Values of Nonconsumptive Wildlife-Related Recreation.* Report 85–2. Washington, DC: Division of Federal Aid, U.S. Fish and Wildlife Service.

Hay, Michael J., and Kenneth E. McConnell. 1979. "An Analysis of Participation in Nonconsumptive Wildlife Recreation." *Land Economics* 55(4):460–471.

Indiana Department of Natural Resources (IDNR). Division of Fish and Wildlife. 1986. "Contributions Fund Nongame Program." *Focus Newsletter* 2(1):1.

Jackson, J. J. 1982. "Public Support for Nongame and Endangered Wildlife Management: Which Way Is It Going?" *Transactions of the Forty-seventh North American Wildlife and Natural Resources Conference* 47:432–440.

Janecek, J. 1980. "The Role of Nongame Programs and Activities of the U.S. Fish and Wildlife Service." *Illinois Division of Wildlife Research Periodic Report 15,* pp.14–17. Springfield, Illinois.

Kallman, Harmon, C. Phillip Agee, W. Reid Goforth, J.P. Linduska, Steven R. Hillebrand, and Nan Rollison. 1987. *Restoring America's Wildlife 1937–1987: The First 50 Years of the Federal Aid in Wildlife Restoration (Pittman-Robertson) Act.* Washington, D.C.: U.S. Department of the Interior.

Kellert, Steve R. 1979. *Public Attitudes Toward Critical Wildlife and Natural Habitat Issues: U.S. Fish and Wildlife Service Phase I Report.* Washington, D.C.: U.S. Government Printing Office.

————. 1980. *Activities of the American Public Relating to Animals: U.S. Fish and Wildlife Service Phase II Report.* Washington, D.C.: U.S. Government Printing Office.

————. 1985. "Birdwatching in American Society." *Leisure Sciences* 7(3):343–360.

Klay, William Earle, and James D. McElveen. 1991. "Strategic Planning in Wildlife Agencies: Theory and Application in a Statewide Context." *Policy Studies Journal* 19(3–4):527–533.

Langenau, Edward E., Jr. 1982. "Bureaucracy and Wildlife: A Historical Overview." *International Journal of the Study of Animal Problems* 3:145–157.

Lime, D. W. 1976. "Wildlife Is for Nonhunters, Too." *Journal of Forestry* 74(9):600–604.

Loomis, John B., and William R. Mangun. 1987. "Evaluating Tax Policy Proposals for Funding Nongame Wildlife Programs." *Evaluation Review* 11(6):715–738.

Lyons, James R. 1982. "A Conceptual Framework for the Identification of Recreational Users of the Wildlife Resource: Who Is the Clientele of Wildlife Management?" Paper presented at the National Symposium on Leisure Research, Phoenix, Arizona.

Madson, J., and E. Kozicky. 1972. "A Law for Wildlife: Model Legislation for a State Nongame Wildlife Conservation Program." East Alton, Ill.: Winchester-Western Division of Olin Corporation.

Manfredo, Michael J., and B. Haight. 1986. "Oregon's Nongame Tax Check-off: A Comparison of Donors and Non-donors." *Wildlife Society Bulletin* 14:121–126.

Mangun, William R. 1986. "Fiscal Constraints to Nongame Programs." Pp. 23–33 in James B. Hale, Louis B. Best, and Richard L. Clawson, eds., *Management of Nongame Wildlife in the Midwest: A Developing Art.* Chelsea, Mich.: Bookcrafters (for the North Central Section of the Wildlife Society).

Mangun, William R., Barbara A. Knuth, Jeffrey K. Keller, and Gary R. Goff. 1991. "Challenges for Public-sector and Private-sector Land Managers in the Conservation of Biological Resources." Pp. 333–344 in Daniel J. Decker et al., eds., *Challenges in the Conservation of Biological Resources.* Boulder, Colo.: Westview Press.

Mangun, William R., and Jean C. Mangun. 1991. "Intergovernmental Dimensions of Wildlife Policy." *Policy Studies Journal* 19(3–4):519–526.

Mangun, William R., and William W. Shaw. 1984. "Alternative Mechanisms for Funding Nongame Wildlife Conservation." *Public Administration Review* 44:407–413.

Martyr, R. 1978. "The Benefits of Nongame." *Proceedings of the Western Association of Fish and Wildlife Agencies* 58:172–184.

Messersmith, J. D. 1976. "A New Dimension for California's Nongame

Wildlife Program." *Proceedings of the Western Association of State Game and Fish Commissions* 56:356–363.

More, Thomas A. 1979. *The Demand for Nonconsumptive Wildlife Uses: A Review of the Literature.* General Technical Report NE–52. Broomall, Pa.: Northeast Forest Experiment Station, U.S.D.A. Forest Service.

Moss, M. B., J. D. Fraser, and J. D. Wellman. 1986. "Characteristics of Nongame Fund Contributors vs. Hunters in Virginia." *Wildlife Society Bulletin* 14:1107–1114.

National Wildlife Federation (NWF). 1980. "Survey Shows More than Half of States Now Funding Nongame Wildlife Programs." News Release 8084. Washington, D.C.

Newcombe, J. 1980. "Nongame Species in Current Policies and Decision Making of the U.S." *Illinois Division of Wildlife Research Periodic Report 15*, pp. 18–22. Springfield, Ill.

Odom, R. R. 1981. "Funding Considerations and Alternatives for State Nongame Programs." *Proceedings of the Nongame and Endangered Wildlife Symposium*, pp. 12–22. Athens, Ga.

O'Leary, Joseph T., and Jean C. Behrens-Tepper. 1985. *Impact of Recreation Activity Specialization on Management and Program Support for Water Resources.* Technical Report Number 114. West Lafayette, Ind.: Water Resources Research Center, Purdue University.

O'Leary, Joseph T., Francis A. McGuire, and F. Dominic Dottavio. 1990. "Recreation Policy and Planning Options with Nationwide Recreation Survey Data." Pp. 123–132 in John D. Hutcheson, Francis P. Noe, and Robert E. Snow, eds., *Outdoor Recreation Policy: Pleasure and Preservation.* Westport, Conn.: Greenwood Press.

Pister, E. P. 1976. "A Rationale for the Management of Nongame Fish and Wildlife." *Fisheries Bulletin, American Fisheries Society* 1:11–14.

Pomerantz, Gerri. 1977. *Young People's Attitudes Toward Wildlife.* Wildlife Division Report 2781. Lansing, Mich.: Michigan Department of Natural Resources.

Ryan, R., M. McCloskey, and R. Lestina. 1978. "Citizen's Advisory Council's Role in Developing State Nongame Programs." *Transactions of the Forty-third North American Wildlife and Natural Resources Conference* 43:53–56.

Scheffer, V. B. 1980. "Benign Uses of Wildlife." *International Journal of the Study of Animal Problems* 1(1):19–32.

Shaw, William W., and D. A. King. 1980. "Wildlife Management and Nonhunting Wildlife Enthusiasts." *Transactions of the Forty-third North American Wildlife and Natural Resources Conference* 43:53–56.

Shaw, William W., and William R. Mangun. 1984. *Nonconsumptive Use of Wildlife in the United States.* U.S. Fish and Wildlife Service Resource Publication 154. Washington, D.C.: U.S. Government Printing Office.

Shaw, William W., William R. Mangun, and James R. Lyons. 1985. "Residential Enjoyment of Wildlife Resources by Americans." *Leisure Sciences* 7(3):361–375.

Talbot, Lee M. 1974. "Nongame Wildlife: A Federal Perspective." *Transactions of the Thirty-ninth North American Wildlife and Natural Resources Conference* 39:81–86.

Thompson, Bruce C. 1987. "Attributes and Implementation of Non-game and Endangered Species Programs in the United States." *Wildlife Society Bulletin* 15:210–216.

Tober, James A. 1989. *Wildlife and the Public Interest: Nonprofit Organizations and Federal Wildlife Policy.* New York: Praeger.

U.S. Department of the Interior (USDI). Fish and Wildlife Service. 1977. *1975 National Survey of Fishing, Hunting, and Wildlife-Associated Recreation.* Washington, D.C.: U.S. Government Printing Office.

———. 1982. *1980 National Survey of Fishing, Hunting, and Wildlife-Associated Recreation.* Washington, D.C.: U.S. Government Printing Office.

———. 1988. *1985 National Survey of Fishing, Hunting, and Wildlife-Associated Recreation.* Washington, D.C.: U.S. Government Printing Office.

U.S. Department of the Interior (USDI). Fish and Wildlife Service, and International Association of Fish and Wildlife Agencies (IAFWA). 1983. *A Summary of Selected Fish and Wildlife Characteristics of the 50 States.* Washington, D.C.: U.S. Government Printing Office.

U.S. Department of the Interior (USDI). Heritage Conservation and Recreation Service. 1978. *Data Book: 1977 National Outdoor Recreation Survey.* Washington, D.C.: U.S. Government Printing Office.

Weeden, R. B. 1976. "Nonconsumptive Users: A Myth." *Alaska Conservation Review* 27(9):3, 15.

Wilkes, B. 1977. "The Myth of the Nonconsumptive User." *Canadian Field-Naturalist* 91(4):343–349.

Witter, Daniel J., and William W. Shaw. 1979. "Beliefs of Birders, Hunters, and Wildlife Professionals About Wildlife Management." *Transactions of the Forty-fourth North American Wildlife and Natural Resources Conference* 44:298–305.

Wright, V. 1976. "Nongame Is Wildlife, Too." *American Forests* 83(12):29–31.

Zwank, P. J., V. W. Howard, Jr., and J. R. Gray. 1980. *Characteristics of State Nongame Management Programs in 1980.* Las Cruces, N.M.: Range Improvement Task Force, Agriculture Experiment Station, Cooperative Extension Service, New Mexico State University.

9

NATURAL RESOURCE HAZARDS: MANAGING TO PROTECT PEOPLE FROM THE RESOURCE

Barbara A. Knuth

Introduction

Contemporary natural resource management policy involves elements of conservation, enjoyment, and protection. Management responsibilities include (1) controlling human actions for the conservation and protection of fish and wildlife and their habitats, (2) increasing fish and wildlife population surpluses for human enjoyment, and (3) protecting humans from potential hazards presented by fish and wildlife resources and their habitats. Each of these responsibilities requires to some extent a focus on both biological and human social systems to be successful. Most state-level management agencies, however, emphasize the importance of activities relating to wildlife habitats and populations, downplaying their responsibilities, activities, and accomplishments involving humans (Knuth and Nielsen 1986). If humans are ignored when managing for the first type of responsibility, fish and wildlife populations may suffer immediately, but at least some people stand to benefit in the short run. If humans are ignored for the second responsibility, people suffer because of missed opportunities for natural resource enjoyment. If people are ignored for the third responsibility, both humans and wildlife will suffer—humans because their health or safety will be endangered and wildlife because reduced human tolerance for wildlife owing to the hazards they present may lead to decreased support for or hostility toward wildlife and their habitats.

Natural resource hazards may be real or perceived. Real hazards include actual risks to human health and well-being such as from rabid raccoons in suburban areas and toxic bacterial infections in marine shellfish. Perceived hazards include real hazards as well as situations that in reality hold no or little risk to humans, such as the common belief that children will be attacked by wolves, or persons' becoming overly concerned after being bitten by the scarlet king snake because they have mistaken it for the poisonous coral snake. Natural resource managers must devise management strategies that will account successfully for differences in perceived and actual risk, protect human health where needed, yet encourage appropriate use, enjoyment, and appreciation of natural resources.

Common to all management responsibilities is a sequence of four events: (1) assessment of *demands* for resource use and protection, (2) specific *activities* conducted by managers toward some end, (3) production of management *outputs* that include immediate and proximate resource uses and enhancements, and (4) creation of *impacts* that are the longer-term ultimate effects of resource management actions (Knuth and Nielsen 1989). Comprehensive evaluations of management successes include each of those stages but should focus particularly on outputs and impacts. Acting to protect people from natural resource hazards, resource managers may produce outputs such as increased or decreased human contact with fish and wildlife or changed wildlife population levels and impacts such as human appreciation and understanding of fish and wildlife populations or protection of human health. The ultimate management goal is to manage natural resource hazards, or human perceptions of those hazards, to produce desirable benefits from the natural resource base. Achieving that goal requires careful selection and implementation of both ecologically and socially directed management activities.

I present here two examples of emerging natural resource management issues in which sound management must include the protection of humans from potential hazards posed by fish and wildlife resources and habitats. The first example is drawn from Great Lakes fishery management and focuses on a fishery beset by human-induced problems with chemical contaminants in the sediments, the water, and ultimately the fish tissue. The second example focuses on a natural pathogen perhaps made more dangerous because of increasing contact between humans and wildlife, arthritis-like "Lyme disease" and its relationship to white-tailed deer and other wildlife. These hazards have clear implications for management actions that will produce socially and ecologically desirable interactions between people and natural resources. The philosophy underlying these management actions is a desire to achieve public health protection coupled with a respect for and continued appreciation (and use) of natural resources. Both management examples involve attempts to influence the way in which people interact with the resource, via communication and education strategies designed to increase public health consciousness and redirect people's attitudes and actions.

Natural Resource Hazard Management

Human health hazards presented by natural resources can be managed with two general strategies. The first focuses on the biota, or managing for specific conditions in wildlife habitat or wildlife populations (for example, removing attractive food sources for raccoons; decreasing deer populations). The second strategy focuses on humans and includes a range of techniques designed to limit human interaction with fish or wildlife resources or their habitats.

Strategies to limit human activities include regulatory and voluntary or advisory approaches. Regulatory strategies imply that some enforcement capability exists and that people will receive some punishment for noncompliance. Voluntary strategies imply no enforcement and no punishment for those who seek to ignore the advice. Regulatory strategies include total closures of harvest seasons or areas, bans on possession of certain species or sizes of animals from designated areas, or prohibition of any human use in particular areas. Voluntary management strategies rely on the use of recommendations or advisories issued to the actual or potential human clientele for a particular natural resource use. The strategies allow individuals to make an informed decision about their exposure to hazards associated with fish or wildlife populations and habitats and seek to accomplish the dual goal of providing recreational use opportunities and associated satisfactions while protecting human health. The use of a voluntary management strategy, however, presumes people are aware of the advice and of the consequences of their decision to comply with or disregard the recommendations. Communicating about natural resource hazards involves several activities: presenting technical and scientific information, presenting possibly traumatic information, presenting uncertainties, and providing professional recommendations (Boyle and Holtgrave 1989).

Relying on a voluntary approach to protect human health demands careful consideration of effective communication mechanisms to describe human health risk potentials, establish realistic attitudes toward the hazards, and influence risk-reducing or risk-mitigating behaviors. Indicators of management success, focusing on both outputs and ultimate impacts of management, may include participation rates in various types of natural resource use opportunities and reported incidents involving negative human health effects from contact with natural resources (Knuth and Nielsen 1989).

Sport-Fishery Hazards: Chemical Contaminants in Fish

One example of real and perceived natural resource hazards comes from contemporary sport-fishery management, the issue of chemical contaminants in fish. Because of industrialization, municipal inputs, and residential uses, chemical contamination of water resources has become commonplace. In some areas, contaminants are of a type or magnitude that they concentrate in fish tissue to such an extent that a human health risk is created. Health risks may include carcinogenesis and developmental, reproductive, behavioral, metabolic, or neurological impairment (Fein et al. 1984; Chen et al. 1985; Kreiss 1985; Humphrey 1988). The magnitude of the health risk generally increases with greater consumption of contaminated fish. Therefore, less exposure to the hazard (that is, less fish consumption) results in reduced health risks.

Marine and inland fishery and human health managers have responded to the problem of toxic substances in fish by issuing "health advisories," which recommend reduced levels of fish consumption from contaminated waterways and may suggest other strategies including fish preparation and cooking techniques to reduce the health hazards to which a sport-fish consumer may be exposed. These actions place management agencies in the uncomfortable situation, in some cases, of promoting a fishery (for example, Pacific salmon fishery in the Great Lakes) while at the same time assuming the responsibility for limiting anglers' potential involvement in and enjoyment of the fishery (for example, all eight Great Lakes states issue some form of a health advisory for fish in those waters). Duttweiler (1983) voiced concerns about fishery management agencies' warning people away from certain uses of sport-fisheries while at the same time implementing management actions to increase those stocks that people are advised to avoid or at least not consume. Advisories are usually developed by or in conjunction with a health department, but often the fishery management agency is the primary disseminator for the advisory itself (for example, Knuth 1989).

Consuming contaminated sport-caught fish is theoretically a voluntary activity, in which a person has a choice regarding the nature and magnitude of exposure to the hazard (Clark et al. 1987). The voluntary nature of this activity depends on how well the public is informed about the risks from fish consumption. People respond to the hazards they perceive (Belton et al. 1986). If their perceptions are faulty, people may not respond in a way they would choose given full knowledge of the contaminant situation.

As advisories rely on a voluntary approach to protecting human health, one of the prime management concerns should be communicating human health risk potentials effectively to anglers, their families, and other probable fish consumers. This management approach requires that careful attention be paid to angler knowledge of advisories, perceptions of risk or understanding of the hazard, and fishing and fish-consuming behaviors. Just as other fishery management strategies recognize differences among various species, habitats, and user groups, health advisories should take into account the diverse needs of the targeted audiences. Educational efforts so far have usually not distinguished between the occasional and the frequent fish consumer, though hazards to which they are exposed are likely different. Their knowledge of the fishery and alternative species and the areas in which to fish also likely differs (Duttweiler 1983).

Health advisories can contain a variety of information, including specific locations, species, and sizes to which the consumption limits pertain, comparisons of sport-fish consumption risks with other types of risk that people face routinely, and assumptions used in developing recommendations such as the annual fish consumption rate assumed or the length of lifetime assumed for fish consumption. Specificity and comparisons may reduce risk "misperceptions," which may have quite significant regional economic and social effects. Controversies over acceptable risk levels can be addressed by providing information on several levels of risk and their associated fish consumption amounts. The health effects considered may include such different endpoints as cancer or developmental disorders and may prompt different reactions from fish consumers depending on their sex and age (Knuth 1990).

Target audiences for a health advisory include a variety of more or less dedicated anglers, as well as fish consumers who may or may not be the anglers themselves. Ultimate changes in individual behavior are related strongly to the match between the advisory recommendations and the attitudes of the targeted audience. Little behavioral change is likely to be elicited if suggested precautions to minimize risk appear too costly. Anglers will be more receptive to the advisory's message if it includes acceptable alternatives or suggestions of ways in which angler behavior can be modified to reduce risks, such as cleaning and cooking procedures.

Discrete behavioral changes possible for reducing exposure to this hazard include: (1) changing the locations fished, avoiding contaminated source waters; (2) changing the target species, avoiding species more likely to accumulate contaminants; (3) changing the size of fish kept to eat, avoiding larger fish more likely to have accumulated contaminants; (4) changing the frequency of fish consumption, attempting to limit the dose of contaminants received; and (5) changing the methods for preparing fish, seeking to remove contaminant-collecting fats (Duttweiler and Voiland 1981).

Research on Lake Ontario salmonid management, angler behavior, and risk perceptions provides several considerations for targeted and specific communication strategies to encourage anglers to make an informed choice about their angling and fish consuming behaviors, while not abandoning the sport fishery entirely. The New York State Department of Health, in cooperation with the Department of Environmental Conservation, prepares and issues health advisories for New York waters. Lake Ontario, as with all New York waters, has a general advisory for all fish consumers to limit sport-fish consumption to one meal per week and additional, more restrictive recommendations for particular species and sizes of fish, or classes of fish consumers, most notably women and children. Studies focused on health advisories for Lake Ontario have included several audiences: (1) a statewide sample of randomly selected licensed anglers to determine general knowledge of and behaviors related to advisories (Connelly et al. 1990); (2) a purposeful selection of opinion leaders from recreational angling associations (Springer 1990); and (3) a purposeful selection of "fishery decision makers," which included state fishery managers and biologists, Sea Grant and Cooperative Extension specialists, and members of county fishery advisory boards (Springer 1990).

A majority of Lake Ontario anglers are aware that health advisories have been issued for the lake, including 98 percent of angling-association opinion leaders and 82 percent of licensed anglers who fish Lake Ontario. However, understanding of and adherence to the advisory is more variable. Most fish caught by Lake Ontario anglers are released, made into trophy mounts, or used as fertilizer (60 percent), but a substantial amount is eaten (23 percent) or given away (17 percent; Connelly et al. 1990) presumably to be consumed by someone else, another potential audience for advisories. Different communication strategies may be needed for the variety of clientele that advisories seek to reach. Based on the statewide angler survey, out-of-state anglers in particular were more reliant for their information about contaminants on the fishing license regulations guide and on information they received from charter boat operators than were in-state anglers. New York City and Long Island anglers, a rather urban clientele, relied more on posted warnings at fishing sites and access points to learn about advisories than did anglers statewide.

One-quarter of licensed anglers who fish Lake Ontario were unsure if they fish in waters where contaminants are a problem (Connelly et al. 1990). This implies either a lack of knowledge regarding where contaminants are found or a potential disbelief that Lake Ontario waters do indeed contain contaminated species. In any case, the implication is that anglers may be exposing themselves to undue hazards because of lack of knowledge or lack of confidence in the sources of information available to them.

Further, even though anglers have heard about or read the advisory, they may not understand or believe the information. Some licensed anglers who fish Lake Ontario for species listed on the advisory were unsure if they fish for potentially contaminated species (23 percent), or believed they usually fished for species in which contaminants are not a problem (28 percent; Connelly et al. 1990).

A majority of Lake Ontario anglers have made changes in their fishing or eating habits to reduce their risks from contaminants in fish (Connelly et al. 1990; Springer 1990). Changes have included switching species or sizes of fish sought, fishing less, changing locations fished, and taking more fishing trips because of a greater feeling of confidence about the relative safety of different water bodies. Anglers can adopt those risk-reducing behaviors without the disruption in their life-style that would come from heeding warnings simply to not eat any fish or not to fish in certain locations.

While not eliminating their consumption of sport-caught fish,

Lake Ontario anglers appear responsive to other risk-reducing recommendations offered by the state. They include the use of certain fish preparation and cooking methods that may reduce exposure to contaminants. On average, Lake Ontario anglers were more likely to use the risk-reducing methods of puncturing or removing fish skin and trimming ventral meat and dorsal fat than were anglers statewide (Connelly et al. 1990; Springer 1990).

Changes in eating habits made by anglers include eating fewer Lake Ontario fish, changing preparation or cooking methods used, eating no sport fish, and eating more sport fish because of a feeling of confidence about the relative safety of fish from particular waters (Connelly et al. 1990; Springer 1990). Again, informed anglers appear willing to make some behavioral changes that still maintain their familiar life-style but decrease the risk to which they are exposed. The response by Lake Ontario anglers regarding changes in cleaning or cooking fish indicates one successful avenue for information and education programs. Few anglers fished more or ate more sport fish, but this must be considered in light of the advisory existing at that time, which did little in the way of actually promoting or emphasizing those New York waters likely to be least affected by chemical contaminants. It does seem possible to encourage positive shifts in angler behavior, given the right information.

Lake Ontario anglers believed that the advisory as issued contains enough information for an angler to understand why limits are recommended on fish consumption and to decide whether or not to eat Lake Ontario fish and that it represents the best information currently available. Fishery decision makers disagreed on all three accounts (Springer 1990). As they are likely to be more informed about the potential information that could be provided to anglers, it demonstrates some dissatisfaction with the information as prepared, which is done largely by the Department of Health (Knuth 1989).

What information did anglers seek from an advisory? Lake Ontario anglers wanted health advisories to indicate which recommendations have changed from the previous year and which sizes of fish in a given species are safer to eat. Fishery decision makers agreed, although they felt less strongly than anglers that information by Lake Basin and a description of specific chemicals causing concern in Lake Ontario were important information to convey. Both anglers and fishery decision makers believed it essential to include information on cleaning and cooking procedures that have been shown to reduce the level of some contaminants in fish flesh and an assessment of how health risks change as a person eats different amounts of fish (Springer 1990). The emphasis seems to be on information that targets risk-reducing behaviors within the normal life-style of anglers and that encourages anglers' abilities to make an informed decision about amount and types of sport-fish consumption.

Both anglers and fishery decision makers felt it would be somewhat important to include the comparison of the risks from consuming sport fish with uncontrollable risks like being in a car accident and with voluntary risks like smoking cigarettes. Judged by both groups to be more important were comparisons with other dietary risks, with fish caught from waters other than Lake Ontario, and with risks or benefits of other protein sources. Both groups felt a description of the health effects posed by contaminants should be included. Anglers felt more strongly than did decision makers that it was important to provide a synopsis of data used in developing the advisories, such as the kind of samples tested for contaminants (for example, whole fish versus skinned fillets) and the name of the agency that actually conducted the sampling and analysis (Springer 1990).

Evidence available from New York's Lake Ontario fishery illustrates that differences do exist between different angling segments in their fishing and fish-consuming habits and in the information they desire about sport-fish contaminants. Natural resource hazard management strategies that rely on information and communication programs should incorporate specific attitudes and behaviors of the target audiences. Rather than offering general warnings about fish consumption and assuming anglers will adopt the entire set of behaviors those general advisories imply, managers can describe an array of possible behavioral changes, each of which provides a probable incremental reduction in risk. Only with consideration of the specific information needs, attitudes, and acceptable behaviors of different target audiences will health advisories successfully attain objectives related both to protecting human health and providing sport-fishery uses.

Wildlife Hazards: Lyme Disease and White-Tailed Deer

The second example of a natural resource hazard that tests wildlife management is the growing public concern about Lyme disease, the most common vector-borne disease in the United States (New York State Department of Health News Release, June 28, 1988). Lyme disease is a nonfatal, but sometimes debilitating, disease caused by a bacterium (*Borreli burgdorferi*) that is transmitted to humans principally by ticks (*Ixodes* spp.). In the United States, the disease is transmitted typically through the deer tick (*Ixodes dammini*). Potential hosts to the tick include white-tailed deer, raccoons, deer mice, other mammals, and some birds (Cochran 1987). Almost fifty thousand cases of Lyme disease were reported in the United States in the 1980s, in forty-three states, and the disease is spreading rapidly. Two factors that may contribute to recent increases in transmission of the disease are the significant increases in regional white-tailed deer populations and the increased proximity of humans and wildlife in a suburban landscape.

The probability of contracting Lyme disease may be associated with a number of human behaviors, including use of given land areas or habitats, frequency of visitation to particular areas, types of outdoor activities engaged in, and interest in land-management practices of both public land-management agencies and private landowners.Outdoor recreation activities contributing to potential wildlife-human interactions involve a wide range, from intensive use of remote wildland areas to more casual contacts in the outdoor suburban or rural/urban fringe. In New York, the state with the highest incidence of Lyme disease, the disease is associated with areas of high human population density (Long Island and the lower Hudson River Valley), resulting in high levels of public concern. That concern is directed partially toward white-tailed deer and other wildlife species known to be hosts of the tick that carries the spirochete responsible for the disease.

Wildlife observation around the home is a major and growing interest of rural, suburban, and urban residents (USDI 1988). State and federal wildlife management agencies and private wildlife conservation organizations have developed management and education programs based on this trend and its projected continuation. Many of the programs emphasize habitat management by individual landowners to maximize benefits to wildlife and thus wildlife attraction to the site for observation (for example, National Wildlife Federation's backyard wildlife habitat program). Private enterprises, including supplemental and alternative uses of agricultural lands, have developed and prospered as a result of current and projected public interest in wildlife recreation (Guynn and Steinbach 1987; Shelton 1987). Public and private money has been committed to support the interest of Americans in wildlife, and many persons and communities depend on that interest for economic survival (Peterson and Randall 1984). Wildlife-oriented business pursuits rest on an assumption of maintenance and even growth in public interest in wildlife recreation. Positive public sentiment, however, may diminish rapidly in the face of growing negative wildlife perceptions due to Lyme disease.

The potential to contract Lyme disease represents a high risk to human health in some outdoor environments, a small risk in others. Whether or not individuals engage in potentially risky activities will depend on knowledge of Lyme disease, perceptions and attitudes regarding the disease, its seriousness, potential vectors, and knowledge of and receptivity to risk-reducing behaviors. In any area, the actual magnitude of the risk may be outweighed by people's perceptions regarding their likelihood of being exposed to or contracting the disease.

Public response to perceived risks from Lyme disease may include shifts in areas used for outdoor recreation or desired for homes, decreased support for certain wildlife management initiatives including habitat protection, and diminished efforts to increase wildlife habitat on private lands. Perceptions about Lyme disease may affect people's use of parks and other natural areas, participation in outdoor recreation activities (for example, camping, hiking, hunting), and attitudes toward hunting. Reactions to Lyme disease pertinent to attitudes toward wildlife may be influenced by the level of commitment and involvement in wildlife resource use activities, the strength of perceptions of personal or economic risk, and the sense of control over the risk. Changes in people's desire to engage in various outdoor recreation activities may lead to undesirable changes in wildlife populations (for example, reductions in hunting may result in an increase in white-tailed deer) and associated habitats (Decker and Gavin 1985).

Perceptions and attitudes resulting from increased incidence or increased awareness of Lyme disease may result in decreased rates of participation in a variety of outdoor recreation activities, perhaps needlessly so if the changes are not directed toward those behaviors most associated with contracting the disease. Perceived roles of wildlife and different habitats in transmitting Lyme disease could also affect public attitudes toward both public and private land-management practices, with important economic implications for those who manage and benefit from those lands. Misperceptions about Lyme disease, therefore, affect not only a person's own potential quality of life if certain enjoyable activities must be forgone but also can create unnecessary economic hardships for those areas dependent on a natural resource/outdoor recreation economy. Natural-resource-related social and economic consequences of Lyme disease are not well understood. The few studies that have been conducted demonstrate that concern about Lyme disease transmission from deer is among the most important fears that the public holds toward deer (Connelly et al. 1987).

In one New York county in which Lyme disease is high in incidence, a majority of residents enjoyed deer but worried about problems such as Lyme disease, plant damage, and deer-vehicle collisions (Connelly et al. 1987). Risk of disease was the problem residents were least willing to tolerate. Of those residents who had concerns about Lyme disease specifically, most viewed deer as a nuisance (Connelly et al. 1987). Residents were almost evenly split as to the desired size of the deer herd, some wanting the herd to remain at its present size and others wanting the herd to decrease.

In a similar study on Long Island, a majority of residents who knew that deer used their property held transmission of Lyme disease to be their primary concern and wanted the deer herd decreased (Decker and Gavin 1985). Most survey respondents favored active deer management to control the size of the deer herd but did not equate management with support for firearm hunting to control herd size (Connelly et al. 1987). Thus, finding a cost-effective deer herd management technique to replace recreational hunting with firearms is the dilemma.

Changes in natural-area visitation rates and human behaviors associated with concern about Lyme disease could have important impacts on generation of revenue and support for programs. For example, tax checkoff donations of New York residents were received at a higher rate from those with the least negative sentiments about wildlife's transmitting disease to humans and about potential damage or nuisance problems caused by wildlife (Connelly et al. 1984). Lyme disease perceptions and the frequency or popularity of wildlife-related recreational activities associated with the transmission of Lyme disease have important implications for resource management programs. Resource professionals must understand (1) how Lyme disease perceptions correspond to resource use patterns, (2) what changes in resource use patterns can be expected to occur because of Lyme disease risk perceptions, and (3) how those perceptions and beliefs can be altered if the use patterns and their impacts are deemed undesirable.

The degree to which managers of municipal, state, or federal lands can design effective policies regarding Lyme disease and wildlife will be enhanced with a broad information base, including an understanding of how people acquire information about Lyme disease. Policymakers should strive to anticipate changes in human attitudes, behaviors, and associated impacts in response to Lyme disease. Timely assessment of perceptions and outdoor recreation participation patterns associated with Lyme disease is needed to develop management policies and educational strategies that are adaptive and responsive to the constituencies most affected.

Negative implications of Lyme disease for natural resource managers include reduced levels of support for wildlife and habitat protection and, in some cases, outright opposition to protection of species and habitats and demands for population reductions. Coupled with this in many communities may be the challenge of reducing wildlife populations when residents are opposed to many or all types of hunting. Educational programs that deal with known instances of Lyme disease but that also recognize and seek to influence misperceptions about disease transmission have the highest probability of producing socially beneficial outcomes (Connelly et al. 1987). Educational strategies that focus on risk-reducing behaviors will be enhanced if they incorporate health and outdoor recreation safety information channels already familiar to the target audiences. Appropriate management responses include surveys to understand public perceptions of risk and programs to influence the amount of control people have over the Lyme disease risk they face. The latter entails public communications about preventing and minimizing exposure to deer ticks, while encouraging continued involvement in wildlife-associated recreation, focusing on the role played by wildlife, ticks, and various habitats in disease transmission, and educating residents about the limited variety of potential population control strategies.

Policy and Management Implications of Natural Resource Hazards

Recognizing natural resource hazards as a management responsibility with both biological and human dimensions will influence resource management programs and research in a few primary ways. First, the focus on limiting human activities for the benefit of wildlife populations or habitats will change to include objectives oriented toward human health protection. Second, decisions to increase wildlife populations or habitats will be considered in light of potential human health effects. Those decisions will not necessarily result in population decreases but may result in appropriate education strategies that increase both wildlife populations and safety for humans having interaction with those wildlife populations. Third, appropriate management objectives must be selected before hazard management strategies are chosen. In general, the objectives of a resource hazard management program can be either descriptive or prescriptive. Descriptive objectives deal with hazard identification and describe options available to avoid the hazards. Prescriptive objectives select and indicate clearly what behavior change should be made to minimize contact with a hazard. Possible objectives include: (1) informing and educating segments of the public about resource hazards; (2) changing behaviors or assisting the public in making a decision to change behaviors; (3) protecting human health and preventing human exposure to hazards via regulation, coercion, or informed choice; (4) mitigating the effects of hazard exposure; (5) protecting economic values of a resource or of resource-dependent communities; and (6) encouraging continued use of a resource in ways that minimize exposure to the hazards.

Choosing voluntary strategies to manage natural resource hazards implies a shift in decision-making responsibility from government agency to individual and so requires informed participation and increased self-determination by the individual (Boyle and Holtgrave 1989). The manager's responsibility, then, is to guarantee that the individual is informed fully about the consequences of any decision she or he makes regarding how to cope with resource hazards. Attaining the objectives will depend largely on developing and using sound communication strategies.

As Boyle and Holtgrave (1989) noted, natural resource hazard communication efforts must be treated as an ongoing dialogue between manager and resource user, not just a "onetime-shot." The communication process should not be considered complete until it is evaluated to determine its effectiveness (Springer 1990). Evaluations should be conducted to determine the correspondence between the hazard warning and the warning as actually understood by resource users. Issued to protect human health, advisories may be misinterpreted as having some biological basis such as population enhancement or habitat protection (Belton et al. 1986). The link between following an advisory and the resulting human health benefits certainly can become obscured.

Experience with other communication campaigns can be applied to natural resource hazards management. Health advisory information transmission will be improved if efforts are made to influence the communication network by which resource users normally obtain information about natural resources, with the intent of providing more accurate information than available otherwise (Heatwole and West 1983). Information disseminated via small interest groups or opinion leaders is often more effective in gaining credibility than information provided by a state agency (Belton et al. 1986). Efforts should be made to identify and use familiar communication channels for those people most likely to be exposed to a natural resource hazard. Educational programming related to natural resource hazards suggests that an effective warning must be reinforced socially and at the local level (Sims and Baumann 1983). Using multiple channels to deliver hazard information and incorporating community or group leaders and media specialists at the ground level in hazard education programs are strategies to enhance success. The impact of any message is greater when it reaches people through a variety of credible channels or in a number of different forms (Sims and Baumann 1983). Subpopulations of resource users may be differentially affected by the advisory message because of inadequate dissemination or the inability of a single message to reach and influence all audiences. Level of education, ethnicity, income, and likely a host of other factors influence the way in which people respond (Heatwole and West 1983; Smith and Enger 1988).

Simply carrying out management activities to protect human health is not enough. Evaluation of management success should be performance-oriented, focusing on desirable outputs and impacts resulting from management programs (Knuth and Nielsen 1989). Health advisories or other communication strategies may be developed and disseminated, but resource users may ignore the advice (Belton et al. 1986). Managers must seek to understand why recommendations are not followed—are they not credible, not understood, not available to specific target audiences? Managers seeking to employ voluntary management strategies should consider characteristics that will affect ultimate compliance and plan to use them to advantage or minimize the effects of those factors likely to detract from successful implementation. Effective warnings must convey an appropriate behavioral response on the part of the individual and not leave such response open to interpretation (Sims and Baumann 1983).

Natural resource hazards such as the aforementioned examples emphasize the need for communication and education programs. The fishery example provides opportunities for encouraging non-consumptive resource uses and support for environmental cleanup programs, while the wildlife example illustrates the need for health protection strategies coupled with ecological education so that the public is not so fearful of the resource that it seeks to destroy it.

Research is needed on fish and wildlife hazards to describe the interplay between human knowledge and natural resource risks, formation of attitudes relative to personal and community characteristics including dependence on the resource base, and implementation of behaviors to cope with or respond to natural resource hazards. Once those tasks have been accomplished, resource managers can identify target audiences and develop educational programs to mitigate negative social and economic impacts.

Acknowledgments

This work is a result of research sponsored in part by the National Oceanic and Atmospheric Administration's Office of Sea Grant, U.S. Department of Commerce, under Grant NA86AA–D–SG045 to the New York Sea Grant Institute and by the U.S. Department of Agriculture under Hatch Projects NYC–147409 and NYC–147420.

References

Belton, T., R. Roundy, and N. Weinstein. 1986. "Urban Fishermen: Managing the Risks of Toxic Exposures." *Environment* 28:19–20, 30–37.

Boyle, M., and D. Holtgrave. 1989. "Communicating Environmental Health Risks." *Environmental Science and Technology* 23(11):1335–1337.

Chen, R. C., S. Y. Teng, H. Miyata, T. Kashimoto, Y. Chang, K. Chang, and T. Tung. 1985. "PCB Poisoning: Correlation of Sensory and Nerve Conduction, Neurologic Symptoms, and Blood Levels of PCBs, Quaterphenyls, and Dibenzofurans." *Environmental Research* 37:340–348.

Clark, J. M., L. Fink, and D. DeVault. 1987. "A New Approach for the Establishment of Fish Consumption Advisories." *Journal of Great Lakes Research* 13(3):367–374.

Cochran, R. 1987. "New York: 'Lyme Disease Outbreak.'" *Outdoor Life,* March, p.13.

Connelly, N. A., T. L. Brown, and D. J. Decker. 1984. *Evaluation of the 1982–83 "Return a Gift to Wildlife" Program Promotion Efforts.* Ithaca, N.Y.: Outdoor Recreation Research Unit, Department of Natural Resources, New York State College of Agriculture and Life Sciences, Cornell University.

Connelly, N. A., T. L. Brown, and B. Knuth. 1990. *New York Statewide Angler Survey, 1988.* Albany, N.Y.: New York State Department of Environmental Conservation.

Connelly, N. A., D. J. Decker, and S. Wear. 1987. *White-tailed Deer in Westchester County, New York: Public Perceptions and Preferences.* Human Dimensions Research Unit Publ. 87–5. Ithaca, N.Y.: Department of Natural Resources, New York State College of Agriculture and Life Sciences, Cornell University.

Decker, D. J., and T. A. Gavin. 1985. *Human Dimensions of Managing a Suburban Deer Herd: Situational Analysis for Decision Making by the Seatuck National Wildlife Refuge, Islip, NY.* Outdoor Recreation Research Unit Publ. 85–3. Ithaca, N.Y.: Department of Natural Resources, New York State College of Agriculture and Life Sciences, Cornell University.

Duttweiler, M. W. 1983. "Communication Human Health Implication of Great Lakes Fish Contaminants." Paper presented to the Twenty-sixth Conference of the International Association for Great Lakes Research, Oswego, N.Y., 25 May, 1983.

Duttweiler, M. W., and M. P. Voiland. 1981. *Fish Contaminants: Minimizing Your Intake.* New York Sea Grant Extension Brochure. Brockport, N.Y.

Fein, G. G., J. L. Jacobson, P. M. Schwartz, and J. K. Dowler. 1984. "Prenatal Exposure to Polychlorinated Biphenyls: Effects on Birth Size and Gestational Age." *Journal of Pediatrics* 105:315–320.

Guynn, D. E., and D. W. Steinbach. 1987. "Wildlife Values in Texas." Pp. 117–124 in D. J. Decker and G. Goff, eds., *Valuing Wildlife.* Boulder, Colo.: Westview Press.

Heatwole, C. A., and N. C. West. 1983. "Urban Shore-based Fishing: A Health Hazard?" *Proceedings of the Third Symposium on Coastal and Ocean Management.* New York: American Society of Civil Engineers.

Humphrey, H. E. B. 1988. "Chemical Contaminants in the Great Lakes: The Human Health Aspect." Pp. 153–165 in M. S. Evans, ed., *Toxic Contaminants and Ecosystem Health: A Great Lakes Focus.* New York: John Wiley and Sons.

Knuth, B. A. 1989. "Implementing Chemical Contaminant Policies in Sport-fisheries: Agency Partnerships and Constituency Influence." *Journal of Management Science and Policy Analysis* 6(4):69–81.

———. 1990. "Risk Communication: A New Dimension in Sport-fisheries Management." *North American Journal of Fisheries Management* 10(4):374–381.

Knuth, B. A., and L. A. Nielsen. 1986. "Content Analysis of Agency Annual Reports with Recommendations for Improvement." *Wildlife Society Bulletin* 14:465–473.

———. 1989. "Social and Institutional Performance Indicators for Wildlife and Fishery Resource Management Systems." *Society and Natural Resources* 2(4):351–366.

Kreiss, K. 1985. "Studies on Populations Exposed to Polychlorinated Biphenyls." *Environmental Health Perspectives* 60:193–199.

Peterson, G. L., and A. Randall. 1984. *Valuation of Wildland Resource Benefits.* Boulder: Westview Press.

Shelton, R. 1987. "Fee Hunting Systems and Important Factors in Wildlife Commercialization in Private Lands." Pp. 109–116 in D. J. Decker and G. R. Goff, eds, *Valuing Wildlife.* Boulder, Colo.: Westview Press.

Sims, J. H., and D. D. Baumann. 1983. "Educational Programs and Human Response to Natural Hazards." *Environment and Behavior* 15(2):165–189.

Smith, B. F., and E. E. Enger. 1988. *A Survey of Attitudes and Fish Consumption of Anglers on the Lower Tittabawassee River, Michigan.* East Lansing: Center for Environmental Health Science, Michigan Department of Public Health.

Springer, C. 1990. *A Risk Communication Model for the Lake Ontario Sportfishery.* Master's thesis, New York State College of Agriculture and Life Sciences, Cornell University, Ithaca, N.Y.

U.S. Department of the Interior (USDI). Fish and Wildlife Service. 1988. *1985 National Survey of Fishing, Hunting, and Wildlife-Associated Recreation.* Washington, D.C.: U.S. Government Printing Office.

10

Exit, Voice, and Loyalty of Wildlife Biologists in Public Natural Resource/ Environmental Agencies

James J. Kennedy • *Jack Ward Thomas*

Introduction

It is not uncommon for natural resource or environmental professionals such as wildlife biologists or foresters to consider resigning from the state or federal agencies in which most are employed. Some do. Those remaining must weigh agency, professional, and other allegiances (for example, family) in managing loyalty conflicts. In the process they develop professional management styles for supporting and confronting their agency, thereby affecting their professional reputation, organizational influence, and careers, as well as the quality of resource management.

Hirschman's book (1970) *Exit, Voice, and Loyalty,* and adaptations of that model (for example, Rusbult et al. 1982, 1988), provides a framework to consider how personal career decisions can produce important group impacts on organizations and society. We employ these concepts to consider (1) the effects of wildlife biologists' entering or *exiting* a traditional multi-use agency, (2) the organizational and career impacts of supporting and challenging the agency with their *voice*, and (3) the impact of *loyalty* in inviting or discouraging employee critique. The agency example is the USDA-Forest Service (FS).

Exit, voice, and loyalty will first be described and discussed at the organizational-employee level, as they interact with each other and impact individual biologists, the FS, and society. Several natural resource issues are then addressed (for example, the role of 1970s' environmental legislation on biologists' voice inside the FS).

Exit, Voice, and Loyalty Defined

Hirschman (1970) defines *exit* as choosing to leave an organization or a nation (we will focus on employee-organization relationships). *Loyalty* is defined as employees' remaining in an organization, passively accepting the conditions of employment, but optimistic about future improvement. Job exit may also be influenced by personal and professional values (for example, sense of responsibility), by investment in position and retirement plans, or by a limited selection of alternatives. *Neglect* was added to the original model to describe another type of loyalty that is *not* as passive and exhibits little optimism—it allows or aids conditions to worsen through reduced effort, cynicism, or absenteeism (Rusbult and Zembrodt 1983). People who remain in organizations, by choice or circumstance, can decide to be active or inactive voices for change (Farrell 1983).

Voice is defined (Hirschman 1970:30) as the most active and risky relationship for those who remain in (are "loyal" to) an organization or a country:

> any attempt at all to change, rather than to escape from, an objectionable state of affairs, whether through individual or collective petition to the management . . . through appeal to a higher authority with the intention of forcing a change . . . or through various types of actions and protests, including those that are meant to mobilize public opinion.

He also stresses that exit, voice, and loyalty are highly interdependent. The need for and effectiveness of one is commonly dependent on the others. The exit of dissidents from an organization or nation, for example, reduces the amount and intensity of voice and can promote sheepish, uncritical norms for the loyal.

Early in this century hunters were among the first citizens to support conservation theories and organizations. Their loyalty to wildlife and other resource conservation and their voice helped create the laws, policies, and budgets upon which game management (later wildlife management) professions and organizations were founded.

Fifty years ago, organizational loyalty issues for game managers also may have been less complex than today. Increasing the number and range of game animals for hunting was the overwhelming focus of their training and management. Most game managers worked for a few single-purpose state or federal agencies. It was probably easier to be loyal to and voice support of game management and hunters' interests in a fish and game agency of the 1940s than in a 1990s' multiple-use agency such as the FS, where wildlife biologists must consider all wildlife species and their habitats, hunters and nonconsumptive users, plus other resource use and development. We now turn to some of these issues.

Exit, Voice, and Loyalty Applied to Issue-Specific Wildlife Management

The general examples above begin to illustrate the interdependence of exit, voice, and loyalty. They also indicate the broad diversity of wildlife conservation and management (and other natural resource/environmental) issues to which the concepts can be applied. Of the many possible natural resource issues, we examine three: (1) the role of environmental legislation of the 1970s on voice inside the FS, (2) the belief of some agency managers that exit of employees merely removes poor-performing misfits, and (3) the possible loyalty conflicts between the FS, biologists' professional values, and family responsibilities.

Environmental Legislation and Changing Voice in the FS

Organizations control and manage voice primarily by (1) the number and type of employees hired, (2) the socializing, nurturing, and training of the recruits, (3) the employee termination practices, (4) the status and reward system, and (5) the distribution of power. For the first half of this century, the FS maintained firm control over these five processes in a "forestmeister culture" (Miller and Gale 1986). Male foresters hired, trained, guided, and promoted other male foresters—producing a cohesive, achievement-oriented, internally controlled agency that dramatically and favorably impressed those who studied it (for example, Gulick 1951; Kaufman 1960; Gold 1982). In the 1960s, however, the environment in which the FS operated changed greatly. Of particular interest to our topic is the increased sociopolitical concern about inadequate voice (and skills) for noncommodity environmental values within natural resource agencies dominated by professional monocultures, such as the FS or the U.S. Army Corps of Engineers.

One of the goals of the National Environmental Policy Act (NEPA, P.L.91–190, 1969) was to redistribute the power (item 5, above) guiding federal natural resource agencies. This was to be accomplished by shifting both internal and external voice from traditional production and utilitarian orientations to include broader socioeconomic and environmental concerns. The NEPA (1969) requirements of public involvement and greater state-local cooperation increased the amount and variety of *external* voice. Consideration of management alternatives and prediction of their environmental and socioeconomic impacts by interdisciplinary teams (including wildlife biologists) increased the amount and type of *internal* voice in agencies such as the FS—confronting "groupthink" tendencies and dominance by one type of professional (Janis 1967; Kennedy 1988). The national mood and the implementation of NEPA (1969) promoted politically significant debate on FS clearcutting practices on the Monongahela and Bitterroot national forests, which led to the National Forest Management Act (NFMA, PL 94–588, 1976). That act endorsed the need for interdisciplinary teams and outlined requirements for long-range planning. It also was the first act to include a requirement (section 6g) to "provide for diversity of plant and animal communities". It is likely to become the major 1990s' national forest wildlife/environmental issue (for example, most recently brought to national attention by the northern spotted owl issue; Thomas et al. 1990). It will likely be a major test of FS loyalties as well.

The FS could have satisfied the NEPA interdisciplinary input requirements by using outside consultants to do environmental impact statement work, but it chose to hire new types of employees (item 1, above). In 1970, there were fewer than 100 wildlife or fisheries biologists in the FS. By 1981, there were about 520, composing 6 percent of the professional work force (Akin et al. 1982); by 1989, the FS employed about 850 wildlife/fisheries biologists (10 percent of the professional work force). Between 1978 and 1981, 25 percent of the natural resource managers hired by the Intermountain and the Pacific Northwest regions of the FS were wildlife/fisheries biologists; 59 percent were foresters, and 16 percent, range-conservationists (Kennedy and Mincolla 1982). In addition, other legislation and policy changes of the era dramatically increased the number of female professionals in the FS (for example, 45 percent of the natural resource personnel hired between 1978 and 1981 by the two western FS regions cited above were women). The new types of employees, working and socializing within the agency, greatly increased the potential for a new and different internal voice. A voice less utilitarian, less male, and more environmentally and recreationally oriented (that is, values more characteristic of urban, postindustrial American society) was heard in the FS as never before (Kennedy 1991).

The NEPA and the NFMA resulted in the hiring of many new "environmental types" and required that their input be evident in environmental impact statements and decisions. However, it gave little guidance on how the new people were to be trained and integrated into the organizational culture—especially into its status and power structure.

Employee Dropout as Elimination of Low Performance Misfits

There is a temptation for leaders of elite, traditional organizations to view the exit of young entry-level employees as a robust and desirable selection process of eliminating poor performers and misfits. Such a view is consistent with American values of competition and self-selection that Herbert Spenser glorified in his theories of social Darwinism (Collins 1889). It allows organizations to perceive recruit dropout as largely healthy and beneficial self-selection and to do little to study or reduce such exit.

Undoubtedly, there may be beneficial effects to the individual, the organization, and the society when some employees resign from an agency such as the FS. Exiting employees may find new opportunities that benefit them and the nation. They may also become a more effective and constructive voice outside the agency—as was the first landscape architect hired by the FS in 1919, Arthur Carhart, upon resigning (Baldwin 1972; Tweed 1980) and as was Aldo Leopold who exited in 1928 (Flader 1974; Kennedy 1984). In addition, dropouts may be replaced by more productive and satisfied recruits, but there are potential liabilities of exiting to be considered.

When abundant job opportunities for a group or profession exist, job mobility (exit) is high. In such an environment it is likely that a disproportionate number of more capable, critical, and risk-taking employees exit rather than stay to voice their concerns and invest their careers in agency improvement. The same process happens in nations. O'Connor (1982:502) describes the result of 250 years of Irish migration as creating a nation "whose youth was escaping from it, out beyond the harbor, and that was middle-aged in all its attitudes and institutions." The mass exodus of East Germans in 1989–90 is a more recent and dramatic display of national exit.

Federal agencies may encounter similar "middle-age" problems with prolonged hiring freezes (for example, the austerity measures of the Reagan administration) or exit of a large segment of its employees. That is especially true if it is the youthful, enthusiastic voices of innovation and change that are lost.

In the high job mobility era of the late 1950s and the 1960s, the exit rate of engineers motivated the FS to examine the problem in one of its first good personnel studies (USDA FS 1967). The results disproved the hypothesis that it was primarily poor-performing misfits who were exiting, for the engineers who resigned usually had above-average performance evaluations and advancement. The loss of high-performance employees probably reduced engineering capabilities and may have diminished FS innovation and adaptability (the latter being more difficult to quantify and measure than simple exit rates). The same phenomenon may also be occurring today with some FS female employees and new specialists. Let's consider wildlife biologists.

The exit rate for FS wildlife biologists between 1977 and 1981 was 3.7 percent. The rate is similar to that of other professionals (for example, foresters, 3.5 percent). However, biologists are five years younger (mean) than FS foresters—5 percent over age fifty versus 14 percent, respectively. A greater proportion of young biologists probably resigned than retired (Akin et al. 1982). Kennedy and Mincolla's (1982, 1985b) study of entry-level wildlife/fisheries biologists, foresters, and range managers found biologists much more strongly committed to their profession and less committed to important agency values or to long-term FS careers. Only 17 percent of biologists had decided to make a career of the FS, compared to 37 percent of their range conservationists and 30 percent of foresters ($\bar{X}^2$, $p = .05$). Not surprisingly, since these professionals had an average of only two years' permanent employment, most were unsure of making a career of the FS.

A second study (Kennedy and Mincolla 1985a) of seventy entry-level FS wildlife biologists and twenty-nine fisheries biologists asked, "Do you want to spend the next 10–20 years of your professional career in the Forest Service?" Thirty-five percent checked *yes*, 7 percent, *no*, and 58 percent, *not sure*. There were no significant differences between men and women who considered leaving the FS, but possible reasons for leaving did differ significantly ($p < .05$). For example, dual-career and family issues (a tension of loyalties) were much more important to women.

Those checking *no* and *not sure* described the reasons they might leave the FS as (in declining frequency): (1) lack of promotion/career opportunities, (2) low status and priority of wildlife/fisheries management, (3) inability to fit into FS culture, and (4) dual-career and other family issues.

Dual careers and other family issues were cited several places in the survey as an increased concern of both male and female professionals, but it was the women who volunteered it as an issue serious enough to cause exit from the FS. Female wildlife/fisheries biologists were also much more likely to have never married (56 percent) than the males (21 percent, p = .05). They found it much more difficult than their male colleagues to balance relationships or family allegiances with FS loyalty and the agency work ethic (Kennedy and Mincolla 1986).

Wildlife/fisheries biologists cited a wide variety of reasons for their difficulties in fitting into the FS—half of which related to a lack of compatibility with the interdisciplinary, multiple-use nature of FS culture. A sample reply was: "I cannot handle the politics and negotiations in the EIS process, guess I'm research or academically oriented." Other reasons in this category often seemed naive: "I'm more compatible with single-purpose state wildlife agencies, where life is simpler and there's less politics." There was less ambiguity and conflict expressed by foresters and range managers in allegiance to their professions and to the FS.

Loyalty and Voice Issues

Loyalty is used by Hirschman (1970) primarily to identify the simple behavior of staying in place. In this section, loyalty is employed in its broader, common usage that includes a variety of attitude and behavioral responses of "the loyal," that is, those who remain employees. Of special concern is critical and constructive voice as a display of employees' concern for, commitment to, and investment in agencies to which they have allegiance or loyalty, even though some traditional employees see such confrontational voice as disloyal.

Several tests of Hirschman's model (1970) indicate that active voice is one of the highest forms of personal investment people make in a relationship—be it a romantic relationship (Rusbult et al. 1982) or an employee-employer relationship (Farrell 1983; Rusbult et al. 1988). They found it was not disgruntled, disillusioned employees (or lovers) who risked voice to improve the organization (or relationship) but those with previously high satisfaction, strong commitment, and considerable investment in organizations. Although a radical departure from traditional behavioral norms of FS employees, Jeff DeBonis's publication *Inner Voice* (1989) may be a display of a "loyal" employee investing himself in voice to change an agency—however untraditional and revolutionary the methods. DeBonis exited the FS about a year later.

There are also obvious types of loyalty or commitment, distinguishable by a criterion such as *focus* (for example, commitment to profession, employer, family, or religion) that can have complementary or competing loyalty aspects for employees. Important to natural resource/environmental management are also the *time* and *space* dimensions of one's commitment. The major time issue is balancing long-term professional and agency commitments to healthy ecosystems and future generations with more immediate target achievements that might make the agency appear more productive and responsive in annual reports. Interrelated with the time dimension of commitments are space dimension issues in natural resource/environmental management, which revolve around local, regional, national, and (increasingly) global allegiances. Kennedy and Quigley (1989) examine such potential employee-agency conflicts.

We employ the labels *dog-loyalty* and *cat-loyalty* to contrast some important distinctions in time and space allegiances. Dog-loyalty is direct, unswerving, immediate loyalty to the *master*, that is, the boss or the agency, whereas cat-loyalty is a less master-oriented, broader, and more diverse loyalty to the *household*. Cat-loyalty is usually not displayed as quickly, obviously, or directly as dog-loyalty.

In general, many new FS employees exhibit more cat-loyalty than the post-World War II "organization man" that Whyte (1956) described and Kaufman (1960) identified in FS district rangers. It is a result of the more diverse and stronger commitments of many new FS employees that compete with job, boss, and organizational allegiances. New employees often exhibit greater loyalty to their professions, health, and life-styles. The greater number of professional women, single parents, and dual-career couples in the work force also has increased allegiance to family. The hiring of new

230 • James J. Kennedy and Jack Ward Thomas

professional types, such as archaeologists and wildlife biologists, also has increased commitments to specific professions and resources. Furthermore, there is the age at which employees join the FS. Kennedy and Quigley (1989) find that 62–67 percent of chiefs, regional foresters, and forest supervisors (that is, top FS line officers) joined the agency at nineteen to twenty-four years of age. In contrast, only 8 percent of the new generation of FS employees, hired between 1985 and 1989, joined the agency at such a young, impressionable age. Becoming employees at an average age of thirty, they are more likely to be set in their ways and their loyalties upon joining FS than were older generations of line officers.

Employees socialized in a dog-loyalty culture are often insulted and threatened by cat-loyal behavior—as were many traditional FS employees by new, post-NEPA employees who characteristically maintained strong and oft-conflicting loyalty to their professions. A survey of twenty FS line-officer colleagues by Davis (1983:1–4) illustrates such district ranger judgments of the first wave of post-NEPA (1969) wildlife/fisheries biologists who joined the agency:

1. "Biologists tend not to 'belong' because they don't support Forest Service programs and often are more loyal to their own wildlife group than their organization group."
2. "They seem to be playing a game all by themselves. Instead of being team members, they view themselves as protectors of wildlife."
3. "Many are not willing to work within the system. If a biologist is not satisfied with a decision, he will often go to the public or Fish and Game to get the decision changed."

Similar results were obtained in a survey by Cutler (1982) when he was assistant secretary of agriculture in charge of the FS.

A study of 590 foresters, biologists, and engineers by Bullis (1984) also illustrates similar and different foci of allegiances by FS professionals today. Asked, in an open-ended question, "the most important *parties* (or groups of people)" they considered in making important FS decisions, all cited "the general public." Similarities ended here, however. The second most frequent group considered by foresters and engineers fit into a "FS system or policies" category;

wildlife/fisheries biologists were unique in replies that fit the "my profession" category. Foresters and engineers considered "their supervisor" third most often, whereas biologists considered "resource impacts." Both the second and third categories considered by biologists were more cat-loyal but were seldom mentioned by their forester or engineer colleagues (Bullis and Kennedy 1991). The biologists' voicing concern about important FS decisions, based on their professional values and concern for resource impacts, might explain why the line officers surveyed by Davis (1983) seem to consider wildlife/fisheries biologists less loyal than traditional professional employees.

There are abundant songs, sagas, and symbols in most societies that glorify dog-loyalty. Many traditional organizations—whether religious or secular, public or private, legal or criminal—have relied and succeeded on dog-loyalty norms and reward systems. But in an era of rapid change, characteristic of the Western world today, cat-loyalty (with its introspection, confrontation, and experimentation) may be an essential catalyst in generating the amount and type of voice an agency needs to adapt to new, different sociopolitical environments. This may be as true today in eastern Europe as in the United States, in the Polish or Russian forest agencies as in the FS.

From the perspective of individuals or groups of employees, voice in an organization is affected by (1) the number and type of professionals accepting employment and staying in the organization, (2) the kind of socialization they receive during the training or development period, (3) their position in the power structure, and (4) their professional and political effectiveness (Thomas 1986) in their positions. Self-perceived and organization-perceived commitments (loyalties) are highly intertwined with all these conditions.

Kennedy and Mincolla (1982, 1985a) found that the majority of entry-level FS foresters and range conservationists selected their university major hoping it would lead to future FS employment. As students, these young people already had a sense of loyalty (precommitment) to the FS. This was *not* true of their wildlife/fisheries colleagues—only 22 percent of FS wildlife/fisheries managers surveyed were looking forward to future FS employment as college students (versus 71 percent of range conservationists and 56 percent of foresters, $p = .01$).

After about two years of permanent employment, wildlife/fisheries biologists also were more committed to their profession and less to the FS than were their forester and range conservationist colleagues. There was no difference between these three professional types in believing they were committed to their profession (over 80 percent for each group), but biologists stood out in *strength* of professional commitment ($p = .05$). On a seven-point scale, 65 percent of biologists checked "extremely strong" or "very strong" professional commitment (versus 22 percent of foresters and 45 percent of range conservationists). Such strong commitment to profession was sometimes in conflict with the values these young professionals believed the FS rewards—especially agency loyalty.

When asked (in an open-ended question) "what values/attitudes are rewarded by the FS," almost all entry-level professionals agreed they were (in declining frequency): loyalty to the FS, work ethic/ productivity, and getting along with people and working well in teams (Kennedy and Mincolla 1982). These three most rewarded FS values accounted for over 80 percent of responses, with about 50 percent providing "FS loyalty" as the *most* rewarded value. The majority of the open-ended loyalty replies were also dog-loyal types, for example, "show strong support of the FS," "never criticize a FS decision in public," "be a FS-man, do your job and go [transfer] where they need you."

In a subsequent study (Kennedy and Mincolla 1985a), entry-level wildlife/fisheries managers were asked the question, "What are the biggest attitude/value conflicts wildlife/fisheries managers have (if any) with the FS in their early years?" In declining order of frequency, their open-ended replies fit the following categories: (1) wildlife/fisheries management has low priority/status (96 percent citing it as a common conflict), (2) economics and politics versus ecology (32 percent), (3) wildlife/fisheries managers' low credibility/ outsiders (30 percent), and (4) need to compromise (17 percent).

It should not be surprising to discover that foresters or range conservationists found it easier to be simultaneously committed to their profession and to FS organizational values. Foresters and range conservationists have been employed by the agency much longer than biologists, and they have shaped FS values to be generally consistent with their professional values. Significant numbers of biologists are new to the FS, and they were essentially thrust upon the agency as a result of 1970s' legislation as "change-agents" (Kennedy 1985b) to expand the FS environmental values, sensitivities, and management skills.

Closing Comment

To be successful FS change-agents, biologist recruits must develop attitudes and skills that facilitate commitment to both their profession and the agency (as well as family and other demands). In addition, they must learn to provide effective voice, find job satisfaction, and influence important FS decisions if they are to remain employees and develop the status/power to effect agency change. This is no easy task for newcomers to an agency they perceive as not very supportive of their professions or wildlife/ fisheries resources. To compound the problem of agency integration and voice effectiveness, FS biologists in the Kennedy and Mincolla (1982, 1985a) studies readily admitted that they were poorly trained and had few role models in college for the change-agent task and had to reeducate themselves as FS recruits to be effective FS professionals (Thomas 1986).

The FS has become a team decision-making organization in the post-NEPA era—as illustrated in its current mission statement (USDA FS 1986) and the "Integrated Resource Management" philosophy (USDA FS 1985). This is also displayed in the "FS attitude/ values" young biologists believe are necessary for them to succeed in the FS (Kennedy and Mincolla 1985a, cited in order of frequency in response to an open-ended question): (1) getting along with people and in teams, (2) being capable and confident in your professional area, and (3) learning how to give and take, to compromise. Entry-level biologists (Kennedy and Mincolla 1982) are also much more likely to have a graduate degree (65 percent) than their forester

(32 percent) or range colleagues (15 percent, $p = .01$). The additional education increases the biologists' professional allegiance and commitment, as well as the probability of their having a biology or wildlife management professor as a role model and mentor. Postgraduate education is also more individually oriented than undergraduate education: it develops independence, a propensity to question, and self-sufficient attitudes and behavior that initially can be a "voice" handicap in teamwork and in the art of compromise (Cutler 1982).

The open-ended responses to questionnaires and in interviews suggest that many FS biologists also develop mythic hero images of themselves, more so than their forester and range management colleagues. Their motivation for selecting their profession is more idealistically described, and they claim much stronger professional allegiance (Kennedy and Mincolla 1985b). Biology or ecology professors and courses dominate their education, and 40 percent judge themselves to be more research oriented than management oriented upon joining the FS. Somehow, many of the entry-level biologists are educated and socialized in universities to consider compromise unprofessional (several males also believed it "unmanly"). Their "exact science" education and biology professor role models, more indirectly than directly, foster bias against compromise—especially those with a graduate degree. Thus, their voice is often communicated in a righteous and unwavering manner, which is not amenable to group consideration and compromise (Kennedy 1991).

In a pro-active response to the studies cited above, the FS has instigated several training courses (Cross 1987) to help entry-level biologists better understand the FS organizational culture, their change-agent role, and the attitudes/behavior that tend to be successful in effecting organizational change. For change-agents must not only have the *will* but also the *skill* to be effective (Thomas 1986). An initial (one-week) orientation course helps entry-level wildlife/ fisheries biologists reevaluate their hero images and develop more effective attitudes about compromise. A second course (two-week) teaches compromise and negotiation skills, namely, communication, consensus-building, and confrontational skills.

The courses do not encourage entry-level biologists to become yes-men or yes-women. That would dampen voice that is needed, even though it might sometimes be disquieting to the agency. After several years of uncertainty about and often resistance to new recreational, amenity, and environmental values thrust upon it by changing social values and lower court decisions, the FS increasingly recognizes its need to adapt to the new and evolving values of a postindustrial, urban American society (that represents the majority of its "stockholders"). For the traditional FS culture to adapt, the power structure must listen and respond to new voice within (and without) the organization. This often requires more open and tolerant norms of agency loyalty and commitment (Twight 1985).

Loyalty norms that accommodate challenge and dissent are apparent in recent FS management guidelines (USDA FS 1985, 1987a 1987b). Similarly, the two aforementioned entry-level biologist short courses focus on the arts of balancing professional and agency commitments and employing professional voice effectively. On an organizational level, the important issue these courses address is how one can be effectively critical of the agency and still be perceived as a concerned, committed, responsible (that is, loyal) FS employee. On a personal level, one must also learn how to confront colleagues (or superiors) of other disciplines and genders without their feeling their basic personhood and professionalism are being judged wrong or inferior.

Also central to both courses is an examination of the wisdom, "rights," and ethics of changing agency cultures (Fitzgerald 1988)— suggesting that one should have empathy and respect for traditional organizational cultures (and individual employees), even though one does not embrace or agree with some values. It seems easy for many well-meaning, intelligent, committed professionals who join the FS today to behave as have some government agents and missionaries who worked among Native Americans in the past. That is, they view traditional FS culture as primitive and heathen (say, relative to gender or environmental values) and in need of immediate salvation. An essential characteristic of wise, caring, effective change-agents is learning (in head and heart) to distinguish between the components of the traditional culture that should be preserved or enhanced and those components that should be changed.

Of course, there is another humbling issue all young, idealistic, impatient professionals must recognize in an organization such as the FS, namely, that proud, old, successful bureaucracies change by evolution, not by revolution. A recent study by Twight and Lyden (1988) offers some sobering evidence that FS district rangers' allegiances are still oriented toward traditional, production-oriented values. Still, one of the most effective forces in evolutionary, organizational adaptation is intelligent, empathetic, and skillful voice from persistent change-agents who do not exit the FS—and who remain committed (loyal) to their profession while developing a reputation for offering caring advice and consent to the agency that employs them.

References

Akin, B., M. Glazer, and T. Marine. 1982. *Work Force Planning Data 1981.* Washington, D.C.: U.S. Department of Agriculture, Forest Service.

Baldwin, D. N. 1972. *The Quiet Revolution—Grass Roots of Today's Wilderness Preservation Movement.* Boulder, Colo.: Pruett Publishers.

Bullis, C. A. 1984. "Communication as Unobtrusive Control: A Re-examination of Identification in the U.S. Forest Service."Ph.D. dissertation, Purdue University, West Lafayette, Ind.

Bullis, C. A., and J. J. Kennedy. 1991. "Value Conflicts and Policy Interpretation: Changes in the Case of Fisheries and Wildlife Managers in Multiple-Use Agencies." *Policy Studies Journal* 19(3):18–36.

Collins, F. H. 1889. *Epitome of the Synthetic Philosophy of Herbert Spenser.* London: Williams and Northgate.

Cross, G. M. 1987. "Continuing Education in Natural Resources: Needs and Opportunities." *Transactions of Fifty-second North American Wildlife and Natural Resources Conference* 52:691–96, Washington, D.C.: Wildlife Management Institute.

Cutler, M. R. 1982. "What Kind of Wildlifer Will Be Needed in the 1980s?" *Wildlife Society Bulletin* 10(1):75–79.

Davis, B. 1983. "Comments by Line and Managerial Personnel Concerning Communications Problems With Biologists in Region 4." Paper presented at Idaho Forest Service Biologists' Workshop, Sun Valley, Idaho.

DeBonis, J., ed. 1989. *Inner Voice*. Vida, Ore.: Association of Forest Service Employees for Environmental Ethics.

Farrell, D. 1983. "Exit, Voice, Loyalty and Neglect as Responses to Job Dissatisfaction: A Multidimensional Scaling Study." *Academy Management Journal* 26(4):596–607.

Fitzgerald, T. H. 1988. "Can Change in Organizational Culture Really be Managed?" *Organizational Dynamics* 17(2):5–15.

Flader, S. 1974. *Thinking Like a Mountain—Aldo Leopold and the Evolution of an Ecological Attitude Toward Deer, Values and Forests*. Columbia: University of Missouri Press.

Gold, K. A. 1982. "Managing for Success: A Comparison of the Private and Public Sector." *Public Administration Review* 42(6):568–575.

Gulick, L. H. 1951. *American Forest Policy*. New York: Duell, Sloan, and Pearce.

Hirschman, A. D. 1970. *Exit, Voice, and Loyalty—Response to Decline in Firms, Organizations, and States*. Cambridge, Mass.: Harvard University Press.

Janis, I. L. 1967. *Victims of Groupthink*. Boston: Houghton Mifflin.

Kaufman, H. 1960. *The Forest Ranger*. Baltimore, Md.: Johns Hopkins Press.

Kennedy, J. J. 1984. "Understanding Professional Career Evolution—An Example of Aldo Leopold." *Wildlife Society Bulletin* 12(3):215–226.

———. 1985a. "Conceiving Forest Management as Providing for Current and Future Social Value." *Forest Ecology and Management* 13(4):121–132.

———. 1985b. "Integrating Professional Diversity into Mainstream Forest Service Organizational Culture." Paper presented at USFS Region 4 Management Meeting, Boise, Idaho.

———. 1988. "Legislative Confrontation of Groupthink in U.S. Natural Resource Agencies." *Environmental Conservation* 15(2):123–128.

———. 1991. "Integrating Gender Diverse and Interdisciplinary Professionals into Traditional U.S. Department of Agriculture-Forest Service Culture." *Society and Natural Resources* 4(4):165–176.

Kennedy, J. J., and J. A. Mincolla. 1982. *Career Evolution of Young 400-series U.S. Forest Service Professionals*. Logan: College of Natural Resources, Utah State University.

———. 1985a. *Career Development and Training Needs of Entry-level Wildlife/Fisheries Managers in the USDA-Forest Service*. Logan: College of Natural Resources, Utah State University.

———. 1985b. "Early Career Development of Fisheries and Wildlife Biologists in Two Forest Service Regions." *Transactions of Fiftieth North American Wildlife and Natural Resource Conference* 50:425–435.

———. 1986. "Women and Men Natural Resource Managers in Early Stages of Their Professional Forest Service Careers." *Women in Forestry* 8(1):23–28.

Kennedy, J. J., and T. M. Quigley. 1989. "How Entry-level Employees, Forest Supervisors, Regional Foresters and Chiefs View Forest Service Values and the Reward System." Paper presented at Sunbird Conference, Second Meeting of Forest Supervisors and Chiefs, Tucson, Ariz.

Miller, M. C., and R. P. Gale. 1986. "Professional Styles of Federal Forest and Marine Fisheries Resource Managers." *Journal Fisheries Management* 6(2):141–148.

O'Connor, F. 1982. *Collected Stories.* New York: Vintage Books.

Rusbult, C. E., D. Farrell, G. Rogers, and A. G. Mainous III. 1988. "Impact of Exchange Variables on Exit, Voice, Loyalty, and Neglect: An Integrative Model of Responses to Declining Job Satisfaction." *Academy of Management Journal* 31(3):599–627.

Rusbult, C. E., and I. M. Zembrodt. 1983. "Responses to Dissatisfaction in Romantic Involvements: A Multidimensional Scaling Analysis." *Journal of Experimental Social Psychology* 19(3):274–293.

Rusbult, C. E., I. M. Zembrodt, and L. K. Gunn. 1982. "Exit, Voice, Loyalty, and Neglect: Responses to Dissatisfaction in Romantic Involvements." *Journal of Personality and Social Psychology* 43(6):1230–1242.

Thomas, J. W. 1986. "Effectiveness—The Hallmark of the Natural Resource Management Professional." *Transactions of Fifty-first North American Wildlife and Natural Resource Conference* 51:217–238.

Thomas, J. W., E. D. Forsman, J. B. Lint, E. C. Meslow, B. R. Noon, and J. Verner. 1990. *A Conservation Strategy for the Northern Spotted Owl.* Portland, Ore: Interagency Scientific Committee to Address the Conservation of the Northern Spotted Owl.

Tweed, W. C. 1980. *Recreation Site Planning and Improvements in National Forests* 1891–1942 (FS–354). Washington, D.C.: USDA-Forest Service.

Twight, B. W. 1985. "The Forest Service Mission: A Case of Family Fidelity." *Women in Forestry* 7(5):5–7.

Twight, B. W., and F. J. Lyden. 1988. "Multiple Use vs. Organizational Commitment." *Forest Science* 34(2):474–486.

U.S. Department of Agriculture. Forest Service (USDA FS). 1967. *Use of Engineering Skills in the Forest Service.* Washington, D.C.

——— 1985. *Working Together for Multiple-Use—Integrated Resource Management.* Eastern Region, Milwaukee, Wis.

——— 1986. *Caring for the Land and Serving People* (FS–402). Washington, D.C.

——— 1987a. *Spirit of the Forest.* Eastern Region, Milwaukee, Wis.

——— 1987b. *Team Excellence.* Eastern Region, Milwaukee, Wis.

Whyte, W. H. 1956. *The Organization Man.* New York: Simon and Schuster.

PART 5
WILDLIFE POLICY FUTURES

11

PUBLIC POLICY ACTORS AND FUTURES: CONSIDERATIONS IN WILDLIFE MANAGEMENT

Joseph F. Coates

The Fish and Wildlife Service of the United States Department of the Interior is a grand old federal agency. It has a solid history of satisfied clients and clear, slowly evolving missions.

Its future is likely to be more tumultuous. The management is faced with broad and deep internal and external forces reshaping its mission. The attitudes, behaviors, values, and needs of its external and internal current and potential constituents are rapidly evolving away from the narrow historic purpose. This chapter outlines some of the factors shaping its role in the future of wildlife management. Emphasis will be given to trends that will evolve over the next ten to fifteen years to reshape the Fish and Wildlife Service through the issues they generate. By concentrating on the Fish and Wildlife Service, many critical issues that will affect state-level agencies and other public and private organizations influencing wildlife management have a clear, incisive focus. The federal policy implications have either their analogs or their conjugate implications for other wildlife management groups.

The Fish and Wildlife Service recently ran a broad public outreach to identify refuge management issues as part of "Refuges 2003—A Plan for the Future." The thirty-five thousand responses broke down into seventeen leading topics as shown below.

- Management of Nongame Species
- The Compatibility Process
- Economic Uses on Refuge Lands
- Role of Hunting and Trapping as Management Tools
- Recreational Activities on Refuges
- Land Acquisition Needs/Goals
- Use of Pesticides
- Predator Management
- Management and Designation of Special Management (Research Natural Areas, Wilderness Areas)
- Habitat Management
- Protection of Biological Diversity
- Enhancement of Environmental Education Opportunities
- Enhancement of Fisheries Programs
- Environmental Contaminants
- Water Issues (for example, Federal Water Rights, Water Quality)
- Threatened and Endangered Species
- Waterfowl Management

Aside from the obvious importance of the issues that came out of that process, it is equally important to notice the absence of certain nascent issues. There was nothing at the level of importance of those seventeen items reflecting:

- Overseas or global concerns for wildlife
- Changing patterns and capabilities coming out of genetics research and molecular biology
- Role and status of the future of ecology as an applied science
- Information technology
- New and declining constituencies

With these conspicuous factors omitted, it is clear that the survey draws only upon people who are already alert, focused, concerned constituents of the traditional Fish and Wildlife Service. What is fed back to the management is an agenda that is compatible with their current plans and programs or, at worst, stressful on the margins where incidental change is likely. If the FWS limits itself to that agenda, it will find itself rapidly drifting away from an awareness of emerging issues and opportunities, and increasingly unprepared for the future. Within the agenda of seventeen items, there are many problems that continue to be important and, in many ways, freshly challenging, such as the competing uses of refuge land, land acquisition needs and goals, and the broad, complex issues of environmental contaminants. The first lesson that comes out of this is that every organization needs to guard against limiting its outreach and exploration into the future to those already familiar with the organization and to those urging incremental change rather than identifying new forces at play and the inevitable, more radical changes the future must hold.

With that point as background, let us look at some of the factors affecting the future of fish and wildlife management. They fall into a half dozen broad categories: demographic trends, social trends, environmental trends, organizational trends, trends in information technology, and trends in science and other technologies. After that let us briefly turn to the constituents of fish and wildlife management and the new or newly important issues they raise.

Demographic Trends

The most important demographic trend affecting fish and wildlife management is the steady growth in U.S. population over the next four decades. From a current population of 250 million, we will grow at about 0.8 percent per year, leveling out around 330 million in the year 2030. For the FWS, as for any other organization dependent to a first approximation on the sheer number of people for its prosperity and growth, this has to be good news. However, in looking at the more specific demographic details, the patterns cut in a number of different directions. The aging of society is having several substantial effects on the future of all federal agencies. Our emerging sixty-five-plus population is, for the first time, a population in which the assumption can be made that the majority have had at least a high school education, and a large percentage have been through college. Therefore, a large percentage of the aging population will be economically well off, with substantial economic reserves. Many have been involved in an extended history of activism, whether that was consumer affairs, environmental affairs, or others of the score of public issues.

The political power of that aging population must be grasped early and effectively to make them friends rather than hostile opponents of fish and wildlife management. Anyone concerned with public policy should recognize that, in the 1988 election, while only 12.6 percent of the population was over sixty-five, 19.4 percent of the voters were over age sixty-five. What do those aging Americans want? They want a broad sense of participation, to be active and engaged, but they want all these things to be safe, reliable, relatively comfortable, and hassle free. With an even older cohort, one must also look at the fact that there is diminished physical vitality, a fading sensorium, that is, weakened eyes and ears. Yet these people want to continue their youthful involvement with the outdoors or enjoy new experiences. They are likely to want to introduce, if not their own children, their grandchildren to the outdoors, to fishing, hunting, photography, or bird watching. They have the time and leisure to make extensive commitments.

In our sedentary society Americans are increasingly made up of white-collar, metropolitan office workers. Even those who are in blue-collar jobs increasingly are spending their time in sedentary or physically nondemanding jobs. Consequently, two trends develop that are at odds with each other. First is a remoteness from rural and natural environmental experiences. Second is a strong desire for more active alternatives to this sedentary life. Whether on weekends or holidays, there is a desire to do something different, including exploring the outdoors and enjoying outdoor living. On the other hand, the experience and capabilities for outdoor living from childhood on are diminished or absent in those sedentary folks. The opportunity is to draw them in in a way that educates and enhances their capabilities to enjoy the fish, the wildlife, and the natural environment.

Two-income households are becoming the mode, particularly with baby boomers moving into the period of rapid family formation and their highest incomes. There is a tremendous amount of discretionary income available, but a greater than ever pressure on time. The two- or three-week vacation is of diminishing practicality for these households. Local tourism and the two- to four-day activity close to home become attractive and even necessary. There is a great opportunity here for fish and wildlife managers.

Another demographic factor is the baby boomers' children, those of the so-called baby boom echo. These wealthy, prosperous, educated families want to take their small children with them into the wildlife situation. The urbanites may not want to take them in the traditional way, but to have the capability to take and use strollers, light vehicles, special backpacks, and related aids. Welcoming small children from households not used to the outdoors into wildlife situations is another new opportunity and challenge. The metropolitanization of America is creating a crosscurrent of opportunities and problems. The country today is about 78 percent metropolitan. Urban wildlife refuges should boom if well-appointed and carefully cared for, offering a special educational experience to metropolitan dwellers and tourists in our cities. Urbanites, however, are increasingly likely to associate animal life with those undesirable aspects of life that they are familiar with in the city, such as the rat and the roach. Consequently, the appeal of fish and wildlife has to overcome that barrier and entice a new clientele into its preserves.

From an international perspective, demographic factors have never been more positive for domestic fish and wildlife. Throughout the advanced nations, Europe, Canada, Japan, and elsewhere, there are millions of prosperous middle-class and wealthy families eager to see and enjoy the wonders of the world. Even throughout the Third World and developing countries there is a crust, albeit a thin crust, of prosperous, westernized people interested in seeing the world. The United States, offering more of everything by way of sights and wonders than any other place in the world, is a universally attractive vacation site.

There is a serious problem with foreign visitors. The United States has traditionally been, if not hostile, at least aggressively indifferent to non-English-speaking people with their different cultures, customs, and values. To be successful, fish and wildlife managers must actively reach out to these foreign visitors to welcome them and to create a hospitable, attractive, and positive experience. The utility of multilingual presentations and signages is unclear. What is clear is that the new customer is here and expects care, attention, and service. As far as foreign tourism goes, fish and wildlife can be an important local factor in stimulating the business and prosperity of rural communities and can make welcoming foreign visitors a positive aspect of local life.

Social Trends

An examination of social trends is always troublesome because sociological theory is not developed fully enough to insure a high reliability of trends, impacts, and behaviors associated with social change. The trends discussed below all meet the criteria, however, of decades or more of continuation, based on empirically well-grounded data. These trends also, by and large, evolve out of our last five decades of continuing prosperity and steadily rising levels of education. And finally, in each case, there is little or nothing in sight that is likely to reverse the trends.

Among the most important social trends for fish and wildlife management is the implicit and explicit conflict between the animal rights people and the gun controllers, and those who wish to fish and hunt. The animal rights people will rise in importance, power, and influence and become a force working against what they see as animal abuse, including not only experimentation but also animal slaughter. On the other hand, in their enthusiasm for preserving animal rights and their natural habitats, they should draw attention to those habitats and form a nucleus of an important and attractive clientele. Similarly, the gun control people, while at odds with one of the most important constituents, the hunter, also offer the promise of a new clientele whose hunting expeditions will not be with guns but with cameras or the naked eye. Their hunting will be for a new experience rather than a trophy. The emerging conflict between those who are antitraditional and protraditional hunting will ultimately have to find a balance point where both can be accommodated, although not necessarily at the same place and definitely not at the same time.

Since one person's positive experience is not guaranteed to be positive for another, a broad range of provisions and alternatives must be made available in significant fish and wiidlife management. A positive experience for some may be encountering an unknown butterfly or the kinesthetic experience of planting a tree or clearing a streambed. For others, a positive experience may be cooking a salmon, felling a deer, or introducing a novice to the glories of the outdoors.

On the larger scale, middle-class values favoring quality, a high degree of service, reliability in the products and services received create a fresh burden and opportunity for fish and wildlife managers. Much of that middle class, particularly those not in their earliest years and not from a rural background, and not fully committed to fish and wildlife, must be drawn into it. They represent the opportunity to create a new constituency. The key is delivering the three values mentioned above. Quality, reliability, and service do not have obvious meaning for fish and wildlife management but must be made obvious through careful and close innovation, experimentation, and constant user surveys. Complicating the matter of middle-class values is the cultural diversity of society. No single message can be expected to appeal to the majority of Americans. It must appeal differently and selectively to men and women, young and old, various racial and ethnic minorities, and various socioeconomic categories. While the opportunity exists with a quarter of a billion people in the United States to create a massive new clientele, it has to be done in the context of cultural and economic diversity.

Further characteristics of the rising middle class are attention to time and risk. Time must be used well and effectively. Even leisure time must be efficient and effective. For any institution in contemporary U.S. society to be a waster of time is to commit organizational suicide. To use time richly and fully by combining tasks and experiences, by doing two or three things at once, is one step toward becoming successful. Even leisure must be in an efficient context. Paralleling concern for time is the broad concern for risk. While in many situations middle-class society chooses to avoid all risks as, for example, in pharmaceutical drugs or public transportation, risks are increasingly acceptable if the person feels that she or he has both the knowledge and the skills to take the risk. The natural environment of the preserve is intrinsically risky, and hence it is important to promote a knowledge base, first vicariously, then with direct experience with those environments. That puts the person in control rather than in arbitrary situations in which the risk is poorly understood, uncertain, or unrealistic in its importance. The middle class, with its commitment to recreation and tourism, is giving increasingly profound emphasis to every aspect of their lives being a positive experience. What is positive in even moderate risks can vary widely, depending on individuals and groups.

Environmental Trends

Trends in the environment and public response to the environment are central to understanding the evolving future of fish and wildlife management. The emergence of green politics on an international scale, a development of the past decade, goes well past traditional special-interest politics. There are seventeen green parties in the world. As they proliferate and focus on their special interests, and elect or influence the election of public officials, the early focus will be on the toxic materials in food, water, air, and terrain. That set of concerns must become a wash over all environmental policies. Every environment must be safe and free of toxics. Where they exist, measures to contain, control, and remove them must be taken. Fish and wildlife preserves are likely to be seen as having the potential to develop into the great water purifiers of the nation. They will be the place where one can enjoy toxic-free environments and the "natural" (really managed) environment.

At the international level, environmental concerns are leading to fresh organizational approaches. Bankrupt countries are finding that trading international debt for nature in the form of land set-asides is not only economically effective but also internationally and politically positive. The debt swaps, as innovations, are enriching the options open to environmentalists and land managers.

It will be interesting to see what happens when our federal and state governments move more dramatically into land swaps and land management, going beyond the present domestic, private programs of The Nature Conservancy.

Rising international environmental concerns also create a need for advice and training throughout the majority of the 143 nations of the world. For the Third and Fourth World nations the need is to teach them how to be more alert to the durable values of their fish, wildlife, and natural habitats and to better innovative environmental management. Domestic agencies at the state and federal level are ideal pools of talent on which to draw. We anticipate that within the decade we will see multiple mechanisms that amount to an international environmental police. The third cluster of environmental elements is the emergence of new issues. Ocean rise, greenhouse effect, water pollution, toxics in solid wastes, mining effects, and the effects of energy generation create the broad public sweep of concern about the environment facilitating concern and opening interest in issues more specific to fish and wildlife. Most notable are the questions of biological diversity, the maintenance and restoration of endangered species, and managing natural resources such as fisheries and elk herds. The broad sweep of global environmental issues should make more sources available for a greater range of experimentation and expanding missions of fish and wildlife managers.

Organizational trends, as with all others, tend to cut in many directions. The declining federal budget, the new penury, the restricted transfer of money to state and local governments will continue to have adverse effects on national programs. The shrinking federal financial role will create more pressure at the state level, where more diversity, more experimentation, and more trial and error can be expected under restrained budgets with greater pressure for accountability.

Coming out of that organizational tension one can see a drive toward more user fees and, at the organizational level, more contracting out for services since they are likely to be cheaper. There will also be greater pressure for innovation, joint ventures, and further alliances.

Alliances is the "in" word in corporate America. The problems of managing complexity and maintaining flexibility have driven many corporations to a new strategy of seeking alliances with every kind of public or private organization. Alliances allow them to have what they need, as well as the opportunity for a break in the relationship if needed. The unprecedented flexibility the new alliances offer is their basic appeal. These lessons are directly and easily transferrable to federal, state, and local governments concerned with meeting analogous problems in the natural environment. If there is one piece of advice I would offer to every administrator of a preserve, it is to seek alliances to achieve what you need.

Innovations are an accompaniment of the alliances. We have mentioned the debt swaps for environment. We also see that many natural preserves will have to move into a strategy of rationing. Not just price rationing, although that is one factor, but rationing by skill, ability, and certifiable competence to move into the more esoteric, removed, or fragile areas of a preserve. Private groups like The Nature Conservancy or newly created public or private groups might be in a better position to manage innovations. It will be increasingly attractive to have as your slogan, "Let The Nature Conservancy do it" or "Let the Audubon Society do it for us." It would be rash to trivialize the significance of the problems and the opportunities innovations offer. At the federal level alone there are 89 million acres, 452 million refuges, and 140,000 square miles of land, the size of Germany, which are the responsibility of the Fish and Wildlife Service.

Information Technology

Information technology is the most important, undeniable pressure for positive change in American society today. Wiring the nation with fiber optics will reduce prices and increase services for all long-distance communication. As every home increases its investment in information technology and as every office continues its decade-long trend toward every white-collar worker's becoming an information worker, easily accessible and richly textured channels for the exchange, solicitation, evaluation, and joint working of data will become routine. Wildlife managers must recognize that the traditional approaches involving paper, processes, procedures, hearings are not obsolescent, they are thoroughly obsolete. The old ways cannot keep pace with the pressures of change, and they cannot satisfy the knowledge needs of current and potential constituencies. If there were a single technological measure to recommend to fish and wildlife managers, it is go totally electronic. At the consumer interface, an example would be sponsoring photo and video safaris; whether to a streamside in Illinois or to a national park in Kenya, there would be an opening up of new constituencies. One must go beyond the old magic of the photograph. One must be able to provide endless depths of information to all comers, at any time, in a menu that the user determines. The age of take-it-or-leave-it information is over. Information must be tailored and delivered in real time.

Information technology also offers the promise for the wilderness, literally, to speak for itself. Wiring up a wilderness area so that, as one tours it, one can get variously detailed explanations of what one is looking at, its place in the ecology, its history, and so on by pressing a button, stepping on a pedal, or manipulating a headphone would enhance the appeal of wilderness for a new constituency and for a substantial fraction of the present constituency. The most vociferous opponents to those kinds of changes are your fading constituents, not your new ones. The ever-larger constituency and more important political constituency are committed to information in all forms. One variation on this is the need to train to see wildlife. In the same way that one cannot understand a Renaissance painting, avant-garde architecture, the significance of a West African dance, or the meaning of the lyrics of a Yugoslav folk song without background knowledge, the reality is that people do not see the environment. Their eyes, their ears, their nose, and their feet must be sensitized and trained. That is one way to build a constituency.

Science and Technology

Aside from information technology, science and technology offer two broad avenues for enhancing fish and wildlife. One is ecology and the other, genetics.

Ecology is the total science of the environment. This science relates all animate and inanimate elements into a seamless web. But ecology is a primitive science. The bulk of ecological research has been directed at small plots over short time periods, rather than developing the full sweep capable of understanding and managing an ecology. Wildlife managers must become more scientifically oriented toward both the needs and limitations of ecology. They must become major advocates of the grand experiment, continuing long-term research on broad, dedicated areas in order to put ecology on a footing where it can meet the missions of fish and wildlife agencies and the needs of society at large.

Ecology is the most promising, but merely promising, science for raising wildlife management to needed levels of sophistication.

Genetics promises to radically alter the concept of wildlife management as we develop the technology of genetic manipulation and the capabilities to better define which DNA elements affect different functions. We will be able to introduce new diversities, including better environmental fitness and better resistance to environmental threats to endangered species. We are also just around the corner from the capability to restore extinct species. From a technical point of view, the critical question is, How does one release the genetic material locked into every somatic (body) cell of every animal and make it effective as a genetic message? It is not unthinkable that in the lifetime of every reader of this chapter, passenger pigeons will fly again and mastodons will once again walk the earth. The tissue is available in museums, and once we learn to unlock that somatic genetic message, the process will be straightforward. The genetic message from mastodon tissue put into the ovum of an elephant, with the elephant as the living incubator, will produce 100 percent pure walking mastodons. Ditto for the passenger pigeon and innumerable others. Every museum is a genetically viable reliquary for endangered and extinct species (assuming we have some tissue). These goals can never be realized and achieved unless new levels of scientific sophistication are introduced into fish and wildlife management services and until these organizations acquire the broad scientific constituency and advocacy base that they need. Useful, effective outreach is not only to the general public but also to highly specialized publics such as the scientific community.

Living and Working in a Fish and Wildlife Agency

The work force of all governmental agencies is changing. It is increasingly nonrural—not the farm boys who from their earliest age have been associated with rural life and have moved into their careers because of their enthusiasm for hunting, fishing, and wild-life. The full-time work force increasingly recruits women, ethnic and cultural minorities, and people who have not had, from their earliest youth, direct contact with the countryside, open space, and wildlife. Agencies are confronted with the dual challenge of recruiting these people by making their jobs attractive and, at the same time, closing a gap of twenty or more years of noneducation in the important aspects of fish and wildlife. On the other hand, these new recruits mirror the new constituencies.

Even among those coming from traditional environments, there is a level of sophistication about fish and wildlife that runs counter to much of the highly bureaucratized attitudes of many present state and local managers. Recruitment, retention, and reinvigoration of the work force will be a major challenge for the next decades, as Kennedy and Thomas point out in chapter 10.

Some Constituents and Some Constituent Issues

As indicated earlier, the constituents for fish and wildlife agencies are growing in numbers and in diversity. Their expansion over the next forty years is good news for every public agency. It means more potential clients for the services. But diversity will dominate, and conflicts over use will increase. Specifically, every fish and wildlife service should give intense attention to recruitment of people living in metropolitan areas, and aging Americans as workers and clients, customers and users. That is where the political power lies.

One could make a case that there are no primary problems in wildlife management itself, but that the primary problems are with people management, particularly people management internal to fish and wildlife organizations. A new management, a new policy, a new orientation, a new agenda would take care of all or most of the primary issues of wildlife management. The old, narrow technician's specialized view of fish and wildlife management is likely to be suicidal to his or her agency.

The reclamation of old and the making of new refuges is a major opportunity facing all services. Jamaica Bay, for example, in New York, is probably one of the largest and most neglected fish and wildlife resources in the country. Decades of off and on, some and none, stop and go have increasingly deprived the vast metropolitan population of an unprecedented resource that should be part of more than one agency's vision. Jamaica Bay, of course, is only exemplary of the hundreds, if not thousands, of opportunities for the development of fish and wildlife resources in or adjacent to our large cities.

Advertising of resources is pathetic and inadequate by FWS. It contrasts badly with the British National Trust's practice of issuing spectacularly attractive catalogs of its holdings. There is no catalog, beautiful or otherwise, of national, state, and local wildlife assets. A lesson can be taken from the publication *Arizona Highways,* which looks to propagandize the state's assets to a striking and strikingly successful degree.

Uses and users in conflict will become more extreme, sophisticated, strident, and universal in fish and wildlife management areas. The opportunity for managers, therefore, is to reach out early in the preplanning and planning stages to all identifiable constituents and bring them into an open process to develop an understanding of all the options and choices and the kinds of tradeoffs that need to be made. Aggressive, positive, early outreach is antithetical to the mentality of many managers but is essential to future success. For every problem that fish and wildlife managers must solve, there are a dozen issues—that is, matters of conflict—they must learn to resolve. You cannot resolve a conflict without intimate knowledge and the confidence of the parties at odds with each other.

Wildlife reserves hold a great promise of being the reverse of NIMBY (not in my backyard). With care and attention to public outreach and users in conflict, wildlife reserves could be the most sought-after governmental asset in thousands of communities in the United States.

Finally, it is timely and appropriate that we have a national commission to address federal, state, and local issues on the future of wildlife resources and their management for the next century.

NOTES ON
CONTRIBUTORS

INDEX

NOTES ON
CONTRIBUTORS

Tommy L. Brown is a senior research associate and leader of the Human Dimensions Research Unit in the Department of Natural Resources at Cornell University. He has published extensively on socioeconomic aspects of fish and wildlife management and has served as an expert witness on wildlife values for the Environmental Protection Agency.

Ted T. Cable is an associate professor in the Department of Forestry at Kansas State University. He received an M.S. in wildlife ecology and a Ph.D. in forest recreation from Purdue University. He has research interests in the study of social and economic benefits of wildlife resources.

Joseph F. Coates is president of J. F. Coates, Inc., which specializes in futures research and technology assessment. He teaches graduate courses in technology assessment and futures research at The George Washington University. He was formerly assistant to the director of the Office of Technology Assessment. At the National Science Foundation he established and directed the first program in technology assessment.

Nancy A. Connelly is a research support specialist with the Human Dimensions Research Unit in the Department of Natural Resources at Cornell University. She received a master's degree in 1986 from Cornell University in resource policy and planning and has worked on a number of studies dealing with fish, wildlife, and other natural-resource-based management issues.

Philip S. Cook is a research associate in the Department of Forestry at Kansas State University. He holds a B.S. degree in natural resources from the University of the South in Sewanee, Tennessee, and an M.S. in forest economics and management from Virginia Polytechnic Institute and State University.

Daniel J. Decker is an associate professor in the Department of Natural Resources at Cornell University. He is the department extension leader and coleader of the Human Dimensions Research Unit. His research interests and publications focus on stakeholder attitudes and values toward wildlife, integration of human dimensions in wildlife management, and evaluation of stakeholder response to wildlife management policies and programs. He is president of the Human Dimensions in Wildlife Study Group.

Jody W. Enck is a research support specialist with the Human Dimensions Research Unit in the Department of Natural Resources at Cornell University. His research experience encompasses both biological and human dimensions aspects of wildlife management. Previous research includes habitat use, survivorship, and food habits of several wildlife species as well as satisfaction/dissatisfaction associated with wildlife-related recreational activities, and acceptance of wildlife and wildlife damage to various publics.

Trellis G. Green is an associate professor in the Department of Business and International Affairs at the University of Southern Mississippi. His economic values studies have been used to help establish harvest regulations for the red drum in the Gulf of Mexico and the south Atlantic.

Cliff Hamilton worked for the Oregon Department of Fish and Game. He has several publications in wildlife conference proceedings dealing with current wildlife issues.

Ann H. Harvey has been a research associate with the Northern Rockies Conservation Cooperative since 1988. She received an M.S. in natural resources policy from the University of Michigan, where her thesis work focused on interactions among wildlife management agencies. She has worked as a wildlife biologist and environment educator in California, Alaska, and northwestern Wyoming.

James J. Kennedy is assistant dean of the College of Natural Resources at Utah State University. He has numerous publications in natural resource journals concerning career development and training needs of wildlife and fisheries managers as well as the role of professional values in wildlife management.

Barbara A. Knuth is an assistant professor of Natural Resource Policy and Management in the Department of Natural Resources, New York State College of Agriculture and Life Sciences, Cornell University. She holds a Ph.D. in fisheries and wildlife sciences from Virginia Polytechnic Institute and State University, an M.En. in environmental sciences, and an A.B. in Zoology from Miami University. She is president of the New York Chapter of the American Fisheries Society. Her research program focuses on resource policy alternatives, human management strategies, and participatory decision making in fish, wildlife, and water resource management programs.

Jean C. Mangun is a visiting assistant professor in the Department of Biology at East Carolina University. She received a doctoral degree in human dimensions of wildlife management at Purdue University. Her publications on wildlife and recreation issues include a coauthored article in *Leisure Sciences* and several proceedings of the Midwest Fish and Wildlife Conferences.

William R. Mangun is a professor and director of the master of public administration program in the Department of Political Science at East Carolina University. He was with the U.S. Fish and Wildlife Service as the project manager for policy analysis and national surveys after serving as the national resource management coordinator. He is the author of *The Public Administration of Environmental Policy,* the coauthor of *Managing the Environmental Crisis* and *Nonconsumptive Use of Wildlife in the United States,* and the author/editor of *Public Policy Issues in Wildlife Management.*

Joseph T. O'Leary is a professor of forest recreation at Purdue University. His research focuses on the analysis of nationwide recreation surveys, recreation specialization, and life-cycle development.

Gerri A. Pomerantz was a research associate with the Human Dimensions Research Unit in the Department of Natural Resources at Cornell University. She also was a visiting assistant professor in the Department of Wildlife and Fisheries Sciences at Texas A&M University. Her research interests include evaluation of people's attitudes and values regarding wildlife, integration of human dimensions information in wildlife management, and environmental education.

Ken G. Purdy was a research support specialist with the Human Dimensions Research Unit in the Department of Natural Resources at Cornell University. He is currently program director of the Solid Waste Research Institute of Northeast Oklahoma. His wildlife research interests are in the area of motivations and dynamics of hunting participation and public attitudes and values toward wildlife and wildlife management.

Debra A. Rose is a doctoral student in the Political Science Department at the University of Florida. Affiliated with the UF Tropical Conservation and Development Program, she specializes in the international and comparative political economy of natural resource use, with emphasis on wildlife issues. In addition to sea turtle conservation, her current research interests include international environmental regimes and U.S. endangered species politics. She is conducting research in Mexico on endangered species policy implementation.

William F. Siemer is a research support specialist with the Human Dimensions Research Unit in the Department of Natural Resources at Cornell University. He received an M.S. in the human dimensions of wildlife management from Michigan State University. His research interests include environmental education, public involvement in wildlife management, and fish and wildlife policy and planning.

Jack Ward Thomas is chief wildlife biologist of the U.S. Forest Service Pacific Northwest Research Station in La Grande, Oregon. He is a noted researcher in the field of wildlife conservation. His publications have provided essential guidance for wildlife managers on numerous critical wildlife resource issues for many years. Recently he served as chair of the Interagency Scientific Committee to Address the Conservation of the Northern Spotted Owl.

INDEX